# A Healthy Business?

# About the author

Andrew Chetley is a Canadian-born research and development consultant, journalist and campaigner. For eleven years he worked for the British development NGO, War on Want. In 1984 he became General Administrator of the International Baby Food Action Network (IBFAN) and for some years played a leading role in the campaign to re-establish the importance of breastfeeding for infant health. He has also worked closely with Health Action International (HAI) on a range of issues, in particular the need to remove some of the more hazardous and useless drugs from the market. He served as editor of *Health Now*, the newspaper published by HAI and IBFAN during the 1986 World Health Assembly. He has contributed articles to numerous publications, including *The Lancet, World Health, Development Dialogue, Development Forum* and the Gemini News Service. He is also the author of a number of reports. His books include:

   *The Baby Killer Scandal* (War on Want, London, 1979)
   *The Politics of Baby Foods* (Frances Pinter, London, 1986)
   *Antibiotics: the wrong drugs for diarrhoea* (Health Action International, The Hague, 1987)
   *Towards Rational Drug Use* (Health Action International, The Hague, 1988)
   *Peddling Placebos: an analysis of cough and cold remedies* (Health Action International, Amsterdam, 1989)

He currently works for the Bernard van Leer Foundation in The Hague, specialising on issues concerning the care and education of young children.

# A Healthy Business?

## World health and the pharmaceutical industry

**Andrew Chetley**

**Zed Books Ltd**
London and New Jersey

*A Healthy Business?* was first published by Zed Books Ltd,
57 Caledonian Road, London N1 9BU, UK, and 171 First Avenue,
Atlantic Highlands, New Jersey 07716, USA, in 1990.

Copyright © Andrew Chetley, 1990.

Cover designed by Sophie Buchet.
Typography by Andrew Chetley.
Printed and bound in the United Kingdom
by Biddles Ltd, Guildford and King's Lynn.

**British Library Cataloguing in Publication Data**

Chetley, Andrew
  A healthy business? : world health and the
  pharmaceutical industry.
  1. Pharmaceutical industries
  I. Title
  338.4′76′51

  ISBN 0-86232-734-2
  ISBN 0-86232-735-0 pbk

**Library of Congress Cataloging-in-Publication Data**

Chetley, Andrew.
  A healthy business? : world health and the pharmaceutical
  industry/Andrew Chetley.
    p.    cm.
  Includes bibliographical references.
  ISBN 0-86232-734-2.—ISBN 0-86232-735-0 (pbk.)
  1. Pharmaceutical industry—Government policy. I. Title.
HD9665.6.C47    1990
338.4′76151—dc20               89-35871
                                 CIP

*For David*

# Contents

# Tables

# Acknowledgements

First, and foremost, thanks must go to the hundreds of people around the world who contributed advice, ideas, information and practical assistance in making this book possible. They include health workers, development workers, community leaders, corporate executives, UN officials, journalists, and patients and consumers of drugs. The list is far too long to acknowledge them all by name.

Special mention, however, is due to two previous authors on the subject of pharmaceuticals – Mike Muller and Dianna Melrose. Their publications, both of which appeared in 1982, were significant in helping me first to coalesce my own ideas about the risks and benefits of medicines. A group of eight Bangladeshis, too, deserves special mention, because of their courageous efforts in formulating a National Drug Policy for Bangladesh in 1982, the significance of which led me first to take a long, hard look at the world's pharmaceutical jungle.

My good friend and colleague David Gilbert played a major role in the preparation of this book, undertaking diligent research during its formative stages. My wife Ana Isabel, who endured several years of living with papers scattered throughout the house, and a husband who at various times was distracted, argumentative, depressed, and elated – depending on how the research and writing was going – nevertheless was consistent in her support and encouragement, and irreplaceable as a proofreader. John Cunnington, Linda Dobraszczyk, Catherine Hodgkin, Charles Medawar, Ian Munro, Philippa Saunders, Prakash Sethi, Ingemar Rexed and Michael Tan, who kindly agreed to read parts of the manuscript in draft form, helped to provide the stimulation to improve its contents. Robert Molteno's excellent editing and patient encouragement have helped to ensure that the book was completed.

# Note on Terminology

*Developing countries*: Many terms are used to describe those nations in Asia, Africa, and Latin America whose gross national products and other economic and social indices are less favourable than those of, for example, the countries of Western Europe. Collectively, they are called the *Third World*, the *poor world*, the *South*, *underdeveloped countries*, or *less/least developed countries* (LDCs). Throughout this book, the term *developing* has generally been used (except where other terms are used in direct quotes) even though it begs the question of whether these countries are actually developing and also the question of the so-called developed countries (the *North*), for all countries are, or should be, developing.

*Transnational corporations (TNCs)*: This term refers to those commercial enterprises that operate across national borders, generally with subsidiaries in two or more countries, and generally refers to the world's largest manufacturing and trading concerns. Other terms that have been used to describe them are: *multinational corporations (MNCs)*, *international firms/companies/enterprises*.

*Pharmaceuticals*, *medicines* and *drugs*: All three terms have been used interchangeably. The best definition of a drug is given by Dr Gunter Lewandowski of Ciba-Geigy: 'a drug is a substance *plus* information'.

*Billion*: This term is used throughout to signify one thousand million.

*Dollars* or *$*: is used to indicate US dollars. Where other currencies have been converted into dollars, the rate used is the average rate prevailing at the time.

# Abbreviations

| | |
|---|---|
| ABPI | Association of the British Pharmaceutical Industry |
| ACE | angiotensin-converting enzyme |
| ADR | adverse drug reaction |
| AIDS | acquired immune deficiency syndrome |
| AMA | American Medical Association |
| AMCHAM | American Chamber of Commerce of the Philippines |
| AMREF | African Medical and Research Foundation |
| APED | Action Programme on Essential Drugs and Vaccines (WHO) |
| APMA | Australian Pharmaceutical Manufacturers' Association |
| ARI | acute respiratory infections |
| ASCEP | Australasian Society of Clinical and Experimental Pharmacologists |
| ASEAN | Association of South East Asian Nations |
| BASS | Bangladesh Aushadh Shilpa Samity |
| BBC | British Broadcasting Corporation |
| BCG | Bacille Calmette-Guerin (anti-TB vaccine) |
| BFAD | Bureau of Food and Drugs (Philippines) |
| BGA | West German drug regulatory agency |
| BgMA | Bangladesh Medical Association |
| BMJ | *British Medical Journal* |
| BPI | West German Pharmaceutical Manufacturers' Association |
| BRAC | Bangladesh Rural Advancement Committee |
| BUKO | German Federal Congress of Development Action Groups |
| C&F | cost and freight |
| CIDA | Canadian International Development Agency |
| CONAMAD | Comité Nacional de Alimentos, Medicamentos y Drogas (National Food and Drug Committee – Peru) |
| COPPTEC | co-operative pharmaceutical production and technology centre |
| DANIDA | Danish International Development Agency |
| DAP | Drug Association of the Philippines |
| DHF | Dag Hammarskjöld Foundation (Sweden) |
| DHSS | Department of Health and Social Security (UK) |
| DMPA | depot medroxyprogesterone acetate (contraceptive) |
| DOH | Department of Health (Philippines) |
| DP | Depo-Provera (brand name for DMPA contraceptive) |

| | |
|---|---|
| DPT | diphtheria, pertussis and tetanus (vaccine) |
| DTB | *Drug and Therapeutics Bulletin* |
| EC | European Commission |
| EEC | European Economic Community |
| EDCL | Essential Drugs Company Limited (Bangladesh) |
| EDL | essential drugs list |
| EPI | Expanded Programme of Immunisation (WHO) |
| FAO | Food and Agriculture Organisation (of the UN) |
| FDA | Food and Drug Administration (USA) |
| FONAME | Fondo Nacional de Medicamentos (National Medicines Fund – Peru) |
| GMP | Good Manufacturing Practice |
| GNP | Gross National Product |
| HAI | Health Action International |
| HAIN | Health Action Information Network (Philippines) |
| HIV | human immunodeficiency virus |
| IBFAN | International Baby Food Action Network |
| IFPMA | International Federation of Pharmaceutical Manufacturers Associations |
| IMS | Intercontinental Medical Statistics |
| IOCU | International Organisation of Consumers Unions |
| IOMS | International Organisations Monitoring Service |
| IUD | intra uterine device (contraceptive) |
| JPMA | Japanese Pharmaceutical Manufacturers Association |
| LDC | less (or least) developed country |
| MaLAM | Medical Lobby for Appropriate Marketing |
| NCE | new chemical entity |
| NCIH | National Council for International Health (US) |
| NEFARMA | Dutch Association of Pharmaceutical Industries |
| NGLS | Non-Governmental Liaison Service (of the UN) |
| NGO | non-governmental organisation |
| NSAID | non-steroidal anti-inflammatory drug |
| OECD | Organisation for Economic Cooperation and Development |
| OHE | Office of Health Economics (UK) |
| OPPI | Organisation of Pharmaceutical Producers of India |
| ORS | oral rehydration solution |
| ORT | oral rehydration therapy |
| OTC | over the counter (drugs) |
| PAHO | Pan-American Health Organisation |
| PDAN | Philippine Drug Action Network |
| PHC | primary health care |
| PhMA | Philippine Medical Association |
| PID | pelvic inflammatory disease |
| PMA | Pharmaceutical Manufacturers Association (USA) |
| PMAC | Pharmaceutical Manufacturers Association of Canada |

| | |
|---|---|
| PPA | Pharmaceutical Products Association (Thailand) |
| PSECP | Philippine Society on Experimental and Clinical Pharmacology |
| R&D | research and development |
| RAD-AR | Risk Assessment of Drugs – Analysis and Response (a Ciba-Geigy programme) |
| RCP | Royal College of Physicians (UK) |
| RDS | revised drug strategy (of WHO) |
| RMCC | Ronald McDonald Children's Charities |
| RMI | Research Medicines Industry (New Zealand) |
| SIDA | Swedish International Development Authority |
| SMON | sub-acute myleo-optic neuropathy |
| SNIP | Syndicat National de l'Industrie Pharmaceutique (French pharmaceutical industry association) |
| TB | tuberculosis |
| TNC | transnational corporation |
| UCI | Universal Child Immunisation |
| UNCTAD | United Nations Conference on Trade and Development |
| UNCTC | United Nations Centre on Transnational Corporations |
| UNDP | United Nations Development Programme |
| UNFPA | United Nations Fund for Population Activities |
| UNICEF | United Nations Children's Fund |
| UNIDO | United Nations Industrial Development Organisation |
| UNRISD | United Nations Research Institute for Social Development |
| USAID | United States Agency for International Development |
| VHSS | Voluntary Health Service Society (Bangladesh) |
| WEMOS | Werkgroep Medisch Ontwikkelings Samenwerking (Medical Workgroup for Development Cooperation – Netherlands) |
| WFPMM | World Federation of Proprietary Medicine Manufacturers |
| WHA | World Health Assembly |
| WHO | World Health Organisation |
| WRAIR | Walter Reed Army Institute of Research |

*Thirty years ago modern health technology had just awakened and was full of promise. Since then, its expansion has surpassed all dreams, only to become a nightmare. For it has become over-sophisticated and over-costly. It is dictating our health policies unwisely; and what is useful is being applied to too few.*

Dr Halfdan Mahler, Director General, World Health Organisation

# Introduction

Mike Muller's book *The Health of Nations* concluded with this comment from
health authorities in Mozambique:

> The battle against the pharmaceutical transnationals will not be easy. But the
> debate must be rekindled wherever possible, since the positive achieve-
> ments to be realised and already in sight will represent an immeasurable
> benefit for the health of all the people in the world, especially those least
> protected: those of the developing countries.[1]

Since that book was published in 1982 the debate indeed has been rekindled
in a multitude of ways. As Muller confidently predicted, during the 1980s the
debate has shifted from an earlier focus on the safety, efficacy and cost of drugs
to the 'gross mismatch between actual drug usage and real drug needs'.[2]

In boardrooms, in health care facilities, in courtrooms, in the corridors of
power within national governments, in conference halls, across the pages of
learned journals and in the headlines of the mass media, more and more
frequently the subject of the rational use of drugs has become a focus of
attention. Slowly, too, in the research laboratories that topic is beginning to
influence the choice of drugs for the future.

Perhaps where the debate demonstrates its urgency most obviously is in the
*barrios* and shantytowns of developing countries, or in their remote rural areas.
Here, the difference between having or not having access to health care and
useful medicines is often the difference between life and death. But the pharmaceutical jungle does not only grow in tropical areas; its presence is also felt in
the confusing array of products on offer in industrialised countries. The twin
spectres of over- and under-medication are two sides of the same coin, and their
adverse effects know no geographical, economic or ideological barriers.

## Future shock?

If we turn our gaze backwards two or three generations to the beginning of the
20th century, we are shocked by the primitive nature of the treatments being
offered to those suffering from illness. Even one generation back, at the
beginning of the 1960s, the idea of routinely prescribing medicines to pregnant
women was still common – an idea which today would bring gasps of horror
from most medical practitioners. One cannot help but wonder what the inhabi-

tants of this planet will think 100 years from now when they, in turn, look back at the medicine of the late 20th century. Will they be appalled at the mishandling of antibiotics, which led to the spread of microbial resistance and perhaps, as some commentators[3] have suggested, so assaulted the human immune system that scourges such as acquired immune deficiency syndrome (AIDS) were able to take root? Will they feel outrage that even in remote jungle outposts the coolers existed to keep sugar-laden soft drinks chilled, but the cold-chain of freezers essential to keep measles vaccines at the right temperature was missing, resulting in some 2 million preventable deaths of young children each year? Will they be shocked to discover that the pain killer dipyrone, which was described by the American Medical Association (AMA) in 1977 as 'obsolete' provided some 5 per cent of the turnover of a leading research-based drug manufacturer in 1987, despite the existence of equally effective and safer products on the market? Will they be stunned by the hard-sell promotion for an anti-arthritic product, benoxaprofen – which triggered enormous sales in its short market life, and a series of unfortunate side effects – and the paltry sum which victims of the drug received in compensation? Will they be dismayed by the practice, widespread for a generation, of starting men and women on the road to drug dependence through the incautious prescribing of benzodiazepine tranquillisers in place of sound counselling and support? Will they be staggered by the poor quality of many of the drug toxicology tests and clinical trials performed, such as the study which found that one product caused no more cancer in chickens than a placebo, but which failed to report that half the chickens died of heart failure?[4] Will they be amazed that in 1980 the World Health Organisation (WHO) said that the antibiotic neomycin 'should *never* be used in the treatment of acute diarrhoea', yet seven years later, 14 per cent of antidiarrhoeals on the market in developing countries contained neomycin? Will they laugh or shake their heads sadly at the promotion of pizotifen in Western Europe for the prevention of migraine headaches with a caution that it may cause slight weight gain in some patients, while in several developing countries the same product promises rapid growth and effective appetite stimulation among malnourished children? Will they conclude that the inappropriate use of medicines was one of the factors which transformed the hope of the WHO strategy for 'Health For All by the Year 2000' into a hollow dream?

The answers to those, and many similar questions, do not have to, indeed cannot, wait for future generations. Throughout the world many people both inside and outside the pharmaceutical industry are beginning to question the wisdom of depending for so much of our health care on mass-produced medicines. Among the voices raised outside the industry is that of the global network of health, development, consumer and public-interest groups Health Action International (HAI), which was founded in 1981. Part of the credit for the continued resurgence of interest in the role of pharmaceuticals rests with the work of HAI, some of which is described later in this book. The WHO, through its Action Programme on Essential Drugs and Vaccines, also born in 1981, has similarly made a major contribution. Individual health workers, often feeling as if they were crying in the wilderness, have persistently raised the issues in medical journals and meetings with their colleagues. Governments, anxious to cut costs and provide the best possible health care within constrained economic limits, have taken a hard look at how to rationalise their use of drugs. And, within the industry, a few brave voices are beginning to urge changes which could have far-reaching impact.

## Challenging perceptions

Now, as we enter the last decade of the 20th century, it is an appropriate moment to pause a little, reflect on the progress made in health care in the past hundred years, and begin to lay the foundations for the next century. This book is one small contribution to that process. It is unquestionably biased, and for that I make no apologies. Rather, had I reviewed the considerable information available about the use and misuse of drugs and formed no opinions or conclusions, then I think I would be obliged to apologise to readers, or not write the book in the first place. Readers do not have to accept my conclusions or opinions, and in virtually every instance where a controversial concept or topic is discussed, I have tried to present adequate data to allow them to formulate their own conclusions. The extensive bibliography at the back of the book provides an ample entry into much of the current literature.

I am reminded of the words of one of the world's most respected and inspiring journalists, the late James Cameron, who said:

> I still do not see how a reporter attempting to define a situation involving some sort of ethical conflict can do it with sufficient demonstrable neutrality to fulfil some arbitrary concept of 'objectivity'. It never occurred to me, in such a situation, to be other than subjective, and as obviously so as I could manage to be. I may not always have been satisfactorily balanced; I always tended to argue that objectivity was of less importance than the truth, and that the reporter whose technique was informed by no opinion lacked a very serious dimension.
>
> It can easily be misrepresented. Yet as I see it – and it seems to be the simplest of disciplines – the journalist is obliged to present his attitude as vigorously and persuasively as he can, insisting that it is his attitude, to be examined and criticised in the light of every contrary argument, which he need not accept but must reveal.
>
> Surely the useful end is somehow to engage an attitude of mind that will challenge and criticise automatically, thus to destroy or weaken the built-in advantage of all propaganda and special pleading – even the journalist's own. The energetic argument for liberal thought must, by definition ... embody the machinery for its own conquest, since it presents itself as equally vulnerable.[5]

In writing this book, I also make no apologies for drawing on a broad diversity of sources rather than constraining myself to the more traditional medical or scientific literature. As Laurence and Bennett put it: 'drugs are much too serious a thing to be left to the medical profession and to the pharmaceutical industry'.[6] Politics, economics, law, sociology, psychology, culture and that most uncommon of human virtues, common sense, all play important roles in determining attitudes to drugs and health. We ignore the inputs of those disciplines at our peril.

In the growing mountain of literature about the medicalisation of health, why produce yet another book? What will it contribute that is new and fresh? Much of the information in this book is relatively freely available, so in that sense it offers little that is 'new' – a dangerous statement for an author to make in the introductory pages of his or her text. Why read further? What is different is the pulling together of often disparate strands of thought in a way which makes the whole greater, I hope, than the sum of its constituent parts.

Essentially, at a time when the pharmaceutical industry appears poised on the threshold of a new wave of discovery not only of products but of ways of both producing and administering them made possible by the research going on in biotechnology, it is a good moment to analyse some of the professional and public scepticism about the role of the industry before rushing headlong into a new era of fulsome praise for its technological wizardry. It is important, first of all, to examine the record of the industry in an up-to-date manner and focus on five key questions which will determine how constructive, or otherwise, will be its role in improving the health of the world's population in the 1990s and beyond.

Drug safety is one of those questions, as is the cost of medicines, both of which cut across geographical boundaries and affect people and governments in all countries. Another universal problem is the quality of drug information available to prescribers and patients alike. Taken together, these three points form the backbone of the current international demand for a more rational use of drugs. Underlying this is the internal decision making of the industry about what research choices to make and the constant tension between the 'money making' marketing divisions and the high spending research departments. It is the outcome of this conflict which usually determines how many and which drugs are available, and that leads to the final question, what is the industry doing in terms of providing the drugs which the bulk of the world's population – those living in developing countries – needs?

While looking back and locating the debate around pharmaceuticals firmly in its recorded and even unrecorded history, the book also looks forward and speculates, perhaps even dreams a little, about a new way of organising the development, production, distribution and use of pharmaceuticals that will bring positive benefit to the health of people everywhere.

Above all, the book is focused on people: their needs and their desires for better health – indeed, their very right to it.

# 1.   The obstacles to world health

*Thirty years ago modern health technology had just awakened and was full of promise. Since then, its expansion has surpassed all dreams, only to become a nightmare. For it has become over-sophisticated and over-costly. It is dictating our health policies unwisely; and what is useful is being applied to too few. Based on these technologies, a huge medical industry has grown up with powerful vested interests of its own. Like the sorcerer's apprentice, we have lost control – social control – over health technology. The slave of our imagination has become the master of our creativity. We must now learn to control it again and use it wisely, in the struggle for health freedom. This struggle is important for all countries; for developing countries it is crucial.*

Dr Halfdan Mahler, Director General, World Health Organisation[1]

Dr M. A. Muttalib's first patient of the morning at his clinic in Dhaka, Bangladesh, was a young boy of six. After a few questions to his mother, and a simple examination, Dr Muttalib made the diagnosis – a parasitic infection – and prescribed the right medicine, a single anti-worm tablet. As the child and his mother left the clinic, Dr Muttalib explained that the drug was very effective. 'By tomorrow the boy will be cured.' He leaned back in his chair and sighed deeply. 'But within six months, he'll be back with another worm. And I'll prescribe another tablet, and so it goes on. You see, the child goes back into the same unsanitary environment and becomes re-infected.'

His next patient was a young baby girl. He checked the simple weight card that her mother presented, weighed the baby and examined her for any signs of malnutrition or other illness, and smiled reassuringly at the mother. The baby was in good health and growing well, but it was time for a measles vaccination. Despite the gentle care he took in administering the shot, the young baby, who had been gurgling happily, burst into tears and howled. By the time he had finished filling in the weight card, the baby was subdued again, cuddled firmly against her mother's breasts.

The third visitor of the morning was a salesman from a drug company, offering three new antibiotic treatments for diarrhoea in infants. Dr Muttalib listened politely to the sales talk, smiling as the representative brought out a dossier with a collection of copies of research studies which were supposed to justify the use of the drugs. Dr Muttalib skimmed through the studies and handed them back to the salesman. 'These are seven, eight years old. Don't you have more recent studies?' he asked. The salesman, whose patter had been perfect up to that point, faltered. He muttered something about more recent experience, but nothing had been published yet. Dr Muttalib pointed out to the salesman that there were very few occasions when antibiotics were required for diarrhoea in children, and sent him on his way without a sale.

As he put away the free prescription pads advertising the products which the salesman had been trying to sell, Dr Muttalib said, 'what we need in this country are simple treatments and basic health education. Our doctors should be able to deal with this. It is a tragedy that we can easily prevent many of the problems of infant health and don't do so. If breastfeeding is there, no antibiotic is needed for the treatment of diarrhoea. If diarrhoea does occur, some inexpensive oral rehydration salts and continued breastfeeding will be enough.'

The telephone rang. It was a mother who had given birth the day before. She called to say that she was fine, the baby was fine and that she was breastfeeding and enjoying it. She thanked him for all the help that he and the clinic staff had given in preparing her for breastfeeding. Dr Muttalib put down the phone and smiled. Another child was started successfully on the road to health.

The events in Dr Muttalib's clinic during less than 30 minutes of that September morning in 1982 encapsulate some of the major problems of health care in a developing country. In a dramatic way, they also highlight the benefits and the failings of drugs. Some drugs, such as the anti-worm tablet that Dr Muttalib prescribed, are effective but cannot get to the root causes of ill health: poverty, lack of sanitation and clean drinking water, low levels of education and understanding about the causes of disease. Some drugs, such as measles vaccine, are both effective and essential in helping to prevent illness, even though in many countries, they are in short supply. Some drugs, such as antidiarrhoeal products containing an antibiotic, may be ineffective, certainly unnecessary and possibly harmful, yet these are often the most promoted products. And in many instances, the solution to health problems depends on non-drug therapies, such as the encouragement of and preparation for breastfeeding.

## The major killers

Today's world presents a grim future for the newborn child, particularly in developing countries. Every year, some 14.1 million children under five years of age die. Diarrhoeal diseases account for approximately 30 per cent of all child hospital admissions and about 40 per cent of all outpatient visits to clinics and health centres in the developing world. In all, an estimated 5 million children a year die from diarrhoeal diseases; about 3.5 million of the deaths are caused by the loss of body fluids (dehydration) brought about by repeated episodes of diarrhoea, usually triggered by unhygienic conditions and a lack of clean drinking water. Measles, now considered a trifling and relatively minor childhood infection in most industrialised countries thanks to effective vaccines, claims another 2.1 million children. Measles and diarrhoea often go hand in hand.[2]

**Table 1.1 Proportion of children who die before their fifth birthday in selected countries**

| Afghanistan | 1 out of every 3 |
|---|---|
| Mozambique | 1 out of every 4 |
| Nigeria | 1 out of every 5 |
| Cameroon | 1 out of every 6 |
| Lesotho | 1 out of every 7 |
| Kenya | 1 out of every 8 |
| Honduras | 1 out of every 9 |
| Botswana | 1 out of every 10 |
| China | 1 out of every 20 |
| Argentina | 1 out of every 25 |
| Portugal | 1 out of every 50 |
| The Netherlands | 1 out of every 100 |
| Sweden | 1 out of every 125 |

Source: calculated from data in UNICEF, *The State of the World's Children 1987*, p.74.

Acute respiratory infections (ARI) such as whooping cough, tuberculosis, diphtheria, pneumonia and bronchitis are estimated to cause over 3 million deaths each year. A further 3 million children die from malaria. Tetanus in newborn babies results in 800,000 deaths a year, while polio kills 265,000 children; both diseases are preventable by immunisation.[3]

Of the children who survive the first five years of life, millions are left physically or mentally disabled for life. Every year, an estimated 250,000 are left paralysed by polio.[4] Another 250,000 go blind as a result of vitamin A deficiency. Children, too, are the principal victims of parasitic infections such as roundworms, which infect some 1,000 million people, and hookworms, which infect nearly 900 million people.[5]

## Malnutrition

At the root of much of the childhood illness and death in developing countries lies malnutrition, graphically portrayed during the 1980s in the harrowing faces of children suffering from famine in Ethiopia, Sudan and Mozambique. It is a daily reality for at least the estimated 800 million 'destitute' people in the Third World today.[6] Probably 500 million of those people are considered severely malnourished – at or near starvation level.[7] Yet many hundreds of millions more suffer from undernutrition. The United Nations Economic and Social Commission for Asia and the Pacific estimates that undernourishment and malnutrition affect some 640 million people in that region alone.[8] Infants and children are usually the hardest hit. Surveys of rural communities in many different countries in the tropics have revealed that about half the children suffer from poor nutrition.[9] Malnutrition has been described by the Food and Agriculture Organisation of the UN as 'the world's principal public health problem'.[10]

There are many misconceptions about malnutrition. Perhaps the greatest is that malnutrition is caused only by the lack of food. Malnutrition can be caused by intestinal parasites, by changing from breast milk to commercial substitutes, by not knowing how and when to begin weaning, and in half or more of all cases, malnutrition is caused by infection. All infections have a nutritional impact. They can decrease the body's absorption of nutrients, induce rejection of food by vomiting, drain away nutrients through diarrhoea, and induce mothers to stop feeding while diarrhoea lasts. And by any or all of these methods, 'infections become a major cause – perhaps *the* major cause – of malnutrition among the world's children'.[11]

Another misconception is that malnutrition is only a problem in developing countries. The US Department of Health says that of the ten leading causes of death in that country, at least six are directly related to malnutrition.[12] In addition, overnutrition is a cause of serious concern in many industrialised countries. The World Health Organisation (WHO) estimates that some 20 per cent of the population of industrialised countries suffer from obesity, a total of perhaps 200 million people worldwide.[13]

## Too many people?

A further misconception related to malnutrition is that the world has too many people to be adequately fed. Through the 1960s and 1970s, the idea of a population crisis gained prominence in development circles, and fertility control became a major priority in both research and aid funding. In 1975–6, for example, population programmes were allocated two-thirds of all US foreign assistance to the health sector,[14] while about half of Britain's multilateral aid contributions were for population control programmes.[15]

According to the World Bank, high rates of population growth 'are holding back economic and social development in many of the poorer countries'.[16] Other population agencies agree and argue for increased efforts to remove this obstacle to economic growth. Admittedly, a rapidly expanding population cannot be adequately supported within the present social and economic system. But the problem is as much, if not more, to do with the distribution and consumption of resources. The total food resources available in the world would be adequate to feed everyone properly if they were fairly distributed among nations and social groups.[17] A Guatemalan teacher points out that 'the problem is not that the Indigenas (Indians) are having too many children. Guatemala could produce everything we need. The problem is the distribution of the land.'[18]

The idea that controlling population is the way to tackle poverty and economic problems has led to some severe distortions in planning. One researcher in India says that a gigantic national birth control programme 'crashed into other social and economic development programmes, causing them considerable damage' and diverted attention and efforts away from work on the country's basic problems of poverty, social injustice, ill health, unemployment and illiteracy.[19]

Population agencies often argue that population policies will bring enormous benefit to women.[20] The promise remains unconvincing. The factors which combine to deny women their equal rights and equal participation are much broader than the simplistic focus on the constraints of childbirth and child rearing would suggest. Furthermore, once contraception has been accepted, women are again forgotten. As one writer puts it:

> While resources are lavished on free medical services for purposes of birth control, those same women who are provided with contraceptives are often unable to obtain skilled assistance in childbirth, or free advice in the event of serious illness. The overwhelming publicity surrounding population control has therefore obscured the broader health needs of women.[21]

Maaza Bekele, a UNICEF consultant in Africa, notes that contraception on its own will not, and indeed cannot, bring about a change in women's position in society that would assure them better opportunities for education, employment prospects, adequate housing and access to proper nutrition. It is the lack of these basic elements that leaves many of the world's women trapped in poverty, and it is poverty that forces many women to rely on having large numbers of children as some sort of guarantee for the future.[22]

The experience of the state of Kerala stands in stark contrast to what has happened in other parts of India. The literacy rate is nearly twice the national average, the crude death rate is nearly half the national average, the infant mortality rate is under half the national average and the crude birth rate is nearly one-third less than the national average.[23] The differences are the result of development strategies based on social equity. John Ratcliffe notes that:

> as the political economy was transformed from one founded on exploitation of the many by the few to one which began increasingly to assume welfare functions traditionally fulfilled by children, fertility declined – and continues to decline – in response.[24]

Slowly now recognition is growing everywhere that parents tend to have smaller families when they are confident that their children will survive.[25]

## The roots of illness

As the Kerala experience shows, the starting point of health policies must be an understanding that a large proportion of ill health in developing countries is a symptom of the more fundamental problems of poverty and deprivation. In the long term, the problems of malnutrition and infection can be solved only through improvements in the social and economic conditions of the world's poor.[26] That does not mean, however, as many development specialists contend, that the improvement in health and reduction of deaths in developing countries will follow automatically if economic development raises the Gross National Product (GNP). Recent experience has repeatedly shown that riding the GNP bandwagon toward improved national income does not necessarily lead to improved health....The optimism of the 1960s over the rapid growth of developing economies has now been tempered by the colossal failure of social benefits to 'trickle down' to the poor.[27]

As economist John Kenneth Galbraith points out,[28] 'no error in the advice given to the developing countries in recent decades has rivalled that which placed investment in industrial apparatus ahead of the investment in human capital'.

Dr Halfdan Mahler, in one of his last speeches as Director General of WHO, was equally hard-hitting about the failure of many past development efforts where the focus was on economic growth with 'no sympathy whatsoever to the concept of social poverty and to the need to support people in extricating themselves from that'.[29]

## The Western approach to medicine

If the solution to better health care and development is to focus on people-oriented strategies, how appropriate is the Western approach to medicine? Although throughout recorded history there are many examples of 'healers' and 'healing techniques', medicine as we know it today had its origins in the scientific revolution of the 17th century.[30] One common thread which stretches from earliest recorded history through to today was the recognition that the ability to 'cure' illness conveyed power and prestige. The 'healers' of the past – with their strange-smelling potions, their rituals, and their mysterious chants – were both revered and feared. Their specialised jargon and 'skills' set them apart from the rest of their community. Even today, the mystique of medicine is maintained by many involved in health care, and acts as an isolating force to remove the understanding of illness from the people, and to create a dependency relationship between those who are ill and those who have the 'solutions' to illness. As Goran Sterky notes, the exclusive right to determine what constitutes sickness has been transferred to the physician, whilst medical technology and professional satisfaction help to erode people's self-confidence.[31]

Whilst in antiquity the 'solutions' may not have always worked, the concept of illness was more holistic. There was a recognition that the environment of the ill person, his or her relationships with others, and even the person's spiritual beliefs, could be implicated in the cause of the illness. As society developed through the 17th and 18th centuries, the conception of illness and its solutions came to mirror the increasing mechanisation of production. People were looked at more as machines than as organically interacting beings. While this mechanistic approach led to the discovery of much of what we now know about the causes of infections and the possible routes for treating some of them, it also led to a focus on curative medicine and on the 'conquest' of the natural world.

Throughout this process, health care – and to a certain extent, health itself – became a commodity to be bought and sold. During the 20th century a thriving 'health industry' has emerged, offering services, equipment and technology, drugs, and a whole ideology and philosophy of illness and health. Paradoxically, the health industry has a vested interest in illness, for as long as illness persists, there is a market for the services and products which it offers. Today's physician often tries to maintain the myth that he or she and the technology and medicines he or she uses are somehow politically neutral. As Illich puts it, 'the assertion of value-free cure and care is obviously malignant nonsense'.[32] Joe Collier points out that medical care in the UK is class, sex and race biased – both because the treatment people receive depends on their social status, sex and ethnic origins, and in terms of their employment prospects and opportunities to influence policies in the medical professions.[33]

## Impact on developing countries

Debabar Banerji notes that the introduction of Western medicine in Third World countries set in motion complex interactions. These included interaction between Western medicine and the pre-existing 'health culture' of the population, comprising cultural perceptions, the cultural meaning of health problems, and health behaviour in terms of various cultural devices available and accessible to the community.[34]

According to UNICEF, the concept of curative rather than preventive medicine is not designed to deal

> with the great alliance of malnutrition and infection which was and is still the most important threat to life and health for the majority of families in the developing world today. In consequence, the steep decline in infant deaths is now slowing down at a much earlier stage, and at a much higher level, than in the industrialised world.[35]

A study of 10 projects which focused on direct attempts to reduce child deaths and improve child health in poor communities with populations of 60,000–70,000 in different parts of the world demonstrated that significant improvements could be achieved with low-cost interventions. Infant and child mortality rates were reduced by one-third to one-half or more within one to five years, at a cost of less than 2 per cent of per capita income – an amount no greater than that being allocated to health in each country concerned. The authors of the study concluded that a major factor which distinguished the more successful from the less obviously successful projects was the degree to which they departed from the Western tradition of hospital-based, high-technology medical services, and instead used approaches which were more appropriate to village conditions.[36]

As well as being inappropriate, Western medicine is costly. Paul Harrison makes the point that

> even in the West, Western medicine is a very expensive and ineffective way of improving the health of the community. It is bankrupting the sick people or government treasuries at the same time as the incidence of the killer

diseases goes on rising. For the poor countries of the world, the Western approach to health has been a total disaster. It has focused on lavish buildings, imported equipment and drugs, and expensively trained personnel. Its cost has put health care of any kind way beyond the reach of the majority in almost every Third World country.[37]

Dr David Morley of the London Institute for Child Health has coined the 'three-quarters rule' to describe the fact that three-quarters of spending on health care in developing countries is for urban-based facilities and staff, although at least three-quarters of the population live in the rural areas, and that three-quarters of the deaths in developing countries are due to conditions that can be prevented by relatively simple and inexpensive measures, but three-quarters of health budgets go on high-cost curative care.[38]

The World Bank noted in 1980 that health care facilities are often expensive and inaccessible to the majority of people with too much emphasis on curative instead of preventive care. Education of physicians and other health workers is inadequate, particularly in terms of the disease conditions and the treatments most relevant to their countries. Community participation is low, and generally, planning administration and training procedures are poor.[39]

The limitations of adopting a curative approach in developing countries are illustrated by a medical school programme in Colombia for the hospital care of premature infants. Survival rates were comparable to those in the USA, but 70 per cent of the infants discharged were dead within three months because of infection, malnutrition and general poverty.[40]

One doctor with years of experience working in developing countries points out:

> It is up to us to recognise that what we do here in Birmingham or in Boston is not only inappropriate but also may be the largest single determinant of medical practice in the developing world. Whereas we can afford to waste resources without a concomitant waste of life, a similar commitment to expensive and inappropriate medical care in a developing country virtually guarantees the deprivation of 75 per cent or more of the population from effective therapy.[41]

## Towards health for all

WHO, which was founded in 1948, in its early years emulated the technical approach to health care that was so prevalent worldwide. Top-down, almost military-like campaigns were formulated and implemented to tackle individual diseases such as malaria, smallpox, yaws, tuberculosis, filariasis, leprosy, yellow fever, trachoma and schistosomiasis.[42] While there was success with yaws and smallpox, and, to a more limited extent, some temporary impact on some of the other diseases, by the mid-1960s it was clear that a more integrated approach was needed. Planning the development of health services became the solution. A decade further on, it became evident that even the best plans were useless unless they were implemented, and unless people participated in their design. Following a study of health systems in nine countries – Bangladesh, China, Cuba, India, Niger, Nigeria, Tanzania, Venezuela and Yugoslavia – a WHO report called for a

> virtual revolution … to bring about changes in the distribution of power, in the pattern of political decision-making, in the attitude and commitment of the health professionals and administrators in ministries of health and universities, and in people's awareness of what they are entitled to.[43]

A key to this 'revolution' in health care was seen to be a new type of health worker – the primary health worker – who would be a community member, chosen by the community and responsible to it. It was a concept which drew heavily on the experience of the so-called 'barefoot doctors' of China – part-time health workers with a minimum of training. Intrinsic to the Chinese approach was strong political commitment on the part of the central government, recognition that health was an integral part of national development, universal access to all levels of health care, the total participation of the community in the health system as an essential factor in encouraging self-reliance, and the use of traditional medicine (including acupuncture and herbal drugs), which made the health system more affordable and acceptable to the Chinese people.[44]

That such an approach can work in different political settings is proved by the example of Costa Rica. In 1970, the infant mortality rate stood at 61 per 1,000. In just 10 years, that figure was reduced to 19 deaths per 1,000 by developing a programme to deliver primary health care throughout the country, with increased surveillance and identification of diseases at an early stage, low-cost immunisation programmes against major killer diseases, use of oral rehydration treatment to combat diarrhoeal diseases, improved water supply and sanitation, and improved education.[45]

By 1977, the rallying cry for the global revolution in health was proclaimed in a World Health Assembly resolution, 'Health for all by the year 2000'.[46] In 1978, WHO together with UNICEF held a landmark conference at Alma-Ata in Russia which drafted the document which defined primary health care as the vehicle for achieving health for all. The Alma-Ata Declaration, only 1,000 words long, was a charter for health rights.[47] One of its key articles was that 'people have the right and duty to participate individually and collectively in the planning and implementation of their health care'.

The declaration said that primary health care

> is essential health care based on practical, scientifically sound and socially acceptable methods and technology made universally accessible to individuals and families in the community through their full participation and at a cost that the community and country can afford.… It forms an integral part both of the country's health system, of which it is the central function and main focus, and of the overall social and economic development of the community.… Primary health care … includes at least: education concerning prevailing health problems and the methods of preventing and controlling

them; promotion of food supply and proper nutrition; an adequate supply of safe water and basic sanitation; maternal and child health care, including family planning; immunization against the major infectious diseases; prevention and control of locally endemic diseases; appropriate treatment of common diseases and injuries; and provision of essential drugs.

Overall, WHO estimates that something in the region of $12.50 per head is all that is needed to save 'millions of lives a year' through the provision of essential health services.[48] In the years since Alma-Ata, WHO has been working with governments to draw up national and then regional plans for achieving health for all through primary health care. A global strategy was approved by 1981, with a detailed timetable added in 1982. By 1987, a first global evaluation of the strategy was complete. It showed that while some progress had been made, the distribution of health services remained inequitable and there was resistance to change among health professionals in many countries. Lacking too in many countries was a determined political commitment. Ironically, it is in the industrialised countries that strategies seem to be making the most progress. Glen Williams points out that the more affluent countries, alarmed by the rapidly rising cost of health care and the recognition that sophisticated medical technology is unable to prevent major health problems, have been increasingly turning to the alternative approaches embodied in primary health care.[49]

## The role of drugs

Although the pharmaceutical industry usually points outs that it cannot solve the problems of health in developing countries by itself,[50] on occasion, it does overstress the value of drugs. The US-based company, Pfizer, for example says that 'drugs are a singular blessing to the Third World'.[51]

Michael Wood, from the Kenya-based African Medical and Research Foundation (AMREF) rejects such a view. He claims that the blind belief in drugs as a panacea for health problems 'tends to obscure even more fundamental issues of the reality of what constitutes health'.[52] Dr John Bryant, a respected authority on international public health, says 'the dismal fact is that these great killers of children, diarrhoea, pneumonia, and malnutrition, are beyond the reach of the great weapons of modern medicine'.[53]

Mike Muller, who spent several years researching the impact of medicines on health in developing countries, says he is

> struck by the grand paradox of the existence of an assertive drug industry with its powerful armoury of products alongside this sanitary chaos with its almost total absence of the physical and economic structures essential for 'health'. Just how relevant to health could the products of the research-based pharmaceutical industry be in a community in which the supply of enough food to meet even minimum energy needs cannot yet be assured?[54]

In this context, it is worth remembering what happened in the industrialised North some 100 years ago, when significant changes occurred in health. By the last quarter of the 19th century, mortality in children aged between one and two years began a steady decline, and infant mortality similarly declined about 20 years later. By the time the first modern drugs were introduced, infant mortality was at about 50 per 1,000 live births in the UK, and falling rapidly. The improvement from the turn of the century figure of about 160 deaths per 1,000 live births has been directly attributed by several medical historians to public health measures and social legislation which improved the living standards of working people.[55]

The trend is even clearer when individual diseases are considered. In the UK, for example, tuberculosis was the largest single cause of death in the mid-19th century. Effective treatment began with the use of streptomycin in 1947 and immunisation with BCG vaccine in 1954. By that time, however, mortality from TB had fallen from four per 1,000 in 1838 to less than 0.5 per 1,000 in 1947. Similarly, deaths from the major childhood killers – scarlet fever, diphtheria, measles and whooping cough – fell to nearly their present level by the time any effective drug therapy was developed. In the United States, deaths from acute rheumatic fever, which were averaging about 6 per 100,000 population at the turn of the 20th century, were down to under 2 per 100,000 by the time that sulphanilamide and penicillin were introduced as a treatment in the late 1930s and early 1940s.[56]

Modern drug therapy has been useful in speeding up the rate of decline in the death rates from many of these illnesses in industrialised countries and in speeding up recovery rates from some diseases, but it neither started the dramatic decreases, nor is it necessarily effective in conditions of sanitary chaos and poor nutrition. Indeed, in some instances, diseases that appeared to be on the wane now seem to making a comeback. Tuberculosis, malaria and even pneumococcal pneumonia are more of a problem today than 10 years ago.[57]

At the same time, developing countries are increasingly facing the non-infective illnesses which cause so much suffering and death in industrialised countries – arthritis, heart ailments, circulatory disorders and cancers. Even here, some doubts are being raised about the effectiveness of drugs. Dr Bernard Perey, president of the Canadian Royal College of Physicians and Surgeons, comments that 'the greatest remaining opportunities for prolonging life and for generally improving health are essentially beyond the grasp of medicine', and that improvements will come instead from changes in lifestyle, social conditions and the physical environment.[58]

Can the products of the pharmaceutical industry help to improve health? *Some* of them can, as Costa Rica has shown through the judicious use of vaccines and a handful of other carefully selected medicines. Modern drugs, used well, can help the less developed countries to speed up improvements in health, but they cannot replace a lack of the necessary infrastructure to sustain better health.

# 2.    From discovery to controversy

*The first thing to understand about the pharmaceutical industry is that it is Big Business. Its executives are not members of one of the pompously labelled 'caring professions', nominally devoted to the alleviation of human suffering (much as they would like to be so regarded in the public eye). They are tradespeople, and trades-people of a particularly hard-nosed kind.*

Dr Donald Gould, *The Medical Mafia*[1]

It was a chill morning in mid-December 1985, and the campus of Notre Dame University was covered with snow. Overhead, the sky was blue and the sun was shining; its rays just beginning to melt the edges of the white blanket along the paths through the campus. It was the last morning of a conference on Third World health problems and the role of pharmaceuticals. The participants – American academics, representatives from US pharmaceuticals companies, some clergy and representatives from US groups who had criticisms of the behaviour of the pharmaceutical industry, and I – made our way to breakfast in the crisp December air.

Paul Belford from the US Pharmaceutical Manufacturers Association (PMA) was sitting at a table with two colleagues from US drug companies. I asked if I could join them. Paul looked at me, shrugged, and said 'Sure, if you don't mind having breakfast with "murdering vultures".'

The reference was to a video that had been shown the previous evening, which had been made by the UK-based development organisation Oxfam, in co-operation with Health Action International (HAI), the global network of health, development, consumer and public-interest groups which, since its founding in 1981, had been campaigning internationally for the rational use of drugs. In the film, Dianna Melrose of Oxfam described her experience in a hospital in Peru where she saw an endless stream of drug company representatives waiting to see the doctors. She said they were lined up like vultures. Somehow, overnight, the extra adjective 'murdering' had become added to the comment, and the atmosphere round the table matched the climate outside: cold and frosty. The video's title, *Hard to Swallow*, aptly described the inability of the pharma-ceutical company executives to accept the image of their industry which had been portrayed.

Less than two weeks earlier, Paul and I had been sitting in warmer climes, in Nairobi, Kenya, where a WHO international conference of experts on the rational use of drugs was taking place. There, although the debate always threatened to match the tropical temperature outside, tempers were kept off the boil, and the pharmaceutical industry, particularly its American wing, was reasonably pleased with the outcome. Gerald Mossinghoff, the president of the PMA, told the PMA Board of Directors that 'the international health activists got a lot less out of the conference than they had hoped for or anticipated'.[2]

Such was the concern of the pharmaceutical industry about public perception of its image and about the attacks on it from an increasing number of sources that, at the end of 1985, British pharmaceutical companies were giving 'serious consideration' to renaming the industry the 'health care industry' or the 'health care products industry'. Senior industry strategists believed that the word 'pharmaceutical' had come to be regarded as 'synonymous with high profits, exploitation of the National Health Service and patients, and unsafe products'.[3]

How a highly successful industry that had supplied the world with some life-saving products had arrived at this crisis of identity is a fascinating story. It has all the elements that a fiction writer could want to create a best seller: the determined dedication of research scientists chasing elusive cures, the grateful relief of patients facing death who are told that a new drug offers hope, political intrigues, vast sums of money, bribery, fraud, corruption, all the hoopla and glamour of the mass-marketing advertising scene, sex, and violence. Indeed, Arthur Hailey has created just such a best seller with his novel *Strong Medicine*.[4] Yet, as powerful as Hailey's fiction may be, it is but a shadow of the facts that underlie the history of the pharmaceutical industry.

## The early years of the industry

Although potions and herbs have been used for centuries to treat illness, the pharmaceutical industry is relatively new. By the middle of the 20th century, the international pharmaceutical industry was making its mark on world history through a series of important drug discoveries that were hailed as the tools needed finally to conquer many killer diseases. The roots of the industry can be traced to three streams of endeavour: pharmacy, chemistry and microbiology.

Pharmacy, the oldest of the streams, although now an accepted science, began life as an art, and its practitioners relied as much on faith and hope as on the efficacy of the potions they offered. Nonetheless, pharmacy provided an important heritage for today's pharmaceutical industry: the knowledge that certain plants had a therapeutically beneficial effect on the sick, even if understanding of why and how was lacking.

In addition to this positive legacy, there was a negative inheritance that the industry also adopted in varying degrees. This was best typified in the 19th century by the proliferation of 'patent medicines' – concoctions which were claimed to treat virtually every known illness. One such remedy even went so far as to claim that it could restore virginity 'as often as desired'![5]

By the beginning of the 19th century, the stage was set for the transformation of pharmacy into chemistry, although already Paracelsus three centuries earlier had expounded the philosophy that not only plants but minerals could play a role in treating sickness. His thinking and experimentation led to the use of mercury, lead, sulphur, iron, arsenic, copper and potassium in medicine.[6] Here was the alchemist at work, not extracting gold from less noble substances directly, but pointing the way to the means by which 'gold' could be later found, and in large quantities.

His ideas, while accepted, were not advanced until the first 30 years of the 19th century, when a flurry of chemical innovation occurred. The first discovery was the isolation of morphine from opium in 1806, which stimulated German and French scientists to extract alkaloids such as emetine, strychnine, brucine, veratrine, colchicine, quinine, cinchonine, caffeine, nicotine, atropine and codeine from natural sources. In 1824, Emmanuel Merck set up a chemical laboratory in Germany to produce these alkaloids in quantity and quality; this later became the German company E. Merck. Other companies with similar roots include: Schering AG; the Glaxo subsidiaries Allen & Hanbury and Duncan Flockhart; Abbott; Eli Lilly; Warner Lambert's Parke-Davis subsidiary; Searle; Sharp & Dohme (now Merck Sharp & Dohme) and American Home Products' subsidiary Wyeth.

In 1828, chemistry moved on again with the successful synthesis of an organic compound, urea, from inorganic material, ammonium chloride and silver cyanate. Here was a challenge few scientists could resist. Whereas before, the work of chemistry had been the extraction and purification of natural substances, now an opportunity existed to *create* substances. A. W. Hofmann, who synthesised aniline, and his pupil, W. H. Perkin, who discovered the first fast synthetic coal tar dye, Analin Purple or 'Mauve' in 1856, provided the link between chemistry and the newly emerging field of microbiology. The dye could be used for staining bacteria, thus proving to a sceptical world that such microbes existed. On a more commercial level, the discovery also led to the development of the synthetic chemical dye industry, through concerns such as Bayer and Hoechst in Germany.

At the end of the 19th century, the German dye industry had come up with some important pharmaceutical products. Research in the UK and Germany in the 1880s had shown that certain pyridine salts could fight fevers, while others could combat pain. In 1883, Hoechst produced antipyrine for fever, and in 1888 Bayer introduced phenacetin for fever and pain. Within 10 years a chemist in Bayer's laboratory, Felix Hoffmann, had developed what is probably the most-used drug in the world, aspirin. A collection of chemicals now existed that were known to treat the symptoms of many forms of illness. The 'snake-oil' concoctions of the patent medicine dealers were giving way to a set of reliable drugs with a clear effectiveness, and the pharmaceutical industry was off and running.

## The search for 'magic bullets'

Still, one factor was missing: the ability to *cure* disease. In France, Germany and England in the latter half of the 19th century, Louis Pasteur, Robert Koch and Joseph Lister pushed the doors of science wide open with their work on micro-organisms. The germ theory of disease was born, and Pasteur's success with vaccines against the animal disease anthrax and against rabies, and Lister's success with antiseptics in surgery, were important milestones. In 1905, the final link in the chain was found by Paul Ehrlich, who was working with Robert Koch. His job was to stain cells and micro-organisms with chemical dyes, and he observed that some of the dyes occasionally killed the bacteria. This gave him the idea of manipulating the molecular structure of some of the dyes to enhance their ability to kill bacteria. After the organism which caused syphilis was identified, Ehrlich set out to modify arsenic compounds in the hopes of finding one which would work. More than 600 attempts later, he succeeded, and in 1910, Salvarsan (arsphenamine) was born.[7] So, too, was the modern drug era. Ehrlich described his discovery as a 'magic bullet', an antibody which could find its target within the body by itself, as distinct from the vaccines which stimulate the body's own immune system to fight disease.[8]

It was another 25 years before the next 'magic bullet' made its impact on the world although, in the interim, Alexander Fleming's 1928 blob of penicillium mould was largely ignored by the scientific world and the new pharmaceutical industry. Instead, the next major 'wonder drug' was a substance called Prontosil, a red dye which its discoverer, Gerhard Domagk, found to be effective against pneumonia, scarlet fever, childbed fever, and several urinary infections. In 1935, it was put on the market by IG Farbenindustrie, the German parent company of Bayer and Hoechst. Two years later, much to the chagrin of the company, which had carefully taken out a patent on the dye, the Pasteur Institute in France demonstrated that the active ingredient of the product was not the dye itself but a chemical called sulphanilamide, which separated from the dye once it was in a living organism. Sulphanilamide had been discovered in 1908 but as no one had recognised its germ-killing properties, the patent on the chemical had passed into the public domain. Soon other chemicals from the same family (sulphonamides) were isolated and on the market and, with the recognition of the importance of penicillin by Florey and Chain in 1939, the age of antibiotics was launched.[9]

This creative burst, coming as it did on the eve of the Second World War, set up the pharmaceutical industry for large-scale production of the new wonder drugs. The opportunities for profit, however, seemed to attract more interest than any patriotic desire to help the war effort. In the United States, the director of the US Office of Scientific Research, who was responsible for encouraging drug companies to produce penicillin, noted that the companies had co-operated 'after a fashion'. Another commentator explained that 'the firms were too busy trying to corner patents on various processes in the production of penicillin to produce much of it'.[10] By 1950, the industry was poised for yet another innovative explosion. But, before tracing that development, it is useful to explore a little the shadowy side of the pharmaceutical trade that existed at the beginning of the 20th century, a world where the sparkling gleam of test tubes and the glistening white coats of scientists were less evident than the seamier street-wise trading of organised crime.

## The industry as pusher

Today, the words 'drug trade' conjure up a single image: the relentless pushing of narcotic and mind-stimulating products such as heroin and cocaine. It is an activity associated with a criminal element in society and one that is fought against by many governments. Yet, in its early years the fledgling pharmaceutical industry brushed with this trade. According to a former president of Hoffmann-La Roche, Elmer Bobst, Roche was 'heavily involved in the supply of morphine to the underworld between the two wars'.[11] A trial in Shanghai in 1925 and a subsequent investigation by the League of Nations Opium Advisory Committee confirmed the trade. The chairman of the British delegation to the committee, Sir John Campbell, said that he 'had no doubt whatever that Hoffmann La Roche and Company was not a firm to which a licence to deal with drugs should be given'.[12] Roche was not alone. At the turn of the century, Bayer was promoting heroin as a panacea for infant respiratory ailments.[13] Similarly, as one of the world's leading cocaine manufacturers, Parke-Davis developed 'coca-cordial, cocaine cigarettes, hypodermic capsules, ointments and sprays'.[14]

Slightly less criminal, but no less cynical or unethical, in the 1930s, Wyeth was selling the pain killer amidopyrine as a cure for tuberculosis.[15]

The war years, a time when morals and ethics tend to disappear completely, provide another example of the more grisly behaviour of pharmaceutical companies. IG Farbenindustrie operated a massive chemical plant at Auschwitz. It made use of the inmates of the nearby concentration camp to build and run the plant, and also provided some incidental income to the camp by paying for inmates to act as 'volunteers' for drug testing. In one such test, all 150 subjects died. Undaunted, the company notified the camp that it would require a 'new load' of inmates for the next test.[16] At the Nuremberg war crimes trials, 12 senior executives of the company were sentenced to imprisonment. In 1955, one of them became chairman of the board of Hoechst; in 1956, another became chairman of Bayer.[17]

Episodes such as these are fragments of the pharmaceutical industry's history that are conveniently forgotten by today's executives as they plot the course of the industry in its modern incarnation as a health *care* products industry. Yet as we shall see in later pages, echoes of this past behaviour still remain, albeit in new forms.

## The golden age of drug discovery

The immediate post-war years brought forth a seemingly endless cascade of products from the laboratories and the industry: more antibiotics such as streptomycin, chloramphenicol, tetracycline, ampicillin, erythromycin, cephalosporin; the first tranquillisers; the polio vaccine; phenylbutazone for the treatment of arthritis; isoniazid for the treatment of tuberculosis; and the first oral contraceptives; the role of vitamin B in treating pernicious anaemia was identified.[18] It was a 'golden age of discovery' in the pharmaceutical industry.[19]

In virtually every field, science was showering the world with new developments. Space travel became a reality. Television brought distant places into your home. Communications improved. The brutal devastation of two world wars and the crippling poverty of the Great Depression between the wars were becoming distant memories. There seemed to be no limits to what could be achieved.

Yet in the midst of this euphoria, storm clouds were building. Some were directly related to the activities of the pharmaceutical industry. Some were related to the inability of science to provide all the solutions, and to a lack of understanding about what caused some diseases. Others were rooted in societal and political change that was occurring throughout the world. All would have a sobering effect on the industry.

## The thalidomide disaster

In 1958, the German company, Grünenthal, launched a new sleeping tablet, thalidomide, on the German market under the brand name Contergan. The promotional literature for the drug claimed that it was 'astonishingly safe ... fully harmless'.[20] As early as December 1958 Grünenthal was receiving reports that the drug could cause peripheral neuritis, a serious condition which can lead to severe muscular cramps, weakness of the limbs, and a lack of co-ordination. Much of the damage is irreversible.[21] Within three years, thalidomide was linked with sometimes causing birth deformities if given to pregnant women. In November 1961, following press reports in Germany, Grünenthal withdrew the drug.[22] In the short time it was on the market, at least 8,000 children in 46 countries were estimated to have been born without arms, legs, ears, partially sighted or completely blind. An equal number, perhaps even twice as many, died at birth.[23]

As the tragedy was unfolding, the behaviour of Grünenthal and two companies which were licensed to sell thalidomide, the UK-based Distillers company and US-based Richardson-Merrell, was far from exemplary. To doctors who reported the peripheral neuritis, Grünenthal's response was that it was the first time such side effects were reported. An attempt by one doctor to publish a critical report on thalidomide was delayed thanks to Grünenthal's 'friendly connection' with the editor of the journal to which it was submitted. In another instance, the company hired a private detective to compile information about doctors complaining about the drug. Distillers' sales representatives were instructed not to 'alarm the medical profession' about the possible side effects of the drug by discussing the matter. Although thalidomide was never approved for use in the USA, Richardson-Merrell distributed 2.5 million tablets to more than 1,200 doctors as part of a clinical testing programme. The clinical data subsequently presented to the US Food and Drug Administration (FDA) were 'misleading and concocted in a variety of ways'. One key paper supposedly written by an independent physician was actually written by Richardson-Merrell's medical director.[24]

A positive result of the tragedy was a general tightening of drug regulatory laws and procedures in most industrialised countries. Both France and the USA already had regulatory procedures in effect as the result of earlier therapeutic tragedies. In 1937 in the USA, the death of at least 73 people as a result of taking a sulphanilamide elixir containing ethylene glycol led to the establishment of the FDA. In France in 1952, the death of at least 100 people from a preparation of diethyl tin diiodide resulted in stricter regulatory rules. As a consequence, both countries had failed to approve thalidomide by the time of its withdrawal elsewhere, and were spared most of the tragedy.[25] In the UK, prior to thalidomide there was no regulation, but by 1964 a voluntary system was put into place until the 1968 Medicines Act, which made statutory the voluntary arrangements. In 1970 the Committee on Safety of Medicines was established and began work the following year.[26] Ironically, in Germany, although there were some changes in the lax drug registration system, it was not until a 1976 medicines reform act that controls were brought up to the level of other European countries. Even then, companies were given a 12-year period of grace before they had to submit evidence of safety and efficacy for any products on the market prior to 1976.[27] In May 1962, the World Health Assembly (WHA) approved what was to be the first of many resolutions urging WHO and governments to pay more attention to the control of drugs.[28]

## Under the magnifying glass

If the 20-year period from 1940 to 1960 had been one of unparalleled success for the pharmaceutical industries, the next two decades were to be a time of considerable difficulty. By the mid-1970s, Alfred Hartmann, then vice-chairman of Hoffmann-La Roche, claimed the industry was in a state of siege.[29]

While drug safety continued to be a topic of concern, the economic and political power of the pharmaceutical industry also emerged as a major issue. In the USA, Senator Estes Kefauver's hearings in the Senate Subcommittee on Antitrust and Monopoly, Senator Gaylord Nelson's hearings in the Subcommittee on Monopoly, and Senator Edward Kennedy's hearings in the Subcommittee on Health revealed 'profiteering, price-fixing, promotion of ineffective drugs, questionable advertising and sales techniques, monopoly trading and suppression of information'.[30] In the UK between 1965 and 1967 the Sainsbury Committee had some critical words to say about drug pricing and the poor quality of drug advertising.[31] In 1963, a parliamentary inquiry in Brazil found that local subsidiaries of pharmaceutical transnationals (TNCs) were paying prices anywhere from 500 to 1,000 per cent higher for raw materials purchased from the parent company than the international market price. However, before any action could be taken, the Brazilian government was overthrown by a right-wing coup which 'had the open support of multinationals as well as most local industrialists'.[32] In Colombia, between 1968 and 1970 the degree of overpricing ranged from 350 to 6,500 per cent of international market prices.[33] Sixteen companies were found guilty and were fined well over a million dollars. More importantly for Colombia, the costs of drug imports fell by $1.5 million a month.[34]

In 1970, an investigation in Sri Lanka found that nearly 70 per cent of the 1969 foreign exchange spent on drugs could have been saved by importing the same drugs in bulk at international market prices (or that more drugs could have been purchased).[35] By 1972, a bulk purchasing programme was introduced and within six months the savings on only 52 drugs amounted to 40 per cent of the prices paid in the previous six months.[36] Despite strong opposition from the TNCs – including a letter from the president of the US PMA to the Sri Lankan Prime Minister outlining numerous objections to the scheme which he claimed 'calls into question the Government's position with respect to all foreign investment in Sri Lanka' – and a visit to the Prime Minister from the US Ambassador who indicated that food aid from the US could be put in serious jeopardy by the action being taken against US pharmaceutical companies, Sri Lanka maintained a progressive and rational policy for five years, until the government changed.[37]

It was not surprising that developing countries were having difficulties with drug prices, when similar accusations of overpricing were being made in the countries in which the major drug companies were based. Two classic cases, one in the USA and the other which was taken up initially in the UK, and later throughout Europe, illustrate the considerable market power the pharmaceutical industry was (and still is) able to exert.[38]

## Cornering the antibiotics market

In the early 1950s, two US companies, Pfizer and American Cyanamid, dominated the broad-spectrum antibiotic market thanks to patents on chlortetracycline and oxytetracycline. Then in October 1952, Pfizer discovered the molecular structure of tetracycline, identified it as being therapeutically superior and filed a patent application. In March 1953, Cyanamid followed suit, and in September and October 1953 two other companies, Heyden and Bristol, also filed patents for tetracycline. There was a major difficulty in deciding whether tetracycline was patentable, as it probably was produced as a result of the process already covered by the patent on chlortetracycline. Realising this risk, and not wanting to open up a prolonged legal battle, Cyanamid bought out Heyden's antibiotic division for approximately twice the book value of its assets. In January 1954, Pfizer and Cyanamid agreed that whichever one got the patent would license the other to sell the drug. The assumption was that Bristol, at that time a fairly small company, would not be able to sustain a tough patent fight. Pfizer won the patent, licensed Cyanamid, and Cyanamid agreed to supply Pfizer with bulk tetracycline until its own production facility was ready for mass production. Bristol did fight back, and in a patent hearing in October 1954, the examiner concluded that tetracycline was indeed part of an 'old' process and there should be no interference with Bristol's right to sell tetracycline. Pfizer was given the opportunity to demonstrate that tetracycline could not be recovered from the chlortetracycline process, and set up some tests. The first tests were supposedly stopped part way through, although US government evidence showed that the tests continued, the results were recorded outside normal laboratory records, and that they demonstrated that the patent examiner had been correct. A second set of tests, however, did not produce tetracycline, and Pfizer was able to hold on to the patent. Subsequent examination of the tests by the US government indicated that the test procedure was rigged to minimise antibiotic production. When Pfizer refused to grant Bristol a licence for tetracycline, the company went into production anyway and sold bulk tetracycline to Squibb and Upjohn. When Pfizer sued, Bristol produced a tightly argued statement that suggested that Bristol was in a strong position to expose the possible antitrust activities of Pfizer and Cyanamid, destroy the patent, and claim substantial damages. Pfizer finally granted Bristol a licence in January 1955.[39]

With five companies selling the drug, it would be reasonable to expect some price competition. Remarkably, during the years 1955–9, all five companies offered exactly the same average annual price to retailers. And that price was high. In 1957, for example, 83.7 per cent of Pfizer's operating profit of $23.9 million came from its broad-spectrum antibiotics. Similarly, while the rest of Cyanamid's pharmaceutical division ran at a loss during the early 1950s, the company's broad-spectrum antibiotics generated profits. Between 1960 and 1963, prices began to come down a little, but still in remarkable unity. In 1964, Upjohn slashed its price by 40 per cent, and within another four years, there was finally some competition on the price of tetracycline.[40]

In 1961, the US government started proceedings against Pfizer, Cyanamid and Bristol-Myers for a conspiracy to monopolise and restrain trade. In December 1967, the three corporations were found guilty on all counts. In 1970, an appeal court reversed the convictions, but called for a new trial. A government appeal to the Supreme Court upheld the decision for a new trial. In 1973, the companies were acquitted in the retrial, because the judge felt that the government's evidence of price-fixing was only circumstantial.[41]

## The price of tranquillity

The British government fared slightly better when it went to court over the high prices Roche was charging for its two tranquillisers Librium (chlordiazepoxide) and Valium (diazepam). The situation had some similarities to the earlier antibiotics case in the USA, in that Roche held the patents for both tranquillisers. This assured Roche a position as monopoly supplier in the UK for Librium from 1960 to 1968, and for Valium from 1963 until 1971. Although both patents still had longer to run, the British Comptroller of Patents had issued compulsory licences to two companies who wanted to manufacture the generic ingredients of the drugs, in an attempt to introduce some competition. Roche had refused to issue any voluntary licences. However, the new companies made little impact on the market, and the prices remained high. In 1971, the Monopolies Commission began an investigation, which was finalised in 1973. This found that Roche was charging its British subsidiary exorbitant rates for the raw ingredients of the drugs. It was estimated that Roche had made at least £24 million profit on the drugs between 1966 and 1972, £19 million of which had been repatriated to Roche's home base in Switzerland. This was during a period when the British subsidiary declared small profits, and in two years, 1971 and 1972, actually showed a loss. The British government, in accepting the Monopolies Commission report, ordered Roche to cut the price of Librium by 60 per cent and the price of Valium by 75 per cent. The UK Department of Health subsequently ruled that Roche should also pay back £12 million in compensation for the excessive prices. After more than two years of legal battles, Roche finally settled out of court by agreeing to pay £3.75 million, joining a voluntary price regulating scheme, and promising to increase investment in the UK. In return, the compulsory price cut was scrapped, and prices for the two drugs were allowed to increase to about half their 1970 level.[42]

The UK case stimulated governments in Canada, Denmark, West Germany, Holland and the USA to look into the pricing and monopoly situation of Roche's tranquillisers. In Canada, when in 1969 legislation removed barriers to competition, Roche fought hard to maintain its share of the lucrative hospital market, even to the point of *giving* Valium to hospitals. In total, the company gave away 141 million capsules. The result was that its main competitor, Horner, withdrew from the hospital market. Some company correspondence that emerged in a subsequent legal case in which Roche was found guilty of unfair competition through predatory pricing explained its action: 'It is our feeling that this tactic will not only abort Horner's efforts but serve as a warning to others who seem to be showing an interest in the product.'[43]

### The high cost of vitamins

At about the same time, the European Commission (EC) was building a case against Roche over unfair trading of its vitamin products. Large amounts of information for the case were supplied by a Roche employee, Stanley Adams, who pointed out that Roche and other major vitamin manufacturers had formed 'an illegal price cartel to fix prices, agree levels of production and share the vitamin market between themselves'. The EC decided to focus on Roche's further activity in setting up 'fidelity contracts' whereby purchasers were tied into exclusive contracts with Roche, thus eliminating sales opportunities for many of its competitors. In 1976, Roche was found guilty of unfair trading practices and given a small fine.[44]

Adams was subsequently arrested by the Swiss authorities, at Roche's instigation, and three weeks after the company was found guilty Adams too was convicted on charges of persistent economic espionage and persistently betraying trade secrets. As a result of his arrest, his wife, who had been told that he faced up to 20 years in prison, committed suicide.

### A new economic order?

The pharmaceutical industry's behaviour during its formative years established both a substantial economic basis from which to operate and a mode of operation which persists in some sectors of the industry to this day. For an industry which espouses the benefits of the 'free market', some of its early dealings were more representative of a belief in a market that was carefully controlled – providing it was the pharmaceutical industry itself which determined the controls.

In 1981, Robert Dee, chairman and chief executive of SmithKline, outlined to his colleagues in the pharmaceutical industry his vision of the world as one in which

> an innovative minority conceives the world's technology, raises most of the world's food and produces most of the world's goods. This minority is being challenged by a hostile majority. In my opinion, this hostile majority does not want to trade on fair terms, it wants to trade on its own terms. And those terms are what most reasonable people could only call extortion.[45]

It would be interesting to have a clear definition of what Dee considered fair. Certainly, throughout the 1960s and 1970s, the abuse of power demonstrated by at least some parts of the pharmaceutical industry meshed with rising anger in developing countries about an unfair distribution of the world's resources. This was a major factor in the hostility to which Dee alluded. After centuries of colonial rule, many of the newly independent states were in no mood to be told that they now faced a new form of 'colonial' control. To have the old colonial political bosses replaced by the new captains of industry was not seen as a change, only more of the same. TNCs were increasingly viewed as negative factors in development. Their interests were not those of the developing nations. In the mid-1970s, WHO's Director General, Dr Halfdan Mahler, began to describe the situation as one of 'drug colonialism'.[46]

The increasingly articulate demands of developing countries for a 'new international economic order' that would provide more beneficial trade terms, a greater share of technology, and generally a more just share in the world's resources found sympathetic ears in the industrialised world. Development agencies, religious organisations, some consumer groups, politicians and political parties, the media, some scientists and health workers and many academics began to come to grips with the development debate. One of the key issues, exacerbated by the role of ITT in the downfall of the Allende regime in Chile and by the controversial role of the major oil companies during the shortages in the early 1970s, was the power of TNCs and the apparent lack of control over their activities. Thus, even if the pharmaceutical industry as a whole had had an unblemished record, it would in all likelihood have been dragged into the controversy in some manner.

## Women and health

At the same time, initially in industrialised countries, but increasingly globally, another important political movement was developing which would become a factor in shaping attitudes about the pharmaceutical industry. During the 1960s and 1970s, as a liberalisation of attitudes began to occur in many societies, a women's movement began to emerge that was concerned with looking at women's position in society and exploring the means by which women could develop a more equitable relationship with society. Madeleine Kunin, Governor of the State of Vermont in the USA, notes that it was the relegation of women to ancillary roles in the 1960s that spawned the women's movement. 'Young women, sharing the passion for rebellion and change that the men in their lives espoused, were nevertheless barred from significant roles, and were left with a deep residue of anger which germinated into feminism.'[47]

Barry Gaberman of the Ford Foundation says that

> one of the most compelling global phenomena of recent decades has been the flowering of women's movements and related efforts to improve women's social, political, and economic status ... the universality of women's disadvantage has led to the rise of feminist leaders, institutions, and political movements in virtually every region of the world.[48]

One important focus of the movement was the question of women's health. Many cultural stereotypes about women were evident in the male-dominated medical profession's attitudes towards women, and consequently in the kinds of 'treatment' that it was felt they needed. The Victorian belief that women were physically inferior, in part due to the functioning of their reproductive systems, had become interlaced with Freud's view that women were psychologically inferior, perhaps also because of the psychological taboos associated with reproduction and sexuality. The perception of a woman as emotional, unable to bear pain, particularly the 'natural' pain of childbirth which is often seen in male eyes as both a woman's duty and her highest pleasure and source of fulfilment,[49] leads to a regular diagnosis of her behaving abnormally, and with a large degree of neurosis. As a consequence, many of the illnesses of women were assumed to have no 'real' physical basis, and were treated in an 'irrational and ineffective' manner.[50] One such method has been the excessive prescribing of tranquillisers and antidepressants. In most developed countries, more women than men take tranquillisers. In the UK, the proportion is two to one.[51] The pharmaceutical industry reinforced this stereotype in its marketing of these drugs. A 1975 study found that women were 15 times more likely to appear in advertisements to doctors for mood-changing drugs.[52] One early advertisement for Librium depicted a young woman about to go to university, with the headline: 'A Whole New World ... of Anxiety'.[53] Research from the Philippines in 1986 demonstrated that this reinforcement of stereotypes is still a problem, not only with regard to tranquillisers, but also for a wide range of other prescription and over-the-counter drugs.[54]

One reason why the industry focuses attention on women in its advertising is the recognition that women are the principal health care providers for the other members of their families. Women purchase drugs or collect the prescriptions for their children, partners, parents and other relatives. At the same time, women use more drugs than men, usually in connection with their reproductive functions.[55] It was this latter factor which most helped to direct the attention of the women's movement to the role of the pharmaceutical industry at the beginning of the 1970s. Once again, the trigger was concern over product safety.

## Contraceptive safety

An initial concern was over the oral contraceptive pill, first introduced in the USA in 1960. The pill was a pharmaceutical company's dream: a product to be used, virtually daily, by perfectly healthy people. Women found it to be an effective and, initially for most, a trouble-free way of preventing unwanted pregnancies. In 1965, oral contraceptives provided G. D. Searle with 44 per cent of its total sales.[56] A market analyst in the USA points out that oral contraceptives 'have an incredible profit margin' and are 'among the most profitable of all pharmaceuticals'.[57] By 1969 however, a study in the UK linked the use of the pill to thrombosis (blood clotting) and caused the first major decline in its popularity, 'from which it has never completely recovered'.[58]

A related concern emerged at about the same time over a much older contraceptive technique, the intra uterine device (IUD). In fact, three times in the 20th century, IUDs have come to prominence, only to fall from grace due to their propensity to cause infections. First introduced in 1909 in Germany, their association with infection soon led to their rejection as a form of contraception. A slightly different design in the 1920s also failed to gain acceptance, and by the 1940s most physicians believed that IUDs were simply too dangerous to use. By the 1960s, as the scare about 'overpopulation' in developing countries swept through development circles in the industrialised world, two new arguments were being used to help repopularise the IUD. First, it was claimed that the development of new plastics would make the insertion of IUDs easier and thus eliminate any injury that might provide a source of infection and, second, that should an infection develop, the new antibiotics provided the perfect answer. Women in industrialised countries began taking an interest in these devices, particularly those who had encountered problems with the daily ingestion of hormones in the contraceptive pill. But by the early 1970s physicians in industrialised countries began seeing large numbers of women with pelvic inflammatory disease (PID), and a correlation between it and the IUD was established. In 1974, the Dalkon Shield IUD, which had been specially designed for women who had not yet had children, was linked to the death of several women and was later found to be more likely to cause PID than any other type of IUD.[59]

It was a bad period for contraceptives because in 1970 a cancer scare emerged about yet another one, the injectable hormone depot medroxyprogesterone acetate (DMPA), better known by its brand name Depo-Provera (DP). DP was developed by Upjohn and first clinical trials began in 1963. In 1967, Upjohn applied to the US FDA for permission to market the drug, but animal trials which demonstrated the possible risk of breast cancer, as well as the lack of a significant need for the drug in the USA, led the FDA to refuse the application. Despite this, DP is widely used by at least 2 million women a year, most of them in developing countries. Although the cancer link has never been conclusively proved, controversy over DP's use has been considerable.[60]

## A new way of organising

The deepening anger that was becoming apparent over the low status of Third World countries in the world economic order became meshed with the increasing frustration and anger of the women's movement faced with women's similar low status in society. The issue of population control and the paucity of acceptable forms of contraception provided a unifying focus for women all over the world. In the absence of clear information from the pharmaceutical industry, from the scientific and medical communities and in some cases from governments, women began talking to other women, sharing their experiences about the treatment they received from the medical system, sharing information about the adverse effects of contraceptives and other drugs commonly used by women. Local, regional and international networks of women concerned with health began to develop. Their first objective was to look for self-help solutions, and from that the concept of solidarity with others was an easy step to make. Here was a new model of bottom-up organising taking shape, one that was forcing those in positions of power to pay attention and begin to consider alternative policies.[61]

For the male-dominated, North-based, hierarchically organised pharmaceutical industry, this emerging coalition around development and women's issues was a severe shock. The age-old policy of divide and rule that has been so important to maintaining power structures was being seriously shaken. In Asia, Africa and Latin America – traditionally countries that had had a subservient role to the industrialised nations – people and some governments were beginning to speak with one voice. Similarly women, who traditionally were seen as quiet, submissive and empty-headed, were uniting with a common voice and with powerful arguments and evidence. These links were developing across class, cultural, national and linguistic barriers. They were developing across diverse disciplines and were using information from previously unrelated sources to portray a more comprehensive picture of health and pharmaceuticals than had previously been permitted by the carefully managed flow of information from the industry. They were working in a non-hierarchical manner, avoiding the traditional channels of power-broking if these were too slow and moribund, or sometimes getting to the very heart of them to achieve rapid change in policies. This was seen as a challenge not just to a few drugs, but to the whole structure of society, its values and its processes.

## Inefficient economics

Lewis Engman, president of the US PMA in 1981, described the situation facing the pharmaceutical industry as part of a

> movement toward a new economic order, a movement which touches health care only incidentally, a movement which has as its real goal the redistribution of wealth worldwide and the seizure – by political force if necessary

– of economic power by those with no respect for the profit incentive and the rights of private property on which our society is based.[62]

Consider for a moment the millions of homeless, landless, hungry people scattered around the world. If our *global* society is based on the profit incentive and the rights of private property, is there not something sadly wrong with the way it operates? In 1980, the United Nations asked whether the world economy was working efficiently. It also answered the question:

> By no measure of efficiency is the world economy functioning well.... Existing systems of production and exchange do not seem to work in the interests of people or of their natural environment.... The great mass of people in developing countries suffer because an inefficient world economy is one that is less productive and fair than an efficient one. It slows all efforts at development and prolongs their poverty, hunger and disease.[63]

Today, that inefficiency is, if anything, even more evident. Third World debt amounts to a virtually incomprehensible one thousand billion dollars. The public debt of the USA amounts to two thousand billion dollars. Coincidentally, the world's top 200 TNCs have a combined annual turnover of a little more than three thousand billion dollars.[64]

Although individual pharmaceutical companies have a much lower annual turnover, nonetheless a comparison of turnover of the top 20 pharmaceutical companies with 25 countries whose Gross National Product (GNP) is roughly similar shows some interesting trends for the years 1983 to 1986 (see Table 2.1). The 25 countries had an average yearly increase in GNP of only 1.6 per cent, while the 20 companies had an average annual increase in sales of 8.9 per cent. In other words, economic units such as pharmaceutical companies are expanding their 'economies' at more than five times the annual rate of expansion of similar-sized national economies. In such a situation, it is no wonder that pharmaceutical company executives see little need for a change in the economic structure of the world.

Indeed, one could argue that it is perhaps the pharmaceutical industry which has as one of its prime objectives 'the redistribution of wealth worldwide'. The somewhat cavalier pricing structure of drugs mentioned earlier in this chapter certainly redistributed wealth. And how fundamental is 'health care' to the motivation of the industry? One industry analyst provides a disturbing answer:

> Drugs are big business. Companies prefer to portray their activities as being above the hurly-burly of the consumer world, but the truth is that most drug research and manufacture is and will continue to be in the hands of marketing men, and not in the hands of those who have sworn to abide by the Hippocratic Oath. Profit-oriented multinationals have become so sophisticated in their knowledge of both marketing techniques and health care that the future of chemotherapy and, as they diversify, general medical technology, is their responsibility.[65]

**Table 2.1 Comparison of growth of sales of 20 leading pharmaceutical companies with the growth in GNP of 25 countries whose GNP is close to the turnover of the companies (1983–6) ($ million)**

| Company or country | 1983 | 1984 | 1985 | 1986 | Average yearly change (%) |
|---|---|---|---|---|---|
| Costa Rica | 2,550.0 | 2,975.0 | 3,380.0 | 3,996.0 | 13.9 |
| Bolivia | 3,060.0 | 3,348.0 | 3,008.0 | 3,900.0 | 6.7 |
| Yemen | 3,410.0 | 3,575.0 | 3,740.0 | 3,850.0 | 4.0 |
| Uganda | 3,212.0 | 3,450.0 | 3,565.0 | 3,680.0 | 4.4 |
| **Merck Sharp & Dohme** (USA) | **2,422.0** | **2,656.6** | **2,824.0** | **3,441.0** | **10.9** |
| Honduras | 2,747.0 | 2,940.0 | 3,168.0 | 3,330.0 | 6.2 |
| Cyprus | 2,576.0 | 2,555.0 | 2,653.0 | 3,052.0 | 5.3 |
| **Hoechst** (FRG) | **2,552.7** | **2,295.4** | **2,396.4** | **3,042.6** | **4.7** |
| Mozambique | 3,059.0 | 3,151.0 | 2,240.0 | 3,003.0 | −4.1 |
| Afghanistan (estimated 1984–6) | 2,414.0 | 2,601.0 | 2,805.0 | 2,924.0 | 6.2 |
| Lebanon (estimated 1984–6) | 2,782.0 | 2,782.0 | 2,889.0 | 2,889.0 | 1.2 |
| **Ciba-Geigy (Swi)** | **2,108.7** | **2,059.3** | **2,277.6** | **2,851.2** | **9.1** |
| **Bayer** (FRG) | **2,430.4** | **2,128.9** | **2,267.3** | **2,787.5** | **3.5** |
| Senegal | 2,728.0 | 2,394.0 | 2,368.0 | 2,772.0 | −0.2 |
| Nicaragua | 2,728.0 | 2,666.0 | 2,464.0 | 2,686.0 | −0.8 |
| Iceland | 2,052.0 | 2,204.0 | 2,143.8 | 2,682.0 | 8.1 |
| Albania (estimated 1984–6) | 2,436.0 | 2,520.0 | 2,604.0 | 2,604.0 | 2.2 |
| Papua New Guinea | 2,660.0 | 2,485.0 | 2,380.0 | 2,592.0 | −1.1 |
| **American Home Products** (USA) | **2,333.2** | **2,416.7** | **2,523.5** | **2,560.4** | **3.0** |
| Nepal | 2,512.0 | 2,576.0 | 2,640.0 | 2,535.0 | 0.3 |
| Madagascar | 2,945.0 | 2,522.0 | 2,400.0 | 2,369.0 | −7.7 |
| Haiti | 1,890.0 | 2,080.0 | 2,046.0 | 2,244.0 | 5.4 |
| **Pfizer** (USA) | **1,866.0** | **1,891.0** | **1,961.0** | **2,203.0** | **5.3** |
| **Sandoz (Swi)** | **1,450.4** | **1,405.3** | **1,592.2** | **2,155.1** | **11.5** |
| **Glaxo** (UK) | **n.a.** | **1,400.2** | **2,118.1** | **2,143.2** | **17.5** |
| **Eli Lilly** (USA) | **1,645.8** | **1,664.5** | **1,786.0** | **2,119.8** | **7.9** |
| **Roche (Swi)** | **1,497.0** | **1,411.0** | **1,546.5** | **2115.0** | **9.8** |
| Zambia | 3,596.0 | 3,055.0 | 2,613.0 | 2,070.0 | −20.3 |
| **Abbott** (USA) | **1,599.0** | **1,705.7** | **1,866.0** | **2,057.0** | **8.0** |
| **Warner Lambert** (USA) | **1,405.0** | **1,717.4** | **1,872.0** | **2,041.0** | **11.6** |
| Guinea (estimated 1986) | 1,560.0 | 1,881.0 | 1,952.0 | 1,984.0 | 7.4 |
| **Bristol-Myers** (USA) | **1,505.0** | **1,586.6** | **1,753.0** | **1,961.7** | **8.4** |
| Jamaica | 2,990.0 | 2,645.0 | 2,162.0 | 1,932.0 | −15.8 |
| **SmithKline** (USA) | **1,463.7** | **1,541.6** | **1,654.1** | **1,896.0** | **8.2** |
| **Upjohn** (USA) | **1,326.0** | **1,487.4** | **1,593.0** | **1,863.0** | **10.7** |
| Rwanda | 1,539.0 | 1,652.0 | 1,708.0 | 1,827.0 | 5.5 |
| Congo | 2,091.0 | 1,938.0 | 1,887.0 | 1,782.0 | −5.5 |
| **Johnson & Johnson** (USA) | **1,175.8** | **1,319.7** | **1,439.8** | **1,731.7** | **12.0** |
| **Takeda (Jpn)** | **1,291.0** | **1,297.4** | **2,226.4** | **1,700.0** | **3.8** |
| **Wellcome** (UK) | **n.a.** | **1,240.6** | **1,235.9** | **1,675.7** | **12.9** |
| Niger | 1,392.0 | 1,121.0 | 1,525.0 | 1,638.0 | 3.1 |
| **Boehringer Ingelheim** (FRG) | **1,238.7** | **1,259.0** | **1,309.4** | **1,616.9** | **8.2** |
| Mongolia (estimated 1984–6) | 1,404.0 | 1,443.0 | 1,482.0 | 1,560.0 | 3.4 |
| **Schering-Plough** (USA) | **n.a.** | **1,199.7** | **1274.0** | **1,557.6** | **12.0** |
| Barbados | 1,215.0 | 1,311.0 | 1,389.0 | 1,545.0 | 7.7 |
| Mali | 1,216.0 | 1,099.0 | 1,215.0 | 1,494.0 | 5.9 |

Note: n.a. = not available

Sources: Company sales figures: various issues of *Scrip*, *Scrip Yearbook 1987*, and some 1984/5 figures from IMS data; Country GNP: calculated from UNICEF's *State of the World's Children* reports, 1986–9.

The way that 'responsibility' has been discharged, both in the early formative years of the industry and in its more recent phase of development, provides ample cause for concern. In 1975, Dr Halfdan Mahler, Director General of WHO, presented delegates at the 28th World Health Assembly with a searing indictment of the industry's performance:

> Developed countries are faced with problems of high expenditure on drugs, often due to over-consumption or misuse, and of avoidable adverse reactions. Expenditure on drugs in developing countries, in both the private and public sectors, is much lower in absolute terms than in the developed countries, but is usually much higher in proportion to the total health expenditure. The need to optimize expenditure on drugs, which is widely felt in the developed countries, is therefore vital for developing countries. Resources are often wasted in the purchase of expensive drugs that are only marginally useful, or even totally irrelevant to the solution of countries' main health problems, whereas large segments of the population are in urgent need of essential drugs for disease control and primary health care. In many instances, the lack of these essential drugs is an important constraint on the solution of the health problems of the populations in need.

> Drugs not authorized for sale in the country of origin – or withdrawn from the market for reasons of safety or lack of efficacy – are sometimes exported and marketed in developing countries; other drugs are promoted and advertised in those countries for indications that are not approved by the regulatory agencies of the countries of origin. Products not meeting the quality requirements of the exporting country, including products beyond their expiry date, may be exported to developing countries that are not in a position to carry out quality control measures. While these practices may conform to legal requirements, they are unethical and detrimental to health.[66]

By the end of the 1970s, the stage was set for an intensified international campaign calling for wide-ranging changes in both the marketing and use of pharmaceuticals.

# 3.  Searching for sales

*Our industry produces the enchanted substances that give health
care professionals their real power to cure. And actually, prior to
the Second World War there really weren't too many things that
would help. Doctors could tell you to stay in bed, keep warm, drink
a lot of fluids, and they can make you feel better, but because of the
investments in research and development that our companies have
made, we really are making many diseases obsolete.*[1]
Gerald Mossinghoff, president, US Pharmaceutical Manufacturers Association, 1989

For many years whenever I thought about the pharmaceutical industry and tried
to look for a good example of a company that was responding to real health
needs and focusing its research on useful drugs, I would inevitably turn to the
UK-based Wellcome. It has consistently been engaged in tropical disease
research and has produced a number of drugs of value, some of which have only
a very limited market. It seemed as if here was a company of which one could
be proud, a company that was more concerned with finding solutions to health
problems than with being part of the problem itself.

What happened on the morning I walked into a small pharmacy in the centre
of Nairobi in November 1985 forced me to modify that opinion somewhat. I
was doing some basic research on drugs used for the treatment of diarrhoea, a
serious problem in Kenya. In the previous year, the Kenyan health care system
had recorded 2.5 million cases of diarrhoea, almost certainly an underestimate,
as many cases would be treated by self-medication.

As I often did when checking on drugs commonly used, I gave the young man
behind the counter a story about a fictional nine-month-old child who had severe
diarrhoea. I asked what he would recommend. Without hesitation, he reached
for a package of Wellcome's ADM. On the predominantly blue label was a bright
yellow star which immediately caught my attention. In bold black type in the
star were the words 'contains special formula DIAREX'.

'What's this Diarex?' I asked. The man in the pharmacy picked up the package
and turned it round to look at the ingredients listed on the back. He was silent
for a few moments as he studied the list. Then he looked up and smiled. 'Very
important ingredient,' he said. 'Very powerful, fast acting. It's a special
formula.'

None the wiser, but certainly much more intrigued, I purchased the mixture
and then spent about half an hour with a colleague who was a trained pharmacist

trying to identify this wonderful ingredient. The list on the back of the package was not much help. It described Diarex as 'purified brand of semi-methoxylated polygalecturonic acids', in combination with kaolin (a chalk-like substance which acts as an adsorbent and which, in theory, will absorb toxins in the stomach or intestines). Diarex, we discovered, was nothing more than pectin, which is a stabilising agent derived from citrus fruit peel or from apples, and is commonly found in gelatin.

## Ineffective and expensive antidiarrhoeal products

WHO says that kaolin and pectin 'are not indicated in the routine treatment of acute diarrhoeal disease'.[2] Other experts agree.[3] The American Medical Association (AMA) describes the use of kaolin and pectin as 'unwarranted'.[4] A study of 204 patients with acute non-specific diarrhoea indicated that treatment with kaolin and pectin was 'no more effective than a controlled diet in reducing the frequency or looseness of stools'.[5] Another researcher notes that 'adsorbents (kaolin, charcoal) have no demonstrated effect on either duration or severity of diarrhoea. While not apparently harmful, they detract from more important therapy and should be avoided'.[6]

A survey in 1985 found that 52 per cent of the antidiarrhoeal products listed in prescribing guides for five regions of the developing world contained ineffective adsorbents such as kaolin and pectin.[7]

Wellcome, like many other companies, both national and transnational, had succumbed to the temptation of a huge market potential for a product which cost very little to manufacture. The fact that it was successful in selling an ineffective product was confirmed by a survey of 43 pharmacies carried out in the Nairobi area in 1985, which found that 50 per cent of people asking for a treatment for diarrhoea for a six-month-old baby were given ADM.[8] It is always dangerous to

**Table 3.1 Antidiarrhoeal drugs containing adsorbents in selected prescribing guides (1985)**

| Country, prescribing guide and date | Number of antidiarrhoeal products | Number and percentage containing an adsorbent | |
|---|---|---|---|
| India (*MIMS*, Jun 1985) | 47 | 21 | 44.7 |
| Indonesia (*IIMS*, Feb 1985) | 49 | 22 | 44.9 |
| Middle East (*MIMS*, Apr 1985) | 37 | 21 | 56.8 |
| Africa (*MIMS*, May 1985) | 28 | 18 | 64.3 |
| Caribbean (*MIMS*, May 1985) | 19 | 12 | 63.2 |
| **Total** | **180** | **94** | **52.2** |

Source: Chetley and Gilbert, *Problem Drugs*, p.5 of 'Antidiarrhoeals' section.

extrapolate figures, but it is interesting to assume that of the 2.5 million cases of diarrhoea in Kenya, half of them are treated with ADM. At a cost of at least 14 Kenyan shillings a bottle, this would amount to a sales potential of 17.5 million shillings (approximately $1 million at 1985 exchange rates). A 1 million dollar market for just one drug in one country is clearly worth having a shot at. A more exact figure to consider is the total world market for all antidiarrhoeal products, which in 1983–4 was estimated at $438 million.[9]

A pharmaceutical industry spokesman said in 1983:

> the market for antidiarrhoeals is a huge market and certainly a challenge to the pharmaceutical industry. It is our sincere hope and trust, that our initiatives together with the programmes carried out by WHO, training programmes in universities, research activities, etc., will result in having better drugs and better means of treatment to control the children's diarrhoea.[10]

A leading textbook on gastrointestinal disease points out that, because most diarrhoea is self-limiting, 'specific drugs are neither available nor required'.[11] However, there is an effective treatment, at least a therapy which prevents death from diarrhoea. The principal cause of death from diarrhoea is dehydration.[12] It logically follows that the treatment of dehydration should be the most important therapy used in diarrhoeal cases. There is a simple solution to the problem: oral rehydration therapy (ORT). In essence, this is the replacement of the fluid and mineral losses caused by the diarrhoea. The intake of any fluid is helpful, but a little salt and sugar added to water, or to rice water is even better. It is a therapy whose basic ingredients are not expensive, and are generally available even in conditions of poverty. For those who doubt that a home-made remedy could work, WHO and UNICEF have developed a packaged formula with the correct balance of minerals and sugars which is becoming increasingly available in many countries. Commercial preparations, usually more expensive, are also now on the market. It has been estimated that at least half of all deaths from diarrhoea could be prevented by using ORT, at a cost of little more than 10 cents a treatment.[13] ORT alone is effective in treating 90–95 per cent of all cases of acute watery diarrhoea.[14] It has been described by the *Lancet* as 'potentially the most important medical breakthrough this century'.[15]

A major textbook on pharmacology states that 'in all cases of severe or prolonged diarrhoea, no matter what the cause, the rapid and complete correction of water and electrolyte loss is of the utmost importance'.[16]

Studies from around the world demonstrate the remarkable ability of ORT to reduce the number of deaths caused by diarrhoea. In regions of Guatemala, Egypt, Honduras and India, child deaths from diarrhoea have been halved following the introduction of ORT. In Costa Rica, child deaths from dehydration have dropped by more than 80 per cent in hospitals since ORT was introduced. In Trinidad, child deaths from diarrhoeal infection dropped by 60 per cent in the General Hospital, Port of Spain, in the five years after ORT replaced intravenous feeding as the main treatment for dehydration. In Haiti, the diarrhoea death rate among children brought into the State University Hospital, Port-au-Prince, fell from 40 per cent to 1 per cent after ORT was introduced in 1980. In the remote Teknaf region of Bangladesh, a three-year study of over 30,000 cases of diarrhoeal infection showed that 95 per cent could be successfully treated by ORT.[17] In the UK, one study found that no treatment was as effective as simple rehydration therapy.[18]

One researcher has suggested that approximately $200–300 million is needed to supply enough oral rehydration salts to prevent the majority of deaths due to diarrhoea-caused dehydration.[19] In other words, if approximately the same amount of money that was currently being directed each year to the purchase of inappropriate and ineffective antidiarrhoeal drugs was instead directed to the promotion of the use of ORT, there would be a significant improvement in child health in developing countries.

## Research versus marketing

In September 1985, Wellcome took a full-page advertisement in the monthly journal of the Kenyan Medical Association which proclaimed the company's 'continued research in pursuit of excellence', and included ADM in the list of products which the company was proud to sell to Kenyans.

A product such as ADM has more to do with the marketing side of a company than with its research capabilities.[20] It demonstrates a perennial problem and tension within pharmaceutical companies, and one which has important implications for the people who use drugs. In Chapter 2 it became clear that companies do not often compete on the basis of price differentials to sell their drugs. This leaves two possibilities for competition: original research which produces significant improvements over existing (or even non-existent) therapies; and product differentiation based on marketing skills.

In considering these two areas, some understanding of semantics is useful. Research is a noble field of endeavour. It has positive connotations. Most people equate it with progress, with development, with exploring new areas of thought, of science, of technology. It speaks of dedication, of service to humanity, of bettering human existence. It is a world of ideas, of seeking after truth. Marketing, on the other hand, is the province of charlatans and hucksters, con artists, people who are out to persuade others to buy things they don't need, don't want, and probably can't afford. It deals with manipulation, coercion, persuasion. It is a world of images, of half truths or perhaps even outright lies.

Of course, neither of these stereotypes provides the real story, but they are widely held beliefs. Given the choice of image to portray, most people would opt to describe themselves as being concerned with research rather than with marketing. The pharmaceutical industry is no exception.

Indeed, the justification for high drug prices is that the funds are needed to finance continued research and development (R&D) of new therapeutic substances. Wellcome's 'pursuit of excellence' is an echo that is repeated in many boardrooms around the world and in many industry press statements. In 1989, the New Zealand Pharmaceutical Manufacturers Association actually changed its name to the Research Medicines Industry (RMI) Association and launched a consumer advertising campaign to draw attention to the importance of pharmaceutical research.[21]

## Uneven drug consumption

In order to explore the importance of R&D and its relation to marketing, it is first of all necessary to complete the global picture of the structure of the pharmaceutical industry. As was noted in Chapter 2, some of the world's leading pharmaceutical companies have an economic power base equal to or greater than that of some countries. Taken together, the pharmaceutical industry generated global sales in the region of $160 billion in 1988. That is roughly equivalent to the GNP of a country like The Netherlands. During the 1960s and 1970s, as Table 3.2 indicates, the world market for drugs expanded at a rapid rate, an average annual increase in the 1960s of some 10.7 per cent, rising to 15.4 per cent annual growth in the 1970s. In the 1980s, predicted sales for 1990 suggest that the growth will probably decline to about 7.2 per cent per year, while the final decade of this century could see a growth in markets of only some 6 per cent. (Figures for the 1988 world market are already above the estimate for 1990, however, so the growth during the 1980s and through the 1990s may well be around the 10 per cent per year level. In both Table 3.2 and the subsequent tables in this chapter, considerable caution should be used in interpreting the data. The data have been drawn from several different sources, and it is often unclear in those sources as to how the data were obtained and/or what precisely is meant by the category pharmaceutical sales. In some cases, it refers only to prescription drugs; in others it also includes sales of over-the-counter products; in still others, sales could include other health care products or equipment. Some data, for example those generated by IMS, are based on an audit of sales in selected countries, and vary widely when compared with information from other sources. For example, comparing IMS figures for individual company sales in 1985 with figures cited by *Scrip* shows that IMS was anywhere from 4 per cent above to 70 per cent below *Scrip*'s figures, although in most cases IMS data were lower than those cited by *Scrip*. A further complication is the use of the US dollar as the standard unit of currency. Because of fluctuations in exchange rates, it is difficult to ensure that year-on-year figures are compatible and accurately reflect true sales, especially if the company is not US-based, or does not report its sales in US dollars. Various commentators use different methodologies to attempt to compensate for currency fluctuations, and it is virtually impossible to standardise these across the span of 40 years and over a global market. A further complication is intra-company trading between subsidiaries and parents and between separate corporate entities. This is exacerbated by the increasing tendency for mergers, acquisitions and licensing agreements within the industry, which could lead to some double-counting of sales figures. Nonetheless, with those constraints in mind, the data do at least give a reasonable picture of trends, particularly over time, even if the data for a particular company, country or year might be suspect.)

**Table 3.2 World consumption of pharmaceuticals 1960–85, with estimates for 1990–2000 ($ million)**

| Year | Industrialised countries | Third World | Eastern Europe | Total | Other estimates b | c |
|---|---|---|---|---|---|---|
| 1960 | 5,680 | 820 | | 6,500 | | |
| 1965 | 9,150 | 1,350 | | 10,500 | | |
| 1970 | 15,600 | 2,400 | | 18,000 | | |
| 1975 | 29,700 | 6,300 | | 36,000 | | |
| 1977 | | | | 48,000 | | |
| 1978 | | | | 53,000 | | |
| 1980 | 52,500 | 10,350 | 12,150 | 75,000 | 76,000 | 80,000 |
| 1981 | | | | 87,920 | 76,278 | |
| 1982 | | | | 81,500 | | |
| 1984 | | | | 89,730 | 101,940 | 88,000 |
| 1985 | 74,479 | 19,600 | | 94,079 | 100,000 | |
| 1986 | | | | 110,000 | | |
| 1988 | | | | 130,000 | 160,000 | |
| 1990 | 100,190 | 28,050 | 21,760 | 150,000 | | |
| 1995 | 133,090 | 44,280 | 27,630 | 205,000 | | |
| 2000 | 143,600 | 92,770 | 33,630 | 270,000 | | |

Sources: **1960–75**, Burstall, Dunning and Lake, 'Multinational enterprises, governments and technology; pharmaceutical industry', OECD, Paris, 1981, summary published as *An Industry Like No Other* by Pharma Information, Basle, 1982; **1977**, UNCTC, *Transnational Corporations* (1979); **1978**, Burstall, Dunning and Lake, 'Multinational enterprises'; **1980**, UNCTC, *Transnational Corporations* (1984); **1980b**, *Scrip*, No. 694, reported in *Drugs and the Third World,* German Pharmaceutical Manufacturers Association (1982); **1980c**, Office of Health Economics, quoted by Peretz, 'Pharmaceuticals in the Third World'; **1984**, *Scrip Yearbook 1987*, prescription drugs only; **1984b**, *Scrip Yearbook 1987*, prescription and OTC drugs; **1984c**, *Scrip*, No. 1166/7; **1985**, WHO, *The World Drug Situation* – Third World includes China; **1985b**, *Scrip*, No. 1270/1, p.6; **1988a and b**, *Scrip*, Review Issue 1989, p.7; **1990–2000**, UNCTC, *Transnational Corporations* (1984).

The table also shows a marked disparity between pharmaceutical sales in industrialised and developing countries. Although approximately three-quarters of the world's population currently live in developing countries, they account for only some 20 per cent of pharmaceutical consumption. This is up from about 12 per cent in 1960, and it is estimated that by the beginning of the next century a little more than one-third of pharmaceutical consumption will occur in the Third World.

## Market concentration within the industry

If drug consumption is concentrated in industrialised countries, drug production is even more concentrated. In 1982, only 11.6 per cent of global production occurred in developing countries.[22] The lion's share of production occurred in the USA (21.6 per cent), which together with Japan (17.8 per cent), Germany

(7.3 per cent), France (6.8 per cent), the UK (4.7 per cent), Italy (4.6 per cent), Switzerland (2.6 per cent) and Spain (2 per cent) accounted for two-thirds of the world's production. As a bloc, the EEC countries accounted for just over one-quarter of world production.

Unlike most other international trade involving TNCs, concentration of the market is not immediately evident at the level of individual companies. Although the industry is made up of at least 10,000 individual companies worldwide, only about 100 companies, the large research-based companies, have a significant share of the market. In 1986, the top 50 companies accounted for 63.2 per cent of world pharmaceutical sales, with the top 25 companies

**Table 3.3 Sales rank of major companies (1977–88) and 1988 sales**

| Company and origin | Rank 1977 | 1980 | 1985 | 1986 | 1987 | 1988 | 1988 $million |
|---|---|---|---|---|---|---|---|
| Merck Sharp & Dohme (USA) | 2 | 3 | 1 | 1 | 1 | 1 | 4,983.7 |
| Hoechst (FRG) | 1 | 1 | 4 | 2 | 2 | 2 | 3,958.0 |
| Bayer (FRG) | 3 | 2 | 6 | 4 | 5 | 3 | 3,712.6 |
| Glaxo (UK) | 18 | 18 | 8 | 8 | 3 | 4 | 3,706.2 |
| Ciba-Geigy (Swi) | 4 | 4 | 5 | 3 | 4 | 5 | 3,531.7 |
| American Home Products (USA) | 6 | 5 | 2 | 5 | 6 | 6 | 3,218.0 |
| Sandoz (Swi) | 9 | 7 | 16 | 7 | 8 | 7 | 3,147.0 |
| SmithKline (USA) | 27 | 14 | 14 | 14 | 14 | 8 | 2,975.0 |
| Takeda (Jpn) | 15 | 9 | 7 | 17 | 7 | 9 | 2,840.6 |
| Eli Lilly (USA) | 10 | 11 | 12 | 9 | 9 | 10 | 2,679.8 |
| Abbott (USA) | 19 | 17 | 11 | 11 | 10 | 11 | 2,599.0 |
| Pfizer (USA) | 8 | 8 | 9 | 6 | 11 | 12 | 2,539.0 |
| Warner Lambert (USA) | 7 | 10 | 10 | 12 | 12 | 13 | 2,509.0 |
| Bristol-Myers (USA) | 14 | 12 | 13 | 13 | 13 | 14 | 2,508.8 |
| Kodak[1] (USA) | | | | | | 15 | 2,500.0 |
| Roche (Swi) | 5 | 6 | 17 | 10 | 15 | 16 | 2,410.2 |
| Johnson & Johnson (USA) | 21 | 21 | 19 | 16 | 17 | 17 | 2,338.0 |
| Squibb (USA) | 13 | 15 | 25 | 22 | 22 | 18 | 2,213.4 |
| ICI (UK) | 26 | 23 | 24 | 21 | 23 | 19 | 2,087.6 |
| Rhone-Poulenc (Fra) | 16 | 16 | 22 | 26 | 21 | 20 | 1,980.8 |
| Schering-Plough (USA) | 17 | 20 | 21 | 20 | 19 | 21 | 1,958.0 |
| Boehringer Ingelheim (FRG) | 12 | 13 | 20 | 19 | 20 | 23 | 1,909.2 |
| Sankyo (Jpn) | 39 | 25 | 18 | 25 | 27 | 24 | 1,894.2 |
| Wellcome (UK) | 28 | 22 | 23 | 18 | 18 | 27 | 1,701.1 |
| Beecham (UK) | 20 | 24 | 31 | 36 | 24 | 29 | 1,555.7 |
| Upjohn[2] (USA) | 11 | 19 | 15 | 15 | 16 | | |
| Meheco[3] (PRC) | | | 3 | | 41 | | |

Notes: 1. Kodak purchased Sterling Winthrop in 1988
2. Upjohn's 1988 sales figures not available
3. Meheco, a Chinese company, does not usually figure in international sales figures; but its 1985 sales clearly demonstrate its large size. 1987 figures are for exports only.
Sources: **Rankings calculated from company sales figures: 1977**: UNCTC, *Transnational Corporations* (1979); **1980**: UNCTC, *Transnational Corporations* (1984); **1985–8**: compiled from various issues of *Scrip, Scrip Yearbook 1987*, and some 1985 figures based on IMS data.

accounting for 46.2 per cent of the market. The leading company, Merck Sharp and Dohme, controlled 3.4 per cent of the market.[23] As can be seen from Table 3.3, the composition of the leading companies changes very little over the years. There may be some jostling for position, usually related to a particular company having a 'best-selling' drug on the market, but there are few surprise entrants or departures from the list of leading companies.

Changes that will become more evident in the next few years relate to the growing tendency for mergers among some of the major companies. The first evidence of this appeared in the 1988 listings, which showed that Kodak, by acquiring Sterling Winthrop to add to some smaller pharmaceutical interests, had entered into the top 15 companies. The recent mergers of SmithKline with Beecham, of Bristol-Myers with Squibb, of American Home Products with A.H. Robins and the planned merger of Rhone-Poulenc with Rorer will affect the listings by displacing some of the German and Swiss companies from the top of the table.

Stability among the market leaders is a common factor in most TNC-dominated industries; but, as Table 3.4 shows, in other fields the number of companies controlling the market is much smaller. One reason for this apparent lack of concentration in the pharmaceuticals market is the nature of the market itself. Individual companies rarely, if ever, compete across the whole range of pharmaceutical products available on the market. Most companies tend to concentrate on specific therapeutic categories: analgesics (pain killers), antibiotics, hormones, vitamins and minerals, cardiovascular drugs, vaccines, anti-cancer products, and so on. In 1985, the top four companies controlled 41.7 per cent of the market for anti-asthma drugs, 49.4 per cent of the market for psycho-therapeutic drugs, 64.4 per cent of the market for anti-cancer drugs and 88.5 per

**Table 3.4 Concentration of TNCs in selected product markets**

| Product | Number of TNCs | % share of market |
|---|---|---|
| Refined oil | 7 | 40 |
| Iron ore | 7 | 50 |
| Copper | 7 | 23 |
| Bauxite | 6 | 45 |
| Aluminium | 6 | 46 |
| Bananas | 3 | 75 |
| Vehicles | 8 | 76 |
| Tractors | 10 | 70 |
| Agricultural machinery | 11 | 73 |
| Tyres | 6 | 70 |
| Cigarettes | 7 | 59 |
| Powdered baby milk | 4 | 67 |
| Nickel | 4 | 60-64 |

Sources: Jenkins, *Transnational Corporations and Uneven Development*, p.40; Chetley, *The Politics of Baby Foods*, p.19.

cent of the market for anti-ulcer drugs.[24] The evidence of concentration is even more striking in the production of bulk drugs or raw materials. Of the 550 bulk medical chemicals produced in the USA in 1981, only six were manufactured by more than three companies, while nearly 430 were available from a single domestic source.[25]

## Financing research from profits

Concentration starts even further back, at the research stage and, not surprisingly, the companies with the highest levels of sales tend to be those which do the most research. The research is financed out of profits and the pharmaceutical industry is extremely profitable. During 1988, for the fourth year in a row, the pharmaceutical industry in the USA led the *Fortune* 500 companies in terms of its net profit on sales and on assets, with median figures of 13.5 per cent and 13.1 per cent respectively. It also topped the *Fortune* list on return on equity for the second year running with a median return of 23.5 per cent.[26] In fact, throughout the period 1970–84, the US pharmaceutical industry consistently outperformed all other manufacturing industries in terms of its pre-tax profit on sales (see Table 3.5).[27] During the period, average pre-tax profits in the pharmaceutical industry ranged from a low of 15.6 per cent in 1981 to a high of 19.3 per cent in the years 1974, 1975 and 1983 against a low of 5.3 per cent in 1982 and a high of 8.9 per cent in 1978 and 1979 for all industries. Earlier data from 1950–65, based only on the 'leading' companies (anywhere from 8 to 12) in each manufacturing group, also indicate a virtually consistent pattern of higher profitability in the pharmaceutical industry in terms of return on equity.[28] These data prompted the director of the US Federal Trade Commission's Bureau of Economics to comment in 1967 that 'the pattern of consistently high profits indicates that large drug companies occupy a unique position in the American economy',[29] a position which they have managed to maintain to the present. In 1988 the 10 most profitable pharmaceutical companies in the world recorded profit margins on pharmaceutical sales ranging from 29 to 66 per cent.[30]

Among some of the leading companies, there is a clear trend towards increased spending on R&D, as Table 3.6 indicates. *Scrip* suggests that among

**Table 3.5 Profit on sales (%) for the US pharmaceutical industry compared to all US industries (1970–88)**

|  | Pre-tax (1970–84) | | | | Net (1985–8) | | | |
|---|---|---|---|---|---|---|---|---|
|  | 1970 | 1975 | 1980 | 1984 | 1985 | 1986 | 1987 | 1988 |
| Pharmaceuticals | 17.2 | 19.3 | 18.6 | 19.1 | 10.4 | 13.1 | 13.2 | 13.5 |
| All industries | 6.8 | 7.5 | 7.7 | 7.1 | 3.9 | 4.1 | 4.6 | 5.5 |

Sources: **1970–84**: Redwood, *The Pharmaceutical Industry*, p.216; **1985–8**: *Fortune*, 27 Apr 1987, 25 Apr 1988, 24 Apr 1989.

the 30 companies spending the most on R&D, the average R&D as a percentage of sales rose from 9 per cent in 1981 to 10.4 per cent in 1984.[31] In the USA, the pharmaceutical industry has increased its R&D expenditure from 3.7 per cent of sales in 1951 to 12.5 per cent in 1985,[32] and 14.3 per cent in 1989.[33] During the 1950s, R&D expenditure averaged 5.8 per cent, in the 1960s it was up to 9.1 per cent and stayed at that level through the next decade, while during the first six years of the 1980s, it has averaged 11.2 per cent. On a more global basis, Table 3.7 indicates what the entire industry spends on R&D in relation to its world sales. Aside from a slightly suspect figure for 1981, it seems clear that the global

**Table 3.6 Percentage of sales spent on research and development in leading companies (1970–88)**

| Company and country | 1970 | 1980 | 1985 | 1986 | 1987 | 1988 |
|---|---|---|---|---|---|---|
| Abbott (USA) | 5.9 | | | | | |
| American Home Products (USA) | | 2.5 | | | 11.0 | |
| Bayer (FRG) | | 4.3 | | | 22.5 | 12.1 |
| Beecham (UK) | 3.6 | | | 12.0 | | |
| Boehringer Ingelheim (FRG) | 9.0 | 11.0 | 16.1 | 18.5 | 20.0 | 19.2 |
| Bristol-Myers (USA) | | 6.8 | 13.8 | 15.5 | 14.5 | 14.6 |
| Ciba-Geigy (Swi) | | 12.0 | 15.0 | 15.0 | 18.0 | |
| Eli Lilly (USA) | 10.3 | 7.8 | | | 15.0 | |
| Farmitalia Carlo Erba (Ita) | 1.3 | | | | | |
| Glaxo (UK) | 3.1 | 8.8 | | | 11.2 | 12.6 |
| Hoechst (FRG) | | 4.4 | 13.8 | 13.9 | 15.5 | 14.9 |
| ICI (UK) | | | 12.0 | 13.0 | 14.0 | 14.5 |
| Johnson & Johnson (USA) | | | 15.1 | 15.3 | 16.9 | 16.5 |
| Merck Sharp & Dohme (USA) | 9.2 | 8.6 | | | 12.0 | |
| Pfizer (USA) | | 5.3 | | | 13.0 | |
| Rhone-Poulenc (Fra) | | 4.5 | | | 15.7 | 12.5 |
| Roche (Swi) | 7.5 | 11.8 | | 22.8 | 20.7 | |
| Roussel-Uclaf (Fra) | 6.7 | | | | | |
| Sandoz (Swi) | 8.9 | 12.7 | 13.3 | 13.6 | 14.1 | 14.3 |
| Schering AG (FRG) | 6.3 | | | | 16.0 | |
| Schering-Plough (USA) | 5.2 | | | | | |
| SmithKline (USA) | 8.9 | 7.7 | 10.9 | 11.9 | 11.7 | |
| Squibb (USA) | | | | | | 12.3 |
| Upjohn (USA) | 10.6 | | | | 18.0 | |
| Warner-Lambert (USA) | | 6.2 | 8.7 | 8.9 | | |
| Wellcome (UK) | 6.8 | | 13.2 | | 18.0 | |
| Average: | 7.1 | 7.4 | 13.2 | 14.8 | 15.5 | 14.4 |
| No. of companies | 14 | 16 | 10 | 10 | 20 | 10 |

*Sources*: **1970**: Redwood, *The Pharmaceutical Industry*, – based on group R&D/group sales, Glaxo = 1971; **1980**: PAHO, *Policies for the Production and Marketing of Essential Drugs*; **1985**: *Scrip*, No. 1,166/7, 25 Dec 1988/1 Jan 1989; **1986**: *Scrip*, No. 1,270/1, 1/6 Jan 1988; **1987**: *Scrip*, Review Issue 1988 and No. 1,393, 10 Mar 1989, p.9; **1988**: *Scrip*, Review Issue 1989.

**Table 3.7 Research and development expenditure as a percentage of total world drug sales (1980–86)**

| Year | World drug sales ($ billion) | R&D total ($ billion) | R&D as % of sales |
|------|------------------------------|-----------------------|--------------------|
| 1980 | 75–80 | 5 | 6.3–6.7 |
| 1981 | 76–88 | 8 | 9.1–10.5 |
| 1982 | 81.5 | 5.5 | 6.7 |
| 1983 | 85 | 5.5 | 6.5 |
| 1984 | 88–102 | 6.5 | 6.4–7.4 |
| 1986 | 110 | 7 | 6.4 |

Sources: World drug sales taken from estimated world market in Table 3.2: R&D expenditure from: **1980**: Taylor, *Medicines, Health and the Poor World*, p.35; **1981**: Peretz, 'Pharmaceuticals in the Third World', p.262; **1982** and **1984**: WHO, *The World Drug Situation*, p.35; **1983**: IFPMA, *The Need To Inform*, p.9; **1986**: IFPMA, *Health Horizons*, No. 1, May 1987, p.1.

average is around the 7 per cent mark, and has consistently stayed there through the 1980s, although a 1989 estimate suggests it has reached 10 per cent of a global sales figure of approximately $150–160 billion.[34] In other words, it is probably running at about 50 to 60 per cent of the net profit figure of the industry and could therefore be increased considerably if necessary.

In the same way that one has to look beneath the surface of the industry to discover the oligopolistic nature of the pharmaceutical market, so too, more careful scrutiny of the research budget reveals some interesting characteristics. The two usual methods of indicating research activity – the amount spent on it and the number of new chemical entities (NCEs) introduced – both have some inherent difficulties.

First of all, even for R&D to remain at a constant 'real' level within the industry, the expenditure would need to increase over time to compensate for inflation and the increased cost of salaries, materials and equipment. As well, the number of safety and efficacy tests now required by leading drug regulatory authorities has increased, as has their complexity. In every country where major pharmaceutical research is carried out, statistics exist that demonstrate the increased cost and time needed to bring new drugs to the market. In the UK, for example, in 1963 it took about three years and £2–3 million to develop and bring a new drug to the market; by 1987–8 the same process was estimated to take 7–10 years and cost £50 million. In the USA, development time has similarly increased from 2 to 7–10 years and in cost from $54 million in 1976 to $75–100 million in 1985. The PMA has suggested that in 1986, the cost was nearer $125 million ($65 million out-of-pocket expenditure and $60 million as opportunity cost).[35] More generally, for the industry as a whole it has been estimated that in constant value the cost has risen from $6.5 million before 1962 to $45–60 million in 1980, excluding capital expenditure, with development times increasing from 3–5 years to 9–12 years during the same period.[36]

Using the PMA's own figures on the amount spent by the US pharmaceutical industry on R&D for each year from 1951 to 1985, it becomes possible to look at what the research dollar could buy. During the 1950s, US R&D expenditure would have been sufficient to turn out 145 NCEs (assuming a cost of $6.5 million per NCE); in the 1960s, assuming a rough average of $25 million per NCE, about 140 could be developed; in the 1970s, with a cost of about $50 million per NCE, a little over 200 could be developed; in the first six years of the 1980s, at a cost of about $100 million each, approximately 170 NCEs could be developed.[37] Actual production however, does not bear out these estimates. Between 1961 and 1985, US-based companies introduced about 424 NCEs onto the global market, against a prediction of 510.[38] While the research dollars spent indicate that NCE introduction should be increasing (from about 14 per year in the 1950s and 1960s to double that number in the 1980s), the actual production suggests a decline. The overall average of NCE introduction during the 25-year period is about 17 per year, but in the 1980s it is only some 14 per year. As Dr Albert Bowers, chief executive of Syntex, pointed out, between 1977 and 1987 R&D expenditure by US companies quadrupled, yet the same number of NCEs were approved by the US FDA in both years. There was no corresponding increase in the availability of new drugs.[39]

That such a slowdown should occur is not surprising, and it is not simply related to the money spent on research. By the beginning of the 1970s, the industry had come to a 'knowledge plateau'.[40] The boom years immediately following the Second World War had exhausted most of the more obvious lines for research investigation. By the beginning of the 1980s, however, signs were evident that the industry was on the threshold of a new 'golden age of productivity', in part due to a better understanding of the way in which the body functions, how disease is caused and what chemicals affect physiological processes. The approach to R&D has also shifted somewhat. Whereas in the past, drugs were generally developed by a screening process whereby a series of chemicals were tested to see what effect they had and whether that effect was both therapeutic and safe, drug development today is more often focused on first deciding what effect is required and then determining what type of chemical will achieve it.[41]

Buried deep in the R&D figures is the fact that very little of the money spent actually goes on this type of basic research. The OECD estimates that only some 9.5 per cent of the industry's total research costs are devoted to basic research.[42] Certainly, the lion's share of the R&D budget is devoted to the 'D', the development of the drug – its clinical testing and preparation for the market. Several commentators have suggested that the time has come to separate the pure research activity from the development process.[43]

## Research on Third World diseases

Also buried is the amount of research expenditure devoted to the disease problems of developing countries. Although some drugs – pain killers, antibiotics, contraceptives, and so on – have applications in both the industrialised and the developing world, some specific disease conditions are primarily sited in the Third World. The most generous estimate of the amount of the total research budget devoted to these conditions is less than 4 per cent.[44] Thus, at today's prices only about three new drugs a year could be developed that are specifically relevant to disease conditions in developing countries. One study in 1981 identified 87 diseases specific to developing countries, of which vaccinations were available for 10 and satisfactory drug therapy was available for another 23. No drugs existed to treat 32 diseases and the remaining 22 could only be treated with very unsatisfactory drugs with toxic side effects.[45]

Mike Muller points out that the industry's research is funded by the profits made on drug sales and the level of research spending is calculated when companies fix their prices. In other words, part of the price of every medicine is effectively a company-imposed research tax.[46] If consumers in developing countries are purchasing just over 20 per cent of the world's supply of drugs at the moment, they are receiving very little return on this 'research tax'.

The drug companies' lack of interest in the problems of the Third World was clearly illustrated by the former president of Parke-Davis. When he took over the direction of the company he found that '50 per cent of the research at Parke-Davis during that time was focused on exotic Third World diseases. I steered it into more commercial applications.'[47] In 1982, the industry-funded Office of Health Economics (OHE) in the UK held a conference on the 'Second Pharmacological Revolution'. OHE director George Teeling-Smith explained that the meeting would only be concerned with 'pharmaceutical innovation relevant to the advanced world'. As Melrose points out, the implication seems to be that the advances in pharmacological innovation foreseen in the industry's new 'golden age' are not relevant to most of the world's population.[48]

The situation was such that WHO's Director General described a conference he attended where an industry spokesman said that

> the production of vaccines and sera is so competitive that they were losing interest in it. What conclusion can you draw from that? When you want health for all and want to prevent six million children from dying from tuberculosis, whooping cough, diphtheria, measles and polio each year. In order to get that you need a vaccine price that is low. But when the price is low, you can't get the products. So the conclusion is that we can no longer treat these vital components of people's health as normal commodities in the market place.[49]

## Determinants of research expenditure

This is touching the heart of the argument. What is the research for? Who makes the choices as to which drugs to develop and market? What influences those choices?

Redwood identifies two possible factors, which he defines as the concept of 'eternal hope' and the much more straightforward 'competition'.[50] Eternal hope springs from the recognition that finding a major new drug can generate enormous profits and encourage confidence in the company from investors. The dramatic impact of drugs such as propranolol, cimetidine and ranitidine in recent years has helped to change the fortunes of three major drug companies – ICI, SmithKline and Glaxo – as well as their positions in the leaders' table in terms of sales. The importance of new drug launches has been underlined in *Financial World*, which in 1984 pointed out that 'the wise investor will look for companies that depend less on mature products that are going off patent and more on a good new-drug flow'.[51] The title of the article, 'Prescription for profits: be selective, be careful', conveys a message to both investors and the people who make the decisions in pharmaceutical companies about how to spend the research dollars.

The impact of the financial community on the pharmaceutical industry is an important one. One of the difficulties with this influence is the short-term vision of most financial institutions. Although Glaxo's chairman, Sir Paul Girolami, argues that 'there is no contradiction between long-term vision and good short-term financial results',[52] for most investors the next quarter's financial returns, or at most the prospects for the next year, figure heavily in the calculations of whether a pharmaceutical company is worth investing in. The simple prospect of Wellcome having a possible treatment for AIDS with azido-thymidine (Retrovir) led to a 260 per cent increase in Wellcome's share price between the first time the drug came to public attention, in late 1986, and March 1987 when it was licensed for use in the UK.[53] Within a year, concern was being expressed in the business press that Wellcome might not be able to secure the patent rights on the drug and over its decision to divert resources away from the development of two other drugs in order to concentrate on anti-viral research.[54] By the end of 1988, although Retrovir was on the market and was demonstrating some usefulness in the relief of AIDS symptoms, Wellcome's share price was lower than it had been before the drug was launched.[55] The expectation was valued more highly than the reality.

## The search for sameness

The other reason for R&D – competition – at first glance could simply be seen an extension of the eternal hope principle. Finding a block-buster drug shuts out the competition in a particular therapeutic market. But at the same time, it stimulates competitors to find another drug that is similar and thereby grab a piece of a lucrative market. This helps to explain why so little basic R&D is done by the industry. Finding a significantly important therapeutic substance is a long-shot. It takes time; it takes money. And the exclusivity of the market is being eroded all the time, thanks to the way patents operate.

A patent is applied for very early in the drug development process, but it may be another eight to ten years before that drug has been through sufficient tests to identify its market niche, demonstrate that it has sufficient efficacy and prove a reasonable degree of safety in order to be licensed for sale. Since many countries only grant patents for a period of some 16 to 20 years, this may leave only another eight to ten years in which to recoup the investment on the R&D. The time involved in developing an original drug, in doing the fundamental research, is all lost time as far as sales potential is concerned. As Charles Medawar points out:

if you want to have the maximum time in the market where you have monopoly advantage, there is obviously an advantage to taking less time in research, and therefore in duplicating existing principles. If there is already a core of information about the kind of drug you are working on, let's say a benzodiazepine tranquilliser or an NSAID [non-steroidal anti-inflammatory drug], that gives you an advantage.[56]

Not only that, but by modifying an existing drug, either by changing a molecule slightly, or by combining one substance with another, it becomes possible to take out a new patent on the product. Thus, much of the R&D expenditure goes on imitative research, producing the so-called 'me-too' drugs.

The story of Sir James Black, the inventor of two of the world's best-selling drugs – propranolol and cimetidine – throws some light on the way in which the industry regards research and where its priorities lie. While working with ICI after discovering the beta-blocker propranolol, which has proven to be of value in treating heart and vascular conditions, Sir James realised that it should be possible to develop other drugs working on similar principles to deal with other illnesses. He was particularly interested in stomach ulcers and wanted to develop a blocker that could prevent acid secretion in the stomach, known to be the cause of ulcers. ICI, however, was not interested in moving into a new area of research. Instead, the company wanted another beta-blocker that offered marginal improvement over the original drug, so that ICI could extend its control of the heart drug market. Sir James left and joined SmithKline, which was prepared to pursue the research on ulcers. Even there, all was not well. Sir James discovered cimetidine only weeks before the company planned to cancel the research work.[57]

When Sir James and two other researchers, Gertrude Elion and George Hitchings whose work on the metabolism of disease organisms and cancer cells has formed the basis for the development of several drugs, were awarded the 1988 Nobel Prize for Medicine and Physiology, the IFPMA proudly stated that this represented 'an important step forward in international recognition of pharmaceutical research as a major area of human progress and a significant indication of the innovative capacity of the industry'.[58] It was the first time in nearly 50 years that the prize had been awarded to researchers from within the industry.

Another Nobel Prize winner, Professor Sir John Vane, who received the award in 1982 for his work on the mechanism of action of aspirin and the discovery of prostacyclin, describes similar corporate short-sightedness over the development of the world's best-selling antihypertensive drug, captopril (Capoten). While at the Royal College of Surgeons, Sir John and his colleagues discovered that an extract of venom from a Brazilian snake inhibited the angiotensin-converting enzyme (ACE). This enzyme transforms an inert blood particle into a potent constrictor, which in turn has an important effect in raising blood pressure. Sir John was acting as a consultant to Squibb at the time and suggested to the company that ACE-inhibition could be the basis of a new antihypertensive drug. Company scientists took up the challenge and managed to isolate a possible injectable substance. But marketing executives tried to kill the project as they could see no commercial future for it.[59] Eventually, subsequent research led to the development of an oral version, captopril, which in both 1987 and 1988 achieved global sales of over $1 billion a year.[60]

One of the statistics which the industry uses to impress on the world the importance of its research activity is that 88 per cent of the NCEs introduced between 1950 and 1969 came from the industry rather than from government or academic research.[61] However, simply counting the number of NCEs introduced each year fails to tell us anything about the kind of research that is carried out. A more qualitative study is required to ascertain the value of this research in terms of improving health care. The *Economist* reported in 1974 that of the 1,500 drug patents filed in 1972, only 45 were genuinely new innovations, while another 150 were major modifications; the remaining 87 per cent were purely imitative.[62] A USAID-financed study in 1981 concluded that as many as 70 per cent of the drugs on the world market are inessential and/or undesirable products.[63] A comprehensive UN study in South East Asia in 1980 said that health priorities were not being properly cared for and that the consumption of drugs in the region was 'extremely inefficient and wasteful'.[64] A 1984 UN study found that in Mexico, Kenya and Malaysia, the products marketed by transnational pharmaceutical companies 'did not correspond to the major health requirements and priorities of each country'.[65] An evaluation carried out by the US Food and Drug Administration between 1967 and 1984 on 3,443 individual drug products which had been licensed prior to 1962 found only 12 per cent that could be rated as effective for all the indications claimed; 40 per cent of the products studied had *no* effective indication.[66] A US Senate inquiry found that of the 348 new drugs introduced by US manufacturers between 1981 and 1988, 292 made 'little or no' contribution to therapy and only 12 (3.5 per cent) were rated as providing an important therapeutic gain.[67] A French study of 508 NCEs marketed in the world between 1975 and 1984 found 70 per cent offered no therapeutic improvement over existing products.[68] An assessment of the 53 NCEs introduced worldwide in 1988 found only 4 (7.5 per cent) which were 'breakthrough products'.[69] In the UK in 1987, 17 per cent of the 2,357 branded products listed in the *British National Formulary* were considered 'less suitable for prescribing'.[70]

Also in the UK, two doctors from the Department of Health and Social Security (DHSS) analysed the 204 NCEs granted product licences between 1971 and 1980 and concluded that they were generally for diseases which are 'common, largely chronic, and occur principally in the affluent Western society'. When they did a further analysis of the 103 applications for product licences between 1973 and 1977, they found 4 per cent were fully innovative, 31 per cent were semi-innovative, and 65 per cent were non-innovative. They concluded that research was being 'directed toward commercial returns rather than therapeutic need'.[71]

One of the authors of the study, Dr John Griffin, left his position in the medicines division of the DHSS in July 1984 to take up a job as director of the ABPI. One of his first tasks was to lead industry opposition to an effort by the British government to introduce a more rational approach to the use of drugs. A strong argument in the campaign, estimated to cost more than £500,000, was that the government was putting 'Britain's research-based industry in jeopardy'.[72]

It could be argued that it is the industry itself that is jeopardising its future prospects. Medawar points out that a further reason why drug research often avoids following innovative tracks is the inability to predict what the world market will be like by the time the drug reaches the market.

> When companies talk about the difficulties of innovation, they're not talking about what happens in the laboratory. It seems to me the *real* difficulty with innovation is knowing how you are going to get back your costs. What are going to be the principles and practices of drug use? How will physicians be behaving? If in 1975 we looked forward and guessed what the market would want, what the market would be, we probably would have got it entirely wrong. We would have missed the growth of HAI. We would have missed the WHO essential drugs programme. You don't know about the political or economic climate. A government may change, or a government may fall. You don't know who your competitors will be. You don't know if company A will have swallowed up or bought up company B.[73]

In that sense, although the 'eternal hope' principle is always there, the bottom line is the far less starry-eyed reality of recovering the investment and putting the balance sheet in order. Playing safe and following old research lines is a way of ensuring reasonably steady returns, even if it means foregoing the spectacular results that an innovative drug can offer.

On the other hand, the US PMA argues that the incremental advances associated with me-too drugs form the basis for future major therapeutic breakthroughs. It argues that the full therapeutic value of a new drug cannot be adequately judged without extensive practical experience, and that experience often demonstrates the value of a drug for a range of additional indications. Also, the effect of the drug on patients and on disease conditions can lead to a better understanding of the disease process and ultimately to new and better therapy.[74] The PMA buttresses its argument by providing a list of 48 drugs approved for use in the USA between 1962 and 1984 for which an additional 82 indications were later approved. What such a list fails to do, however, is clarify whether the drug is significantly better than an existing treatment.

WHO offers a different slant on the argument. It says that the fact that in 1982 there were 78 benzodiazepine tranquillisers, 53 NSAIDs similar to ibuprofen, 57 penicillins and 42 cephalosporin antibiotics at an advanced stage of development

> offers revealing insight into the prevalence of repetitive research patterns. The thesis that molecular manipulation not infrequently offers dividends in terms of improved therapeutic performance is a valid but vulnerable argument. Large numbers of essentially interchangeable marketed products render effective therapeutic comparison impracticable. They create a situation in which therapeutic choice is determined by advertising pressure rather

than objective evidence and, in the longer term, they threaten to frustrate evaluation of therapeutic performance.[75]

Clifford Jellett, of Louis Harris International Medical Surveys, confirmed this from a marketing perspective when he said that '*real* therapeutic advance will be a rare event. It will become increasingly difficult to differentiate new products from existing agents.'[76]

# 4. The importance of marketing

*Companies who peddle drugs unrelated to real health care must be exposed and excluded from the market. Advertising must be controlled in the common good. This is draconian but where health means money and profit there is no other better way.*
Barry Desmond, Minister for Health and Social Welfare, Ireland, from a speech at the 12th World Conference on Health Education, Dublin, 1 September 1985

In November 1983, while I was attending a Health Action International (HAI) meeting in Penang, Malaysia, a colleague passed me a current copy of the *Philippine Index of Medical Specialities* (PIMS). He made a comment about how difficult it was to achieve a rational use of drugs with so many products on the market, and with many of them being so badly promoted.

The topic under discussion during that particular session was how to respond to the voluntary code of pharmaceutical marketing introduced by the IFPMA in 1981.[1] The IFPMA claims that its code is the 'visible, public declaration of the commitment of industry to ensuring that its products are marketed responsibly and on the basis of sound scientific information and principles'.[2] Like most such industry-drafted voluntary codes, it tended to simply codify existing practices.[3] As a former director of Shell pointed out, voluntary codes of conduct 'tend to be placebos which are likely to be less than a responsible company will do of its own volition and more than an irresponsible company will do without coercion'.[4]

Many of the 'provisions' of the IFPMA code are vague generalisations that are open to wide interpretation and are thus difficult to use as guidelines. The most straightforward provision is that 'the word "safe" must not be used without qualification'.

In a few minutes, I flicked through the copy of PIMS and found 11 advertisements which I considered did not meet even this most minimal of provisions. A short time later I submitted the 11 advertisements, along with a few others, to the IFPMA as a complaint.

The reply I received from the IFPMA was illuminating. In six of the cases, both the companies concerned and the IFPMA agreed that the code had been ignored and 'corrective action' was taken. In the remaining five cases, the companies and the IFPMA argued that the word 'safe' had been sufficiently qualified so as not to be a breach of the code. One such example of qualification was in an advertisement for Boehringer Ingelheim's Bisolcillin (bromhexine and ampicillin) which was described as 'remarkably safe'.[5]

During the course of research for this book and for some other publications on pharmaceuticals between November 1985 and April 1988, I came across 106 instances when that provision was broken in advertisements in prescribing guides and medical journals around the world.[6] These were not the result of a comprehensive survey, but rather the obvious manifestations of an industry unable to avoid the use of a word which has powerful marketing potential.

## Defining a difference

The sameness of so many drugs explains the fundamental importance of marketing. It is a slightly paradoxical situation: because drugs are very similar, marketing helps to define a supposed difference, and therefore becomes important; and because marketing is important, it helps to identify the niches into which new drugs could fit and begins to identify the type of research that should be carried out. It is an endless loop, backwards and forwards. As Hans-Peter Hauser, head of international marketing at Ciba-Geigy, said in 1983, 'it used to be that R&D came up with products and said "You sell them". Now, as competition gets fiercer and the industry approaches maturity, the marketing end becomes more important.'[7]

According to the *Wall Street Journal*, 'the very survival of a drug in today's highly competitive marketplace often depends as much on a company's marketing talents as it does on the quality of its medicine'.[8]

There are about 100,000 brand-name drugs in the world.[9] In some countries it is not uncommon to find more than 200 brands of products such as analgesics or antibiotics. In 1984, in the Philippines for example, 185 cough preparations were available, 111 of which contained exactly the same ingredients. Similarly, there were 95 brands of penicillin, 85 brands of tetracycline, and 50 brands of ampicillin.[10] Ironically, this proliferation makes price competition difficult, despite industry claims that such practices have price advantages.[11] Most physicians tend to use only a few of the more widely promoted and generally more expensive products, as these are the names they are more likely to remember. And, as the physician does not bear the final cost of the medicine, price differentials seldom enter into prescribing considerations.[12]

What does figure strongly as an influence on prescribing is the promotion of drugs by the industry. The reason is obvious, as a former Squibb medical director points out: 'The incidence of disease cannot be manipulated and so increased sales volume must depend at least in part on the use of drugs unrelated to their real utility or need'.[13]

Figures on the amount of money spent on drug promotion are less easy to find than those for R&D. Interestingly, in a booklet about the role of promotion in the provision of medicines in the Third World published by the IFPMA in 1985, no figures are given for how much the industry spends on promotion, but a figure is given for the amount spent on R&D.[14] It is generally accepted that the amount spent on promotion is about 20 per cent of sales turnover[15] – some two to three times the amount spent on R&D. Table 4.2 gives some promotional data from

**Table 4.1 Number of drug formulations on the market in selected countries**

| Country | Year | No. of formulations |
|---|---|---|
| Argentina[1] | 1988 | 7,000 |
| Bangladesh[2] | 1982 | 2,700 |
| Belgium/Luxemburg[3] | 1985 | 6,353 |
| Brazil[4] | 1975 | 23,500 |
| Colombia[4] | 1981 | 15,000 |
| Cuba[5] | 1979 | 855 |
| France[3] | 1985 | 8,300 |
| India[6] | 1986 | 45,000 |
| Italy[6] | 1986 | 12,000 |
| Japan[6] | 1986 | 39,500 |
| Mexico[4] | 1981 | 18,000 |
| Mozambique[5] | 1980 | 1,200 |
| Norway[7] | 1984 | 1,900 |
| Pakistan[8] | 1988 | 9,500 |
| Philippines[9] | 1987 | 12,000 |
| Spain[8] | 1980 | 13,620 |
| Sweden[7] | 1984 | 2,500 |
| Switzerland[6] | 1986 | 35,000 |
| Thailand[10] | 1985 | 22,169 |
| UK[3] | 1985 | 10,322 |
| USA[6] | 1986 | 45,000 |
| West Germany[6] | 1986 | 70,000 |

Sources: [1]'Argentinian pharma spending questioned', *Scrip*, No. 1,289, 9 Mar 1988, p.20; [2]Tiranti, *The Bangladesh Example*; [3]German and European industry statistics, cited in: BUKO, *Fewer drugs – Better therapy* p.60; [4]UNCTC, *Transnational Corporations* (1984), pp.88, 94, 111; [5]*World Development*, Vol. 11, No 3, Mar 1983, pp.205, 209; [6]Organisation of Pharmaceutical Producers of India (OPPI), advertisement in *Hindustan Times*, 28 Nov 1986; [7]Medawar, *The Wrong Kind of Medicine?*; [8] 'Pakistani pharma industry defends itself', *Scrip*, No. 1,292, 18 Mar 1988, p.19; [9]Tan, *Dying for Drugs*; [10]Srinivasan, S., 'The drugs charade', *Economic and Political Weekly* (India), 18 Jan 1986

several countries which seem to confirm that the proportion is about right. In at least three of those countries, Argentina, Brazil and Thailand, research shows that the lion's share of the promotion budget – anywhere from 45–60 per cent – covers the cost of company sales representatives.[16]

## Influencing doctors and patients

The impact of drug industry promotion is far-ranging. Certainly, it alters the prescribing habits of physicians.[17] One commentator[18] concludes that the published evidence shows that

**Table 4.2 Promotion as a percentage of sales in selected countries**

| Country | Year | % of sales |
|---|---|---|
| Argentina[1] | 1978 | 25 |
| Australia[2] | 1988 | 18 |
| Brazil[1] | 1978 | 22 |
| Canada[3] | 1983 | 17 |
| Colombia[1] | 1978 | 26 |
| Denmark[4] | 1982 | 11 |
| France[4] | 1982 | 18 |
| India[5] | 1976 | 19 |
| Italy[5] | 1976 | 22 |
| Sweden[5] | 1976 | 18 |
| Thailand[1] | 1979 | 5–20 |
| UK[5] | 1976 | 15 |
| USA[5] | 1976 | 22 |
| West Germany[5] | 1976 | 22 |

Sources: [1]UNCTC, *Transnational Corporations* (1984), pp.88, 94, 111; [2]Margo, 'Medicine men bewitch doctors'; [3]Lexchin, 'The pharmaceutical industry in Canada', p.2; [4]Lind, M., *Report on the Sale of European Pharmaceutical Products in the Countries of the Third World* (Council of Europe, reproduced by IOCU/HAI, The Hague/Penang, 1984); [5]Lall, S., 'Economic considerations in the provision and use of medicines', in Blum, et al (eds.), *Pharmaceuticals and Health Policy*

the more doctors rely on commercial sources for their information about drugs the less rational they are as prescribers; that is, they are more likely to prescribe the wrong drug in the wrong formulation for the wrong reason in an incorrect dosage for an inappropriate length of time.

Promotion also affects the buying habits of consumers for OTC medicines. Television advertising in the UK for cough medicines in late 1985 has been cited as playing a large role in a 24 per cent increase (in terms of value) over the previous year's sales.[19] Yet these are the very same products that the *British National Formulary* says:

have no place in the treatment of respiratory disorders ... [and] are to be *deprecated* not only as irrational but also for administering a large number of drugs to patients in inappropriate dosage and in excess of their needs.[20]

## Excessive advertising

For nearly 20 years now, there has been extensive criticism of the industry's promotional practices. The following comment is not unrepresentative:

When the pharmaceutical revolution began, some 40 years ago, industry was under few constraints. Advertising was flamboyant and aggressive; excessive claims were common. In the long run, this did a wholly disproportionate amount of damage to the credibility, reputation and esteem of the industry.[21]

What makes it remarkable is that it was published by the IFPMA, not one of the industry's critics. The implication of the industry making such a comment in 1985 is, of course, that those wild days are long past and that today, such extravagances do not occur. Unfortunately, that is not the case.

The Medical Lobby for Appropriate Marketing (MaLAM) is an international organisation for health professionals concerned about misleading drug advertising. It has about 650 subscribers in 40 countries and each month issues a thoroughly researched letter based on current scientific medical opinion to its subscribers to sign and forward to a particular company requesting further information about the claims made in an individual advertisement. The aim is to encourage companies to provide sufficient, consistent and accurate information about products. As MaLAM has said to the pharmaceutical industry:

> MaLAM's questions are an opportunity for you to promote your products and your company. Our hope is that you will either justify the advertising or tell us that you are going to improve it. We wish to see properly designed, conducted and reported double-blind, randomised controlled trials to justify claims. If the claim was an error, we will be reassured if you tell us how similar errors will be prevented in the future.[22]

In analysing the information supplied by six manufacturers (Ciba-Geigy, Farmitalia Carlo Erba, Glaxo, Janssen, Organon and Roche), MaLAM found that out of 67 studies, only 31 provided original data relevant to the questions asked. Of these 31, only 13 were controlled studies, and only 3 were randomised double-blind studies. Even these had one or more serious methodological flaws, leading MaLAM to conclude that none of the companies supplied clinical trial reports that both were scientifically valid and supported the advertising claims.[23]

In January 1987, MaLAM referred 208 advertisements to the IFPMA, complaining that they failed to meet the technical requirements of the IFPMA code to provide a succinct statement of side effects, precautions and contraindications in all advertisements, unless they were 'reminder' advertisements. In April 1987, MaLAM submitted a further 254 advertisements. By March 1988, the IFPMA had reported on 308 of the advertisements, accepting 168 of the complaints as valid. The IFPMA said it was not able to act on 48 of them as they involved non-member companies, and rejected 42 of the advertisements referred to in the second complaint as being invalid because they were identical to some dealt with in the first complaint, even though they appeared in different publications.[24]

One of the major drawbacks of the code, in any case, is that it acts as a symptomatic therapy after the fact, rather than as a preventive measure. While companies which agree that some aspect of the code has been breached take remedial action to change the offending information or advertising material, the code does not prevent such materials from being circulated in the first place.

In two countries where the industry operates national voluntary codes – Australia and the UK – concern has been consistently expressed about the ability of those codes to deal with advertising. In Australia in 1985, four senior clinical pharmacologists from the Australasian Society of Clinical and Experimental Pharmacologists (ASCEP) undertook a review of advertisements in Australian and New Zealand medical journals and prescribing guides. They found 53 per cent of a total of 138 advertisements to be unacceptable according to the requirements of the Australian Pharmaceutical Manufacturers' Association (APMA) code of conduct. Nearly one-third of the advertisements contained unjustifiable claims or were misleading. The pharmacologists concluded that the implementation of the APMA code was 'unsatisfactory'.[25]

Further evidence of the unsatisfactory nature of the the APMA code's implementation came in 1989 when SmithKline resigned from the APMA rather than comply with the requirements imposed on the company after it had been found to have breached the code. The APMA had ruled that a promotional campaign to schools suggesting that all pupils be vaccinated with the company's Engerix B hepatitis vaccine broke the code in that it involved promotion to the public and also gave unbalanced information. SmithKline withdrew its resignation after the adverse publicity it caused. But a joint statement from the company and the APMA made no mention of what the company intended to do about the ruling that it had breached the APMA code.[26]

In the UK in 1975, 17 years after the ABPI first introduced a voluntary code, a survey of 3,895 advertisements over a 3-month period found the code regularly being broken. The study concluded that the advertisements give 'very little information and generally do not provide enough for the practitioner to make a decision on prescribing'.[27] In 1984, research in the UK showed that 56 per cent of full-page drug advertisements breached the ABPI voluntary code.[28] A study of the legibility of the small print in UK advertisements (where the warnings are given) found that most doctors had great difficulty in reading the information. The researchers concluded that some pharmaceutical companies were 'ignoring advertising regulations and making a mockery of the idea that advertisements should inform doctors about unwanted as well as wanted effects of drugs'.[29] The Secretary of the British Medical Association noted that 'there is a pressing need to resolve the current unsatisfactory situation in medical advertising, some of which is not in the best interests of patient care'.[30] In 1989, two clinical pharmacologists reviewed the cases dealt with by the ABPI between 1983 and 1988 both formally and informally, and concluded that the code 'is commonly broken'. They estimated that about 100 breaches of the code per year were detected, and of those, more than 70 per cent were also breaches of the UK Medicines Act.[31] Between 1968 and 1986, the British Department of Health prosecuted drug companies on only five occasions for advertising and marketing infringements.[32]

Arthur Yellin of the US FDA says that 'the vast majority' of promotional material submitted for consideration by the agency is 'false and/or misleading' but the FDA is able to take action on only some 5 per cent of cases mainly because of a lack of resources.[33] One company which the FDA has taken to task in recent years is Wyeth-Ayerst, which it claims has an 'intolerable record of compliance with the law'. During 1988 and 1989, the FDA sent the company 18 notices of violations in its promotional activity and said the company had 'in case after case … disseminated promotional materials that are clearly false and misleading', indicating a 'general and wilful disregard for legal and regulatory limitations upon drug promotion'.[34]

One advertising expert in the UK notes that 'it would be impossible to control advertising if one couldn't start with the assumption that the role of advertising is to persuade the consumer and the fact that it consists of partial statements'.[35] An ABPI official in 1984 admitted that false claims and inadequate warnings in advertisements were so common that the industry would collapse if drug company directors were forced to resign every time a breach in the ABPI code was found.[36] As the senior attorney for the *New York Times* has pointed out, 'all advertising is inherently misleading. That's how you sell things.'[37]

## Sales representatives

Printed advertising is only the visible tip of a huge promotional effort undertaken by companies to persuade doctors to prescribe their drugs. In 1983 in the UK, the average general physician received a barrage of more than 100 lbs each month of advertising literature and assorted free gifts, including notepads, diaries, pens and records, all of which prominently displayed brand names of drugs.[38] In 1984 in Bangladesh one doctor received a television set from a drug company so he would prescribe its products. Another was presented with a refrigerator. A female doctor in the capital city, Dhaka, who received an expensive gold necklace, commented, 'they offer gifts like this. I'm obliged to help aren't I?'[39]

Yet the most important element in the promotion push is the drug company sales representative. In 1983 in the UK, 55 per cent of company promotional budgets went towards paying for the sales representatives, enough to ensure that there was one sales representative for every eight general physicians.[40] In the same year in Canada, over 55 per cent of the local promotional budgets went on sales representatives, and there was one representative for every 18 doctors.[41] In Australia in 1987, the figure was 46 per cent.[42]

An Australian sales representative who worked for two medium-sized multinational companies for a total of four years explained that a great deal of training and effort went into ensuring that doctors only heard positive messages about drugs.[43] Representatives are briefed thoroughly by the medical and marketing departments of their company so that they believe in the product. In some cases, they may rehearse a prepared script. The first step is to gain some information about doctors' prescribing habits by paying a visit to the local pharmacies. A small gift – a notepad, a pen – might persuade the pharmacist to be talkative. Also, the pharmacist might need encouragement to stock a particular drug, so a bonus offer might be negotiated, whereby the pharmacy receives one or two free packages for every dozen packages of the drug ordered. Next, the doctor's receptionist may need a little gift in order to ensure the representative gets in to see the doctor. After making a short presentation to the doctor, the representative may leave behind a few scientific papers with positive statements highlighted in yellow, or a video in which an eminent person discusses the drug's merits. Also left are the reminder items – the pens, prescription pads, notepads, coffee cups, rulers, calendars, calculators, clocks – with the brand name clearly visible.

Then, perhaps, an invitation may be issued to a meeting where the company will 'trot out an opinion leader who is on our side and where the drinks and eats are on us'. The representative said:

> I don't think reps intentionally mislead doctors as a general rule. I think they are just reflecting the training they've received. They are given selective information themselves because companies, in order to maintain motivation, only want them to know the real positives.

A Canadian sales representative said that his job entailed 'perceiving needs, or creating them'.[44]

Jody Perez, a former sales representative for Johnson & Johnson's McNeil subsidiary in the USA, explained that he had an expense account of several hundred dollars a month with which to entertain doctors.

> Once you build up relationships with certain physicians, you're able to go out socially with them, go out to eat, go out to certain functions, maybe to a football game or to a boxing match, things like that, and then they always remember you. On more than one occasion … over drinks or a meal or whatever … I could bring it up just real, real casually: 'Oh, by the way, could you start writing some more [prescriptions], let's say Zomax, for me' or whatever in a non-threatening manner. It's asking a friend. I'm not asking a doctor to do me a favour. And let's say we just finished eating, you know a very expensive steak dinner, and things like that – they remember that.[45]

An indication of how seriously companies take the work of their sales representatives is evident from the decision by Ciba-Geigy to equip its US sales force with portable computers to enable them to call up profiles of physicians and pharmacies and obtain data on prescribing habits, sales trends and to identify physician opinion leaders. Ciba estimates that for every 1 per cent increase in a sales representative's effectiveness, 'the company's revenue will increase by $6.7 million annually'.[46]

The West German Pharmaceutical Manufacturers' Association (BPI) says that 'the most important link between doctor and manufacturer has proved to be the specially trained pharmaceutical representative'.[47] Just how special the training is is revealed in a 1977 study from Finland which analysed the content of presentations to doctors by representatives from 30 drug companies. It found that side effects and contraindications of the drugs were often neglected in the presentations.[48] The study concluded that 'the success of the representatives' work is measured by the volume of sales, and not by improvements in the knowledge of physicians'.[49] A follow-up study in 1986 which monitored 69 presentations reported almost exactly the same results.[50] Squibb's former medical director, Dr A. Dale Console, summed up the sales representatives' approach to doctors as: 'if you can't convince them, confuse them'.[51]

A doctor at the Johns Hopkins University School of Medicine in Baltimore, USA, found some interesting ideas in a page of a sales manual a sales representative had inadvertently left behind. It suggested using 'attention getters' such as cookies in the shape and colour of drug capsules, pizzas with drug initials picked out in pepperoni, Easter baskets containing eggs painted to resemble drug capsules and Halloween baskets containing free samples. The instructions pointed out that any of these items could be made into an annual event and that the doctors 'really enjoy them'. The doctor commented that the document contained

> grammar and spelling that suggests that the standard of education among this company's sales force cannot be high.... This drug company, and perhaps others, obviously regard us as idiots who respond to Easter baskets and italicized pizzas by prescribing more of their products. Could it be that they are right?[52]

In April and May 1982, sales representatives of Johnson & Johnson's McNeil subsidiary in the USA were told not to 'bring up the subject' or 'spend selling time initiating discussions' on the adverse effects of the company's NSAID Zomax (zomepirac).[53] In 1985, Ciba-Geigy bulletins for its sales representatives told them not to mention adverse effects or possible lack of efficacy of some of the company's drugs with doctors: 'on no account initiate a discussion with the doctor'.[54] Also in 1985, following the publication of an article in the *Illustrated Weekly of India* about the case of Stanley Adams and the accusations of Roche's restraint of trade practices with vitamins, the Roche subsidiary in India circulated a briefing of the 'facts' of the case to its sales representatives which noted that Adams had been found guilty of criminal charges in Switzerland, but failed to mention the decision of the European Commission about the company's own behaviour. The representatives were told: 'you may deal with this subject only if a query is raised by a doctor. You are requested not to volunteer any information on the subject.'[55] The pattern of not volunteering information is a constant one over the years.[56]

Clearly then, both in its printed material and in the verbal presentations made by sales representatives, the pharmaceutical industry provides 'information' which is far from complete. The IFPMA disputes this. It claims that the information from the industry 'provides prompt, detailed and accurate information for the benefit of both doctor and patient'.[57]

In 1968, a World Health Assembly resolution noted that 'if it is not objective, pharmaceutical advertising in whatever form is detrimental to the health of the public'.[58] The IFPMA code says that the industry undertakes

> to provide scientific information with objectivity and good taste, with scrupulous regard for truth, and with clear statements with respect to indications, contraindications, tolerance and toxicity;
> to use complete candour in dealings with public health officials, health care professionals and the public.[59]

Pharmaceutical promotion abounds which is far from candid or objective, is obviously lacking in good taste, and is what could perhaps be politely called 'economical' with the truth. In 1986, the Philippine Medical Association's Committee on Drugs was highly critical of companies which were 'bribing' doctors by 'entertaining them in lewd shows, financing trips of doctors abroad, holding scientific meetings in five-star hotels, giving lavish gifts such as appliances, and stating unfounded information in advertisements'.[60] One woman drug representative in the Philippines noted that 'charm' was an important qualification for the job. She said that she had to 'boost the doctor's ego' by commenting appreciatively on his attire, taking him out for snacks, or 'going further'.[61]

## Prizes for prescribing

Recently, competitions have caught on as a means of providing doctors with 'objective' information. In 1987, Servier sent a letter to physicians in the Philippines inviting them to see how many words of three letters or more they could make from the brand name Arcalion (sulbutiamine). The winner was offered a trip for two to Paris with the flight and five days' accommodation paid for.[62]

In 1987 in Thailand, a lecturer at Chulalongkorn University Hospital in Bangkok was the lucky recipient of a return trip to Singapore, courtesy of Pfizer. The prize was drawn in a lottery held at a scientific symposium on rheumatology.[63]

Dr D. R. Hay of the Princess Margaret Hospital in Christchurch, New Zealand, was outraged when he received a letter in 1987 from ICI inviting him to fill in a form for a free bottle of champagne or sparkling apple juice to celebrate the market leader status of one of the company's beta-blockers. He commented: 'I am prepared to listen to representatives of pharmaceutical companies provided they know their subject but I don't want to be bribed.'[64]

Also in 1987, paediatricians attending the 25th Brazilian Congress of Paediatrics were offered the chance to win bicycles, surfboards and skateboards in a prize draw as part of the promotion for Searle's Benzitrat drops (an anti-inflammatory product containing benzydamine hydrochloride). The paediatricians were given a 'BenziCard' as an entry form for the draw. The promotional material described the product as 'balanced': hence, the prizes requiring balance.[65]

This particular incident was reported to the IFPMA by Health Action International (HAI) in August 1987, more than a month before the Brazilian Congress was due to be held. HAI demanded that the promotion and the prize draw be stopped. In May 1988, the IFPMA replied, saying 'whilst we do not feel that this constitutes a specific breach of the IFPMA code, the company have taken note of the criticism and this promotional campaign has been discontinued'.[66]

It was not clear whether the campaign had been 'discontinued' before, or after, the prize draw. And, while Searle may have 'taken note' of the criticism, it did not take too much note. In February 1988, Searle invited Australian doctors who were prescribers of its antidiarrhoeal product, Lomotil (diphenoxylate and atropine), to enter a prize draw for a nine-day trip for two to the Olympics in Seoul, South Korea. The prize, which included the flights, accommodation and tickets to the opening ceremonies and other events, was valued at Aus$6,000.[67]

The president of the Royal Australian College of General Practitioners, Dr Eric Fisher, said:

> Advertisements like this one do not reflect credit on the drug company or the practitioners. The college cannot support any advertising which bears no relation to standards of patient care or which does little to increase the education of the prescriber.[68]

Searle was found to be in breach of the APMA code and was forced to cancel the promotion, after 6,000 doctors had responded.[69]

## Bogus clinical trials

Another practice by which the industry brings discredit on itself is the sponsorship of bogus clinical trials. In 1986, the ABPI took the unusual step of indefinitely suspending Bayer's membership of the association after it was revealed that the company was offering doctors gifts and money to conduct bogus trials with its heart drug Adalat Retard (nifedipine). One doctor who put patients on the drug received payments towards a colour television, while another was given money to pay for a trip to the USA to attend a medical conference.[70]

Beginning in 1986, Ayerst, a subsidiary of American Home Products, promised US doctors who prescribed Inderal LA (propranolol) to at least 50 patients and filled in a seven-question 'marketing survey' a free economy air ticket to any USA destination. There were escalating prizes for prescribing for more patients, up to a maximum of 200. One doctor from the Bowman Gray School of Medicine in Salem, North Carolina, said that he was 'very concerned about this form of marketing in medicine; I believe it creates a clear conflict of interest for physicians in their prescribing habits.... I believe that this type of program is questionable ethically.'[71] So too did the Attorney General's office in the state of Massachusetts, which launched an investigation of the programme to see if it violated the state's Medicaid False Claims Act. No charges were brought, but in 1989 Ayerst agreed to pay the state $195,000 'in order to put the matter to rest without incurring additional legal fees and expenses'. The company said the programme was scrapped in 1987. Attorney General James Shannon said:

> it is important that medical decisions be made solely on the best interests of the patient and not on the basis of inducements offered by third parties. While this investigation was resolved without litigation, pharmaceutical companies should be on notice that we will not hesitate to bring criminal charges for such practices.[72]

In 1988, Squibb offered Canadian doctors who put 10 of their patients on its anti-hypertensive drug Capoten (captopril) the use of a personal computer. This was part of a nation-wide survey of the effects of the drug. Although Squibb would retain ownership of the computers, doctors would be permitted to keep them after the study was concluded.[73] The College of Physicians and Surgeons of Ontario subsequently issued a statement saying that it considered the acceptance of special benefits such as computers a conflict of interest.[74] Squibb made a similar offer to Australian doctors in 1986.[75] In 1990, the French Health Minister decided to take legal action against Squibb for offering doctors who took part in a survey intended to assess the attitude of the profession to a new hypolipaemic drug, pravastatin, a number of 'material benefits', including free membership to a discount club which provided significant discounts on cars, computers, and leisure and electrical goods.[76]

Australian doctors who agreed to put their patients on May and Baker's NSAID Orudis SR (ketoprofen) in 1988 were offered Aus$20 for each patient, to reimburse them 'for their investigative work'.[77] In 1986 in the UK, the Royal College of Physicians (RCP) noted that doctors had been offered as much as £100 per patient by companies to put their patients on a particular drug and monitor the results.[78] In 1984, Johnson & Johnson's UK subsidiary Ortho-Cilag sponsored a clinical trial for its NSAID Suprol (suprofen) and offered doctors up to £70 to take part in using the drug as a treatment for sprains, strains, sciatica, and pain after childbirth and surgery. The UK *Drug and Therapeutics Bulletin* (DTB) criticised the trial as encouraging doctors to overprescribe a product which was already known to be no more effective than established pain killers. The DTB pointed out that it would be impossible to gauge the frequency and severity of side effects because there would be no control group with which to compare results. In 1986 the drug was withdrawn from the market following reports linking it with kidney damage. The company said it was being withdrawn because it was not selling well.[79]

Dr John McEwen, the head of the Australian Federal Government's Drug Evaluation Support Branch, said he

> would rather the companies wouldn't do these trials, as they are little more than marketing exercises. These studies produce results which appear superficially to reflect the situation in general practice but which, because of their design, are often far removed from the real world.[80]

When the US FDA took Wyeth-Ayerst to task at the beginning of 1990, one of its demands was that the company provide a listing of all studies 'that are currently referred to in support of any promotional claim for any prescription drug' marketed or distributed by the company. The FDA demanded that the company also 'identify those studies that are adequate and well-controlled'. The FDA was concerned about the company using uncontrolled studies to back up some of its promotional claims. In 1988, the company was 'specifically advised' that studies of this type were insufficient to support any substantive promotional claim about safety or efficacy.[81]

## Altruism or marketing?

A slight variation of the prize competition was tried by the Bristol-Myers subsidiary Mead Johnson in the USA for its paediatric acetaminophen (paracetamol) preparation Tempra. In 1986, the company ran an advertisement in the

*Journal of Pediatrics* that drew attention to the financial contribution the company had made to the Ronald McDonald House and Ronald McDonald Children's Charities (RMCC) in the USA and told doctors:

> for every unit of Tempra purchased in 1986 … *above and beyond* unit sales recorded in 1985 … we'll donate 25c toward making the dream of Ronald McDonald House and RMCC a reality in bigger and better ways. It takes a moment to *specify Tempra* when acetaminophen is indicated. A moment that can and will last a lifetime. [original emphasis]

A complaint about the advertisement was sent to the IFPMA in July 1986. In June 1987, the IFPMA responded that the advertisement was 'in accordance with the requirements of the US Federal Trade Commission, and is therefore not considered to be in breach of national ethical criteria'.[82] Whilst on the face of it Mead Johnson appears to be behaving in a humanitarian manner by donating money to children's charities, encouraging the use of a particular drug as the means by which to do so is a highly suspect form of altruism. Indeed, *Fortune* magazine is much more frank about the real purpose of such donations:

> Cause-related marketing is a strategy for selling, not for making charitable contributions.… Funds for do-good pitches come from marketing budgets, and are tax-deductible as business expenses.… When cleverly planned, they not only produce a charity-begins-at-home increase in sales, they also seem to encourage … brand loyalty.[83]

## Continuing medical education

Another form of promotion involves drug company sponsorship of 'continuing medical education' for health workers. One study[84] compared two courses on calcium channel blockers funded by two different calcium channel blocker manufacturers, and concluded that 'there appeared to be evidence of bias in the content of the courses related to the funding sources'. Both in the USA[85] and the UK,[86] concern has been expressed over the influence drug companies have on continuing medical education. A minimum demand is that the programme of any industry-sponsored courses or seminars must be drawn up by an independent panel.

Gay Beauchemin of the Pharmaceutical Manufacturers Association of Canada (PMAC) says the industry believes that the sponsorship of continuing medical education 'must be entirely divorced from marketing'. In 1985, a grant from Hoffmann-La Roche paid for a national inter-active satellite symposium on benzodiazepine tranquillisers which was telecast in 10 Canadian cities. None of the nine speakers challenged the general pattern of tranquilliser use, nor had any of them written anything in the previous five years that was critical of tranquilliser use. The two publications given out at the symposium both originated with Roche.[87]

In the USA, the FDA sharply criticised Schering-Plough's series of 'scientific and educational' seminars in 1989 which compared some of the company's branded products to generic versions. The FDA said the seminars contained a number of 'falsehoods and misrepresentations'.[88]

A problem also exists with the publication of proceedings of industry-sponsored symposia, which often appear as supplements to learned journals. As the UK *Drug and Therapeutics Bulletin* noted, they are 'seldom vetted as rigorously as articles published in the regular issues of the same journal'.[89] In the USA, the FDA strongly criticised Schering-Plough for sponsoring a special supplement in a May 1989 issue of *Internal Medicine World Report* which presented in a 'purportedly scientific/educational context' the results of an un-blinded study about the company's Nitro-Dur (nitroglycerin absorbed through the skin from a plaster). The FDA said the supplement was 'false and/or misleading' about the benefits of the product. Although it had paid for the supplement, the company was not mentioned by name.[90] The UK RCP recommends that such supplements should clearly indicate that the papers were presented at a sponsored meeting and that they should only be published if the meetings were of educational or scientific value and the content was selected independently of the sponsors.[91]

## Managing the news

A less obvious form of promotion – the use of the news media to broadcast information about prescription-only drugs to patients – can also have impact on sales, and unhappy consequences. In 1982, Eli Lilly distributed 6,500 press kits for its anti-arthritic, benoxaprofen (Opren/Oraflex), with the result that prescriptions increased from 2,000 to 55,000 a week.[92] Within 12 weeks, the product was withdrawn because of its adverse effects.

More recently, in several countries companies have begun to place general advertisements in the popular press, usually without any mention of a specific drug. The ads are designed to encourage patients to ask their doctors for the newest treatment for particular conditions. In New Zealand, the Department of Health said in 1989 that it was 'unhappy' about this trend. SmithKline had taken an advertisement in a leading national magazine promoting vaccinations against hepatitis B. Similar to its promotional activity in Australia, the company had also gone direct to schools to set up private vaccination programmes, side-stepping the government's vaccination programme, and had used general practitioners' lists to direct mail to patients. Wellcome took ads in several national magazines which promoted 'an effective shingles treatment', although no mention was made of the company's Zovirax (acyclovir). People were simply urged to consult their doctor as soon as the first signs of the disease appeared. New Zealand's Principal Medical Officer, Dr Ralph Risely said of the ad that 'to just say a medicine is a marvellous cure for shingles without providing the other information is not responsible and is misleading'. Wellcome, on the other hand, argues that since the product is not named, it is not really an advertisement.[93]

The drug companies also attempt to suppress or downplay any bad news about a particular drug or the industry in general. In some cases, third-party rebuttals are used. When Ciba-Geigy's Transderm Nitro (nitroglycerin absorbed through the skin from a plaster) was criticised in a *Lancet* article in 1984 as being ineffective, the company told its sales representatives that a reply was being organised 'from an eminent British source'.[94] In June 1981, a British Broadcasting Corporation (BBC) television series, *Man Alive*, broadcast a documentary called 'Trouble in Paradise' which examined the links between companies, the banking community and the government in Switzerland. Included in the programme was a 12-minute segment about the Stanley Adams/Hoffman-La Roche case. In December of the same year, the BBC received a strongly worded memorandum from the Swiss Ambassador complaining 'about the treatment given to Hoffmann-La Roche'.[95]

At other times the industry intervenes on its own behalf, as this extract from confidential minutes of a meeting of the ABPI in October 1982 shows:

> Speaking from the floor, Dr. E. A. Stevens (Pfizer Ltd.) referred to a meeting with the Editors of the *Lancet* and *British Medical Journal* a number of years ago, concerning adverse reaction monitoring. He felt that the time had come to meet those editors again. It was essential that matters were reported in a responsible manner. In reply, Dr. Snell [ABPI director of medical affairs] said that this point had already been taken and was being pursued. It was not possible to suppress reports, but the way in which things were reported was important. Mr. J. Whitehorn (Lilly Industries Limited) supported the point made by Dr. Stevens; treatment of the 'Opren' situation in certain publications had been less than satisfactory.[96]

In June 1982, Dr Stevens and Dr Alan Wilson, Pfizer's director of clinical regulatory affairs, visited Dr Stephen Lock, the editor of the *British Medical Journal* (BMJ) to 'make him aware' of deficiencies in a report submitted to the BMJ by a group of doctors from a Yorkshire hospital about the possible high incidence of gastric ulcers associated with the use of Pfizer's NSAID Feldene (piroxicam). The company had already tried to persuade the doctors not to submit the paper. The paper was never published, but the BMJ said the reason was statistical flaws, not industry pressure.[97]

A British journalist, Martin Weitz, had his 1980 book *Health Shock* serialised by the London *Daily Mirror*. In the second edition of the book he reported Michael Hellicar, the *Mirror*'s special writer in charge of serialisation, as saying that in 25 years of journalism he had never come across an industry so defensive and bullying as the drug industry:

> Many newspapers would have been intimidated by the drug industry's barrage of legal and psychological pressure designed to stop publication. Constant phone calls at home, threatening cables and telexes sent to the *Mirror*'s chief lawyer and editor put immense pressure on the newspaper, but this just encouraged us to go ahead.
>
> On a worldwide scale the drug industry must be intimidating many hundreds of editors with the result that the public rarely hears about useless and hazardous drugs.[98]

In Australia, legal threats made by the drug industry prevented the book's national syndication.[99]

## Double standards?

One of the most frequent criticisms levelled at the pharmaceutical industry is that it operates double standards in its marketing of drugs in industrialised and developing countries. WHO's Director General, Halfdan Mahler, put it very gently when he told the industry:

> some of your promotional practices in the developing countries are perhaps excessive. And some of your double standards of marketing are perhaps dubious. And I only beg of you to see these practices in the background of the health and economic situation in the developing countries.[100]

In many ways it might be better to argue that the industry operates a single standard, albeit an abysmally low one, no matter what the part of the world. The only difference between Searle's offer of bicycles and skateboards in Brazil and its trip to the Olympics in Australia is one of scale. The principle (or lack of it) is the same: do what it takes to get the drug prescribed. The key consideration is that the industry does whatever it can get away with. Or, as the IFPMA puts it, 'the claims and comments made by manufacturers are subject to the control of government agencies in many countries'.[101]

Clinical pharmacologist Andrew Herxheimer puts that comment into perspective:

> Multinational pharmaceutical companies usually take the view that if it is legal to sell a drug in a particular country, then it is proper to sell it there, preferably in large quantities. In their country of origin many potentially hazardous drugs may be promoted only for a restricted range of uses, and with certain mandatory warnings. If an importing country has no such requirements, the company can omit the warnings and can promote many more uses, no doubt sincerely believing that the local regulatory authority must surely know what is right for the country, and that it is not for the company to usurp its function.[102]

If the laws in a country are lax, if there are loopholes to exploit, or if the enforcement mechanism is faulty and overstretched, then corners will be cut. Imagine for a moment that a country had no law prohibiting theft. Would it therefore be proper and ethical to steal? The absence of a particular restriction is not an automatic approval of a practice. One of the most obvious examples of this is the information given about new drugs. When a new drug comes onto the market, there are obviously gaps in the knowledge about its positive and negative effects, no matter how rigorously it has been tested. Some effects only become apparent after it has been used in a large number of patients or over a long period of time. Yet a common statement in information about new drugs is 'no known contraindications'. Although a seemingly reassuring statement, this should actually be read as a very strong warning that not enough is known about the drug, that it should be used with caution and with careful monitoring of the patient. It is almost inevitable that, the longer a drug is on the market, the longer the data sheet about that drug becomes as more information becomes available. But to place a warning on the information about a new drug that it should be used with care might not sell as many drugs as telling doctors that there are no known contraindications.

On a wider scale, the quality of product information provided by the industry in developing countries is generally lower than that available in industrialised countries. There is no shortage of documentation on this, and there is little reason to dwell on the point here.[103] One series of studies that does bear looking at in some detail, however, is that carried out by Milton Silverman and his colleagues,[104] partly because the studies were extremely comprehensive and systematic, and partly because the industry claims to have taken the criticisms on board. Here is how the IFPMA describes the industry's response to one of Silverman's early studies:

> An example of the way publicity can influence multinational pharmaceutical companies may be found in the worldwide response to the publication in 1976 of the book *The Drugging of the Americas* by the American pharmacologist Milton Silverman. He analysed the promotional claims made for 28 of the most important products of 20 multinational companies published in a US compendium [the *Physician's Desk Reference*] and compared [them] with the claims made for the same products in the compendia of 12 Latin American countries. Silverman found that claims of efficacy were sometimes broader in the Central American markets than in the USA, while some information on side effects and contraindications did not always appear in the Latin American publications.
>
> This became the subject of widespread attention in the industry and beyond. Companies were quick to respond and took steps to revise their marketing, so that within a short time, companies that had come under criticism applied a worldwide policy of consistency in making claims of efficacy and in disclosing side effects. Subsequent monitoring has seldom shown claims to have been overstated or side effects to have been omitted in any market they served.[105]

The last paragraph is the key one: the industry was 'quick to respond' with a global 'consistency' and subsequent monitoring has shown few problems. True or false? Silverman's second study, carried out in 1980 in Africa and South East Asia, noted that 'in comparison with the information given to American and British physicians, the promotion presented to physicians in the Third World was again found to be marked by grossly exaggerated claims of efficacy and a glossing over of hazards.'[106] In 1984, Silverman carried out another study, comparing USA and UK information to that provided in Africa, Asia and Central America. This time he was able to say that there was a 'marked improvement' in promotional practices in the Third World. However, this statement was qualified by the comment:

Although some drug companies have made gratifying changes in their labeling and promotional policies, for which they deserve full credit, the problem of irrational, inaccurate, or even dishonest promotion has not yet been solved. There are still many instances of puffed up claims and glossed over dangers of drug products.[107]

Silverman points out that it is not simply a case of double standards between the industrialised and developing countries. There is no consistency anywhere:

The marked variations between promotional material presented, for example, in the United States and that published in the Third World – a clear case of double standards – do not represent simply a difference between the possibly harsh restrictions of the US Food and Drug Administration and the more tolerant attitudes of Third World drug regulatory agencies. There are glaring differences concerning the identical product *within* the Third World. Thus, what a pharmaceutical company tells physicians in New York or San Francisco may differ from what it says in Nairobi, which in turn may differ from what it says in Kuala Lumpur or Manila, which finally may differ from what it says in Mexico City or Calcutta.[108]

In West Germany, the German Federal Congress of Development Action Groups (BUKO) carried out a similar study of Hoechst's approach to marketing in developing countries in 1984–5. It concluded: 'in most cases, the information given to the user is less adequate than in the FRG; to a large extent, risks are simply concealed. Instead, Hoechst "invents" new, unjustifiable ranges of use for the Third World.'[109]

Preliminary data from a similar study carried out in 1988 on all German pharmaceutical companies indicate findings that are not very different.[110] Studies carried out by Swiss and French organisations found similar behaviour among Swiss and French companies.[111]

Perhaps the IFPMA should re-read its own code, particularly the passages about using 'complete candour' and having a 'scrupulous regard for truth'.

As a 1986 editorial in the *British Medical Journal* put it:[112]

The industry should shoulder much of the blame for the current inappropriate and excessive use of medicines in developing countries. And it must produce more convincing arguments to support its thesis that the voluntary code of practice of the International Federation of Pharmaceutical Manufacturers Associations (designed to protect consumers against unethical drug promotion) is working. It is encouraging to see that the industry is showing concern, but it must show its critics that this is more than skin deep.

# 5.  Struggling for clear policies

*It cannot be said that the more drugs the better; national lists with
thousands of drugs have no advantage over more limited lists.*
WHO and UNICEF, *But Some Drugs Are More Essential Than Others*, 1986

For eight of the ten years of the 1980s, I spent the better part of each May in
Geneva in Switzerland. Geneva is a pretty city on the shores of Lac Léman in
the southwestern corner of the country. In the distance, on a clear day, the
snow-capped peak of Mont Blanc can be seen. Usually though, I saw little of
the pleasant scenery. Instead I roamed through the corridors of the Palais des
Nations – the main United Nations building in Geneva – which for some two
weeks during the first half of May is the site of the annual World Health
Assembly (WHA).

Each year health ministers, their advisers, and a few non-governmental
organisations – including the IFPMA and the WFPMM which both have official
NGO status with WHO – gather to discuss international health policies. Officially,
the WHA is the governing body of WHO and the representatives of the more than
160 member states theoretically have the opportunity to set the directions WHO
should take in its work. In practice, like most meetings which touch on the
politics of power, the discussions in the corridors, over the dinner table, at the
receptions in the various embassies, or in the hotel rooms are where many of
the most important decisions are made. The plenary sessions tend to drone on
with speeches about the efforts being made by governments to improve health,
while WHO's staff work behind the scenes to ensure that the meeting flows
smoothly along to the concluding session which adopts a series of resolutions,
preferably by consensus.

Two plenary committees try to delve a little more deeply into some of the
specific topics on the agenda. In a half or a full day's discussion, government
representatives have the opportunity to pass on politically coded signals to WHO
about their views on particular issues. If resolutions appear to be controversial,
a drafting committee is usually called for, and generally it is open-ended. This
means that a few countries indicate their interest, but others may join in.
Watching the faces walking into a drafting committee session it is usually easy
to spot a large number of delegates from the industrialised countries, a few from
the Soviet bloc, and a small number from developing countries. This composition reflects the major contributors to WHO's general budget: the USA, Japan,
West Germany, France, Italy and the UK together were assessed to provide 58
per cent of WHO's budget in 1986–7.[1]

As Robert Dee, chairman and chief executive of SmithKline, told his colleagues at an IFPMA assembly in 1981:[2]

> For this year and next, 70 per cent of WHO's budget will be paid by 13 industrialised countries – 13 out of [the then] 156 WHO member countries. Certainly this entitles the industrialised world to stand up to WHO. We must have the will to do so.

The WHA in May 1981 and events which followed in the days immediately after it have a particular meaning in the history of the global debate on the rational use of drugs.

## The baby foods campaign

The 1981 WHA adopted an International Code of Marketing of Breast-milk Substitutes,[3] the result of some 18 months of intensive negotiations at the international level among governments, the baby foods industry, international organisations, health workers and NGOs. The background to the Code lay rooted in nearly a decade's worth of campaigning to draw attention to the negative impact that the promotion of powdered baby milk and the whole concept of artificial infant feeding was having on breastfeeding rates and subsequently on infant health. Breast milk helps to protect a baby against diarrhoea, coughs and colds and many other common childhood illnesses. Nutritionally, it is the best food for an infant. Research has indicated that the act of breastfeeding helps to improve the emotional and psychological bonding between mother and child. It also inhibits ovulation in the mother which helps to increase the intervals between the birth of children, something which has been recognised as an important criterion for both maternal and infant health. Finally, it is less costly than the use of artificial feeds.[4]

Perhaps the only real drawback to breastfeeding is that it is difficult to make money from it; hence the desire of baby milk manufacturers to aggressively push their products. Some of the companies which manufactured and sold baby milks, such as Wyeth, Abbott Ross, Bristol-Myers and Nestlé, also had interests in pharmaceuticals. They, and many of the other pharmaceutical companies, were clearly worried that a code on pharmaceutical marketing would be the next item on the international agenda. The former executive vice-president of the IFPMA commented at the time: 'Nestlé and the other companies made a lot of mistakes to get to the point they did. We won't ever get to that stage if I can help it.'[5]

One of the driving forces behind the baby milks code was the International Baby Food Action Network (IBFAN), a loose coalition of NGOs that was set up in 1979. Ernest Saunders, then the vice president of Nestlé's nutrition division, pointed out in a 1980 memo that IBFAN's 'professionalism' and its skill in mobilising support among governments and health workers were a clear threat to industry interests.[6]

## Health Action International

Immediately following the 1981 WHA, IBFAN held an international congress in Geneva, bringing together 88 campaigners and health workers from 39 countries to plan its future activities. At the end of May, more than 200 women from around the world were also in Geneva for the third International Women and Health Meeting. Sandwiched between these two events, and borrowing some participants from both, was a meeting on pharmaceuticals organised by the International Organisation of Consumers Unions (IOCU), the West German Coalition of Development Action Groups (BUKO) and the United Nations Non-Governmental Liaison Service (NGLS). The 50 participants from 27 countries agreed to set up Health Action International (HAI), a coalition loosely modelled on IBFAN, as an 'international antibody' to the worst effects of international pharmaceutical marketing. It called for an end to the 'commercial anarchy of prescription drug competition', an end to patent protection for the most essential drugs, the progressive replacement of proprietary brands with generic drugs, and the development of regional or national production and bulk-buying arrangements.[7]

Fundamentally, HAI's basic objective was to act as an advocacy group, in much the same way as IBFAN had done with breastfeeding, to bring the major issues related to pharmaceuticals much more into the public spotlight for critical examination and to help speed up the process of finding solutions to the problems. Many of the organisations involved in HAI were also involved in IBFAN, as were some of the individuals (myself included).[8] One lesson that had clearly been learned from the baby foods campaign was that leaving the debate to scientists, governments and the industry was unlikely to move it forward quickly. First, the discussion would in all likelihood be conducted in private and would focus on what was technically possible and politically expedient for those concerned. Second, any agreements made were liable to remain somewhat secret, so that monitoring the progress of change would be difficult. HAI instead sought to inject a shot of reality into the debate by publicising what was actually happening and the impact that was having on people in the field. It was an attempt to bring a countervailing force to bear on the power structure that government and industry constituted and to challenge the often cosy relationship which existed between the industry and health workers. By being closer to the ground and to grassroots health workers and their patients, HAI had access to powerful information about the ways in which drugs were being misused and mispromoted and the likely impact of any national or international policies to improve this situation. By being independent of both government and industry finance, it was freer to be more openly critical and to mobilise popular support for more sensible and workable measures.

The Washington-based *Food and Drug Letter* noted in July 1981 that HAI could be viewed as 'somewhat anemic' in its early stage of development as it had only conducted an organisational meeting, issued a few press releases and distributed a leaflet drawing attention to the problems of using Searle's anti-diarrhoeal drug, Lomotil (diphenoxylate), for young children. However, its potential was clearly worrying the pharmaceutical industry. A member of the staff of the US PMA said 'we take it as a serious potential problem, both from a marketing threat here and now and for a WHO resolution in the future'. A Searle official said it represented 'a worldwide resurgence of consumer organisation activity focused on the pharmaceutical industry, and particularly multinational corporations'.[9] By September of that year, the industry was clearly seeing HAI as part of a global conspiracy of considerable dimension against TNCs. Jay Kingham, the PMA's international vice president, said that it was in the 'Eastern bloc's interests to diminish the power of multinationals' and that those countries, 'UN bureaucrats, activists and some LDCs' had formed an alliance whose objective was to control the world's major corporations. 'This is an item of great concern to business. The infant formula code brought it home.'[10]

## A conspiracy of critics?

The conspiracy theory ran and ran, fuelled in part by the coincidental hosting of a conference on drugs by the World Federation of Trade Unions in Moscow in November 1981. In 1982, the West German Pharmaceutical Manufacturers' Association (BPI) published a document which mentioned the development of HAI and followed it up with a reference to the Moscow event, which had called for the introduction of state controls over pharmaceutical companies. Although no direct link was explicitly made by the BPI, the juxtaposition of the two facts provided ample room for the reader to conclude that the two events must be in some way connected.[11]

In 1985, an article by Dr Claus Roepnack of Hoechst[12] talked about 'a purposefully planned international campaign ... the intention and the contents of the campaign can rather be compared with the "Trojan horse"'. He went on to say that

> the activists of HAI should therefore be asked whether their true intention is not the overthrow of existing social and economic systems in favour of authoritarian regimes. Even if the terminology of the usually young critics is full of expressions which suggest they could have anti-capitalistic and revolutionary aims and even if, perhaps not purely accidentally, the start of their campaign coincided with the World Congress of the Free International Trade Unions Association in Moscow (November 1981), it would certainly be wrong to classify the critics as from the left, to regard them as under remote control, and to see them just as reds.... This campaign is undoubtedly carried on by numerous idealists who are firmly convinced of the correctness of their arguments without noticing, however, that they are acting as a front for professional ideologists and that in the end they run the risk of becoming victims of demagogues.

In 1987, the 'Trojan horse' theme emerged again, this time in Thailand in an article in the English-language newspaper, *The Nation*.[13] The author, a Thai journalist who had benefited from an IFPMA-sponsored study tour to Europe to meet with members of the pharmaceutical industry, posed the question of whether the Thai Drug Study Group or the pharmaceutical industry operating in Thailand was the 'Trojan horse'. He referred to the fact that the Drug Study Group was a participant in HAI and went on to point out that HAI's 'weakness lies in its past association with the Soviet Union and alleged political objectives both of which it has denied'. In September 1986, the Thai Pharmaceutical Products Association (PPA), a member of the IFPMA, told Thai Foreign Ministry officials that the Drug Study Group 'was comprised of activists' and their link with HAI and IOCU had 'ulterior motives, given alleged previous associations with communist countries'.

## Discrediting critics

This strategy of discrediting criticism and critics has a long history. In the early 1970s, when the United Nations set up a Committee of Eminent Persons to enquire into the high profits of the pharmaceutical and chemical companies in the aftermath of the Hoffmann-La Roche case, a small subcommittee of at least six Swiss companies (including Ciba-Geigy, Sandoz and Roche) was established to weaken the impact of the inquiry and avoid the introduction of an international code of conduct for TNCs. During one meeting, the companies outlined a five-point strategy for dealing with critics:[14]

1. The critic is identified as an opponent of the system and thus discredited as a discussion partner.

2. Dubious motives are attributed to the critic: ideological or nationalistic prejudices, envy, stupidity, ignorance and lack of experience.

3. When criticism is global or circumstantial: the contrary is 'proved' by means of isolated instances (e.g. description of an individual project).

4. When criticism is indisputable (e.g. in the case of ITT in Chile): emphasis is put on the fact that it is an individual case, moreover still under investigation.

5. In any case, it should be said in public that defending free enterprise was in everybody's interest. Therefore, it should be shown, especially in the mass media, that criticism of multinationals was basically criticism of free enterprise and that behind it were the enemies of the free world, whose view of life was based on Marxism.

## Movement in the UN system

This approach towards critics was very much in keeping with the political climate of the 1970s. Many of the newly independent nations were looking for an appropriate forum in which to flex their muscles, and the United Nations system was to provide them with many opportunities. Much of the impetus for work on pharmaceuticals came from the Fifth Conference of Heads of State or Government of Non-Aligned Countries held in Colombo, Sri Lanka, in August

1976. A resolution adopted at the conference called for the preparation of a list of 'priority pharmaceutical needs' of each developing country and 'formulation of a basic model list' of such needs as a guideline; the establishment of national buying agencies for pharmaceuticals; either the exclusion of pharmaceuticals from patent protection or a limit to the duration of pharmaceutical patents; the use of generic instead of brand names; the provision of information about drugs only from 'official sources'; the establishment of a local pharmaceutical industry in each developing country as appropriate to its production capabilities; and the creation of regional co-operative pharmaceutical production and technology centres (COPPTECs) to draw up drug lists, co-ordinate research and development, facilitate the transfer of technology, collect and disseminate information on pharmaceutical uses and prices and on technological capabilities of countries, and co-ordinate the production and exchange of drugs. The conference called on the United Nations Conference on Trade and Development (UNCTAD), the United Nations Industrial Development Organisation (UNIDO), WHO and the United Nations Development Programme (UNDP) to assist in the achievement of these objectives.[15]

Both UNCTAD and UNIDO issued several publications during the late 1970s designed to help developing countries deal with the technological issues involved in pharmaceutical supply.[16] The UN Center on Transnational Corporations (UNCTC) published a major report on pharmaceuticals in 1979,[17] and followed this up with another major report in 1984.[18]

A special task force on pharmaceuticals was established by UNCTAD, UNIDO, WHO, the United Nations Department of Technical Co-operation for Development and the United Nations Action Programme for Economic Co-operation which prepared a project financed by UNDP and carried out by the government of Guyana. The report of the project, published in August 1979, contained 26 practical recommendations for governments to follow both individually and in co-operation on a regional basis to develop drug policies, lists and regulations; ensure quality control; reduce prices; improve information flow; and develop local production capabilities. The report was endorsed in its entirety by the Sixth Conference of Heads of State or Government of the Non-Aligned Countries held in Havana, Cuba, in September 1979.[19]

That many of these ideas were echoed in HAI's first meeting is not surprising. They represented the clearest analysis at that time as to what some of the major problems were, and provided possible solutions that were seen to be acceptable to the representatives of the majority of the world's population. Also, several representatives from the UN system participated in the HAI meeting. Among them was Surenda Patel, then director of UNCTAD's technology division. In 1988 he said of the meeting:

> I was privileged to be there. The enthusiasm of the participants was infectious, had confidence and power. We in UNCTAD by then had already started a bit of work on pharmaceuticals. I was pleased, indeed all of us were pleased that now on the world scene there was another voice in support of national and international action.[20]

**The role of WHO**

While what were primarily trade and technology issues were under discussion in other parts of the UN system, WHO was also developing strategies on pharmaceuticals. In 1975, a Certification Scheme on the Quality of Pharmaceutical Products Moving in International Commerce was adopted by the 28th WHA.[21] The scheme requires that health authorities of participating export countries provide, on request, a certificate stating that the product is authorised for sale in the exporting country and that the manufacturing plant in which it was produced follows Good Manufacturing Practice (GMP). Although the scheme was a useful measure, one problem was its slow uptake by WHO's member states. In 1980, less than one-third of member states were participating;[22] by 1985 about two-thirds were participating, although WHO noted that though the original intention of the scheme was to assist the flow of information to developing countries 'it was most extensively used between countries within the European region', and the scheme was 'not functioning effectively in all countries';[23] by 1988, some three-quarters of member states were participating.[24]

Apart from the slowness of participation, a major difficulty with the certification scheme was its attempt to equate 'quality' of pharmaceuticals with what went on inside a manufacturing plant. There are two flaws in that argument: first, it implies that so long as a drug is manufactured under carefully controlled conditions, it must be of value in health care; and second, that upon leaving the factory, the drug will be correctly used. The development of the scheme seems to fall into an approach initially taken in its work on pharmaceuticals by UNIDO, whereby it concentrated on increasing production within the existing structure of pharmaceutical trade, according to the established rules of the game. By 1976, however, UNIDO began to look at ways in which the rules could be changed somewhat, and began to take a more critical look at the ramifications of the existing system.[25]

**Essential drugs**

At about the same time, WHO also was beginning to challenge the system. In 1977, after careful study and partly in response to the calls for action which had been made in other parts of the UN system, WHO issued a guideline for governments, an essential drugs list (EDL), which set out some 220 preparations.[26] WHO suggests that the drugs on this list, which is regularly reviewed to keep pace with the development of useful new medicines, are adequate to meet more than 90 per cent of pharmaceutical requirements of developing countries.[27] One commentator notes that the whole concept of essential drugs represented 'a brilliant symbolic strategy on the part of WHO for mobilizing opinion and resources'.[28] Dr Ernst Lauridsen, the former director of WHO's Action Programme on Essential Drugs and Vaccines (APED) – which was officially approved at the May 1981 WHA – described the concept as 'a peaceful revolution in international public health'.[29]

A revolution it may be, but it was certainly not peaceful. Since the publication of the first essential drugs list, the industry has maintained consistent opposition to the whole concept, particularly if it is applied to the private sector. In 1978, the IFPMA called the medical and economic arguments for such a list 'fallacious' and said that adopting it 'could result in suboptimal medical care and might reduce health standards'.[30] Joseph Stetler, then head of the US PMA, said it would be 'poor business practice' to support the essential drugs list. Michael Peretz explained the IFPMA's opposition by saying 'You can't expect us to support policies which run counter to our own interests'.[31] In 1981, Jay Kingham of the US PMA said the list 'will have everybody go third class in drugs. It won't save money and it won't meet real health needs.'[32] In 1985, a PMA pamphlet claimed there was 'no convincing evidence' that restricting the number of drugs would be of benefit, adding that such restriction 'would have a very adverse impact on the practice of medicine, the level of competition in the pharmaceutical industry, the rate of pharmaceutical innovation and the overall cost of illness in human and economic terms'.[33] In late 1984, the Association of the British Pharmaceutical Industry (ABPI) launched a major campaign to oppose the introduction of a limited list of drugs for the UK National Health Service. It claimed that the proposal would put 'Britain's research-based industry in jeopardy' and take away a doctor's freedom to prescribe.[34] At the 1986 WHA, IFPMA Executive Vice-President Dr Richard Arnold said that 'arbitrary limitations on the number of medicines could only lead to sub-optimal treatment for many patients'.[35] In the years 1986–9, industry associations in Argentina, Australia, Brazil, Bolivia, Denmark, Finland, France, the Federal Republic of Germany, India, Ireland, Italy, Japan, The Netherlands, New Zealand, Nigeria, Pakistan, the Philippines, Portugal, Spain, Sweden, Thailand and the UK have all protested strongly against attempts to introduce more rational drug use.[36]

The Japanese Pharmaceutical Manufacturers Association (JPMA) said in 1989 that neither it nor the IFPMA objects to WHO's APED 'provided it is limited to the public sector in developing countries'.[37] This statement is consistent with a comment made by Jay Kingham of the PMA in early 1982 when he said that 'the industry feels strongly that any efforts by the World Health Organization and national governments to implement this action program should not interfere with existing private sector operations'.[38]

Here is the key to the industry's position: it will accept some tinkering with the public sector, but only in developing countries, provided the private sector (and the public sector in industrialised countries) is left wide open for the 'free' market to determine what drugs should be used. Economics, not health care, is the clear determinant of such a position. The major world markets are in the industrialised countries and any interference in those markets was seen as being detrimental to the economic health of the industry. In developing countries, the public sector is generally smaller than the private sector.[39]

## Drug shortages

A common theme in the protest over efforts in industrialised countries to introduce limited lists of drugs is the exaggerated and completely distorted claim that this will lead to a situation analogous to the conditions in the Third World.[40] The only value in such a claim is at least the recognition that there are severe problems with drugs in many developing countries.

A major problem is often the shortage of the most essential products.[41] For example, before an essential drugs programme began in Kenya, it was estimated that up to 25 per cent of rural health centres were closed at any one time due to drug shortages.[42] In Kinshasa, the capital of Zaire, most people obtain their medicines from small neighbourhood health clinics and/or pharmacies. A survey of 25 health clinics and 37 local pharmacies revealed that:

> the multinational drug companies had a great impact on the quality of treatment offered by these clinics and pharmacies. Accordingly, these facilities routinely lacked essential drugs, such as antiparasitics and antibiotics, while they stocked hazardous and expensive drugs such as aminopyrone-dipyrone drugs.... It is apparent that the multinational drug firms exert a major and adverse influence on the quality and cost of health care in Kinshasa.[43]

The attempts by some governments to introduce a measure of sanity into their countries' similarly chaotic situations through the establishment of essential or rational drug programmes show there is increasing recognition that improvements in health care will only be possible by overcoming essential drug shortages.

There is a danger, however, in only focusing on the supply of the 'right' drugs, without also tackling the enormous problem of the glut of less appropriate products on the private market. WHO estimates that some $500 million have been mobilised to support national drug programmes.[44] At first glance, that seems an impressive figure, but it is only about 5 per cent of the total amount being spent by the pharmaceutical industry to promote drugs.[45] And if we take into account the statistics cited earlier (page 48) about the large percentage of products which offer no therapeutic improvements, it becomes clear that considerably more effort is going into the promotion of non-essential drugs than of essential drugs. Although money alone is not the only criterion, that imbalance is one of the reasons why the struggle to achieve a more rational use of drugs has proven so difficult, and is likely to remain so, unless steps are taken to concentrate much more effort and resources on the promotion of essential drugs and the removal of less than essential products.

## Antibiotics: the end of an era?

Even with what are considered to be essential drugs, there are considerable problems, as the marketing and use of antibiotics demonstrates. Because antibiotics actually do what they are supposed to – attack infections and lead to the rapid recovery of patients – in many ways they have laid the foundation for the reputation of the pharmaceutical industry as being able to provide the world with 'miracle' cures.

Today, thanks to gross mishandling of antibiotics, the age of miracles may be drawing to a close. In 1982, 150 scientists from more than 25 countries pointed out that antibiotics were losing their effectiveness because of the spread and persistence of drug-resistant organisms. They warned: 'we may find a time when such agents are no longer useful to combat disease'.[46]

While the development of resistance to antibiotics is a complex factor, one of the major determinants is the indiscriminate use of antibiotics in both humans and animals.[47] In 1984 WHO warned that 'unless steps are taken to check the misuse of antibiotics, which leads to resistance, one of the best weapons humanity has devised for the protection and restoration of health could be placed in jeopardy'.[48] As a class, antibiotics have been described as 'the most improperly used drugs'.[49] An estimated 22 per cent of antibiotics used in hospitals are prescribed unnecessarily. In one study, no infection was present nor deemed likely to occur in 50 per cent of patients on antibiotic courses in a hospital. A US study found that 60 per cent of the prescriptions given to patients with a common cold – a viral infection that does not respond to antibiotic treatment – were for antibiotics.[50] Similar studies in Iran, Brazil, Bangladesh, Mexico and other Latin American countries, and Australia provide equally disturbing evidence.[51]

Of the 506 different antidiarrhoeals on the market in 11 regions of the world during 1986, 60 per cent contained an antimicrobial, as the table below shows, even though WHO says that antimicrobials are not indicated in the routine treatment of acute diarrhoea.[52] Even by 1988–9, nearly one out of every two antidiarrhoeal preparations contained an antimicrobial. More than 160 companies are involved in this trade – ranging from small, national ventures trading only in their own country up to the large transnationals.

The uncontrolled availability of these products inevitably means that many people are receiving the wrong therapy for diarrhoea. A survey carried out in 75 pharmacies in Bangladesh, Sri Lanka and the Yemen Arab Republic (25 pharmacies in each country) during 1984 and 1985 found that only 21 per cent gave the correct advice for diarrhoea – oral rehydration or consultation with a health worker. Instead, most pharmacies were dispensing combination antibiotics. In Yemen, for example, over 40 per cent of the treatments given out contained neomycin.[53]

WHO said as long ago as 1980 that neomycin 'should *never* be used in the treatment of acute diarrhoea',[54] yet 12 per cent of the antidiarrhoeal preparations available during 1986 contained neomycin. A two-year international campaign by HAI about this problem has helped to reduce this figure to about 7 per cent of all antidiarrhoeal preparations, which is encouraging.

The connection between the pharmaceutical industry's exuberant promotion of antibiotics and the poor prescribing and use of the drugs has been clearly identified.[55] Dr Enrique Fefer, the regional adviser in drug control for the Pan American Health Organisation (PAHO), said in 1982 that 'the ready availability,

**Table 5.1 Antidiarrhoeals containing antimicrobials (1986 and 1988–9*)**

| Country/ Region | Total anti-diarrhoeals | | Total containing antimicrobials | | | | Total containing neomycin | | | |
|---|---|---|---|---|---|---|---|---|---|---|
| | 1986 No. | 1988–9* No. | 1986 No. | % | 1988–9* No. | % | 1986 No. | % | 1988–9* No. | % |
| Africa | 29 | 22 | 16 | 55.2 | 3 | 13.6 | 7 | 24.1 | | |
| Caribbean | 18 | 18 | 10 | 55.6 | 5 | 27.8 | 5 | 27.8 | 2 | 11.1 |
| Hong Kong | 26 | 21 | 7 | 26.9 | 6 | 28.6 | | | | |
| Indonesia | 53 | 62 | 33 | 62.3 | 32 | 51.6 | 8 | 15.1 | 8 | 12.9 |
| India | 63 | 59 | 51 | 81.0 | 47 | 79.7 | 7 | 11.1 | 4 | 6.8 |
| Middle East | 41 | 23 | 22 | 53.7 | 6 | 26.1 | 7 | 17.1 | | |
| Malaysia and Singapore | 29 | 19 | 13 | 44.8 | 1 | 5.3 | 6 | 20.7 | | |
| Mexico* | 72 | 69 | 46 | 63.9 | 44 | 63.8 | 5 | 6.9 | 5 | 7.2 |
| Philippines | 62 | 46 | 38 | 61.3 | 25 | 54.3 | | | | |
| Pakistan | 56 | 53 | 36 | 64.3 | 17 | 32.1 | 6 | 10.7 | | |
| Thailand | 57 | 72 | 29 | 50.9 | 38 | 52.8 | 10 | 17.5 | 11 | 15.3 |
| **Totals** | **506** | **464** | **301** | **59.5** | **224** | **48.3** | **61** | **12.1** | **30** | **6.5** |

*Mexico data are from 1986 and 1987
Sources: Africa: MIMS *Africa* (Nov 1986 and Jul 1989); Caribbean: MIMS *Caribbean* (Nov 1986 and May 1989); Hong Kong: HKIMS (Aug 1986 and Dec 1988); Indonesia: IIMS (Jun 1986 and Oct 1988); India: MIMS *India* (Jun 1986 and Feb 1988); Middle East: MIMS *Middle East* (Oct 1986 and Aug 1989); Malaysia and Singapore: DIMS (Jun 1986 and Oct 1988); Mexico: *Diccionario de Especialidades Farmacéuticas* (1986 and 1987); Philippines: PIMS (Aug 1986 and Dec 1988); Pakistan: QIMP (Mar–Sep 1986 and Sep 1988–Feb 1989); Thailand: TIMS (Jul 1986 and Nov 1988)

widespread promotion and indiscriminate use of powerful drugs for minor ailments adds up to a major public health problem, particularly with respect to antibiotics'.[56] An Australian doctor notes that the powerful marketing techniques of the industry often undermine appropriate antibiotic prescribing habits,[57] while an American doctor points out:

> While the boldface ad advocates 'blind' use of their product, the fine print embodies the spirit of conservative practice. This classic double message, i.e., 'use our product without hesitation' and 'use our product only with great caution', is typical of many drug company circulars containing prescribing information.[58]

Between July and December 1988, one of the 17 acknowledged breaches of the Australian Pharmaceutical Manufacturers Association Code of Conduct concerned an advertisement by Eli Lilly for Keflex (cephalexin) which 'implied that Keflex was the first drug of choice for tonsillitis, even though this was negated by a warning in small print at the bottom of the advertisement'. In total, 9 of the 17 breaches of the code acknowledged by the APMA concerned antibiotics. A Wellcome advertisement for Septrin (cotrimoxazole) was termed 'misleading' in its claims about resistance; whilst another advertisement failed to include a caution about use in the elderly; a booklet produced by Roche entitled *Cotrimoxazole in Perspective* was 'assembled carelessly and was mis-leading', as was an advertisement for Bactrim (cotrimoxazole), and an entire advertising campaign for Bactrim was termed 'unbalanced and misleading by implication and omission'; a Glaxo advertisement for Ceporex (cephalexin) made unsubstantiated claims about efficacy; a Beecham advertisement for Augmentin (amoxycillin) was regarded as 'misleading', whilst another Beecham advertisement for Floxapen (flucloxacillin) used 'unqualified superlatives'.[59]

Perhaps even worse than being implicated in the cause of the problem, the pharmaceutical industry has also been accused of actively discouraging efforts to find a solution. A major international conference to review antibiotic use around the world, due to be held in the USA, was first cancelled and then turned into an unproductive small workshop. The cause of this change of plans is attributed to the pharmaceutical industry in the USA which saw the conference as 'a threat to profits'.[60] In both 1987 and 1988, articles in the *Side Effects of Drugs Annual* drew attention to this problem.

> Alarm bells should go off in the board room of every large pharmaceutical company: Let us not be foolish, let us gain understanding. The only way to save profit beyond the year 2000 is simply to co-operate in a program for a more rational usage of antibiotics.[61]
>
> We should all keep a closer eye upon the pharmaceutical companies. If a company is marketing obsolete antimicrobials in developing countries or conducting policies which will promote resistance to the newest agents the prescribers and regulatory agencies in other countries should simply ask: Why? Marketing antimicrobials is not only a matter of money; it is a matter of ethics as well.... The question of the worldwide increase in resistance is too serious to be hampered by concerns about freedom and profits.[62]

The pharmaceutical industry can hardly claim that it is unaware of the problem. In 1988 alone, there were eight articles in the journal *Scrip*,[63] recog-nised as one of the most important and widely read publications within the industry. For example, a meeting of a WHO working group on multiresistant bacteria in the Western Pacific region found that bacterial resistance was a prob-lem in Australia, Brunei, China, Hong Kong, Japan, Malaysia, New Zealand, Papua New Guinea, the Philippines, South Korea, Singapore and Vietnam.[64]

## A drugs code?

Thus, even the fact that a drug is considered 'essential' and is included in the WHO list, or even in a national list of essential drugs, does not mean that it will not be used irresponsibly or irrationally. The drugs on the WHO list are there because of their proven efficacy in *particular* disease conditions, their relative safety, and usually their reasonable cost.

As Dr J. E. Goyan, dean of the University of California, San Francisco, School of Pharmacy and past Commissioner of the US Food and Drug Administration

(FDA) put it: 'I would be willing to bet that we could get along with about half the number of prescriptions that are written each year.'[65]

Such sentiments are not regarded highly within the pharmaceutical industry. In addition to carrying out political lobbying to prevent the essential drug concept getting a stranglehold in national settings, the industry deemed it important to preserve its 'right' to use its considerable marketing skills to ensure that drugs continued to be used for much wider indications and more frequently than was recommended by independent experts. The idea of limiting the number of drugs by means of essential lists coupled with restrictions on marketing through some sort of code appeared like a two-pronged attack.

By 1981, the essential drugs concept was being accepted, at least at the international level and at least in theory, even if in practice there was still some way to go. In the wake of the baby foods code, a pharmaceutical code was an obvious next step. Indeed, one of HAI's first publications was a detailed criticism of the IFPMA's voluntary code of marketing practice.[66] This was rapidly followed up with a very detailed proposal for a strong code, which covered not only marketing practices, but drug registration, patents and the encouragement of local production.[67]

The HAI draft code – described by Charles Medawar of Social Audit as 'a discussion document, whose main political significance was to demonstrate that the IFPMA's code barely began to scratch the surface'[68] – appeared just in time to catch the last major wave of the debate within the UN system about the need for a New International Economic Order. Within six months of having been set up, and barely a month after the first draft of its code was published, HAI was mentioned by an UNCTAD regional workshop in Africa as one of the organisations playing a major role in developing pharmaceutical policies. The workshop, which was attended by senior government officials from Benin, Burundi, Cameroon, Central African Republic, Chad, Comoros, Congo, Guinea-Bissau, Ivory Coast, Madagascar, Mali, Mauritania, Morocco, Rwanda, Senegal, Togo and Upper Volta, called upon international bodies, 'in particular WHO and UNCTAD, to take the necessary steps for the formulation of a code of conduct in the pharmaceutical sector'.[69] Another UNCTAD-sponsored meeting, held in Geneva in February 1982, repeated the call for international norms on promotion, distribution, trade and technology in the pharmaceutical sector.[70] At the end of 1982, IOCU – which has consultative status with UNCTAD – officially presented the HAI draft code to a meeting of the UNCTAD Committee on Transfer of Technology. The move was welcomed by the Group of 77, which represents the majority of Third World countries. Despite this support, however, a resolution calling for further action failed to be passed by the committee.[71] By June 1983, at the UNCTAD VI conference in Belgrade, all hope of a code proceeding through UNCTAD had faded. Although developing countries had come to the conference firmly committed to such a code, a strong resolution calling for regulations in the international pharmaceutical trade was watered down in final negotiations to a call for UNCTAD's participation in a programme to improve drug distribution in which WHO would take the lead.[72]

WHO, meanwhile, had carefully side-stepped the code issue in its 1982 WHA. Several government representatives, including those from Chile, Cuba, Ghana, The Netherlands, Romania, Samoa and Sudan, stressed the importance of WHO controls to enable developing countries to defend themselves from double standards and high drug prices. A surprisingly strong resolution called on WHO to implement the APED 'in its entirety'. HAI, which had lobbied strongly at the WHA for a code, took this to mean that the possibility of working on a code was still wide open.[73]

## Encouraging drug supply

By the 1984 WHA, when the APED came up for debate again, it had begun to show some signs of action, due in no small part to the recruitment of Dr Ernst Lauridsen as its director. Previously, he had been working for the Danish government aid agency, DANIDA, and in his new job at the APED, he reported directly to WHO's Director General, Dr Halfdan Mahler. Clearly, WHO was serious about making the APED work, and Lauridsen threw himself into the job with great relish.

The main focus in those early years was to encourage national governments, who had all voiced support for the APED at the 1981 WHA, to develop realistic plans and programmes to put theory into practice. A key area was seen as the supply of essential drugs, and measures to ensure that, particularly in rural areas, health posts were stocked with at least a basic armoury to deal with prevalent disease conditions.

Within the industry, there had been a recognition for many years that it was necessary to play a game of 'carrot and stick' with the international organisations. The 'carrot' came early. Virtually at the same time as the industry began its war of words against the concept of essential drugs, several European pharmaceutical companies made an offer to WHO to supply some essential drugs to the poorest developing countries at a 'favourable price'. By 1977, companies in West Germany had made such an offer, followed shortly afterwards by the three major Swiss companies, and by the beginning of the 1980s some 50 to 60 companies around the world had joined in the offer.[74] The offer initially caused some problems for WHO. First, WHO is not an operational agency, that is, it does not operate projects or programmes, but relies on supplying technical advice to governments who wish to introduce such programmes. Thus, it was in no position to buy the drugs and pass them on. Second, the offer of a 'favourable price' was vague: no details were given by the industry as to what the final price might be. The industry pointed out that it was impossible to quote actual prices until the level of demand was known and delivery schedules were worked out on a country by country basis.[75] Third, the question of which countries the offer applied to was also left hanging. When WHO assumed that the original German offer was for all countries in Africa, the industry responded in 1979 that it was only for the 'most needy countries and then only with some of the most essential drugs'.[76] When WHO asked the IFPMA if it would consider Peru an acceptable country, the IFPMA said that it did not consider Peru one of the least developed countries.[77] Fourth, the industry insisted on sending its own experts together with the drugs, ostensibly to train health workers to ensure the drugs were properly distributed, although some observers suspected that the industry simply hoped to use the WHO APED as a way to improve access into Third World markets.[78] Finally, WHO had to be careful not to appear to be recommending a particular company's drug over anothers by accepting the offer.

Thus, for nearly five years the offer lay on the table virtually untouched. One commentator notes that perhaps the 'carrot' was really a 'stick'; it allowed the industry to proclaim its desire to act responsibly and at the same time to chastise WHO for its inefficiency in failing to act on the offer.[79] In January 1982, at WHO's Executive Board meeting, it looked as if, at long last, some progress was going to be made. The IFPMA reiterated its offer and WHO issued a press release with the heading 'WHO Director General welcomes industry offer of drugs for developing countries'.[80] The press release spoke of 'a new era of close co-operation' with the pharmaceutical industry and hinted at 'exciting new developments' which could be expected from 'this generous offer and renewed co-operation between industry and WHO'.

## A changing political climate

What had changed? Essentially, nothing. By January 1984, one report noted that the companies had 'failed to deliver on their 1982 promise'. At the most, one million dollars' worth of drugs had been contributed to WHO's anti-malaria programme and a handful of small-scale bilateral schemes had been negotiated directly between the industry and African governments.[81] The global political climate had changed: conservative administrations were in power in several Western European countries and in the USA, the global negotiations on the New International Economic Order were rapidly getting bogged down, high inflation and rising debt were rampant in many developing countries, and the focus of political attention was moving from international policies to national efforts to contain economic difficulties and prevent local unrest. The message was coming across clearly to WHO that the time for confrontation with industry was over, and WHO heard it. Although support for the APED was still strong within WHO, the shifting political climate meant that it would have to appear more even-handed in its dealings with the industry and the industry's critics.

To reinforce the message, at the 1984 WHO Executive Board meeting, Neil Boyer from the US State Department complained that WHO officials were monitoring the IFPMA code of marketing, something, he said, that WHO should not be doing. The 'monitoring' consisted of the submission of five separate advertisements noticed by WHO staff while travelling in developing countries.[82] He also signalled that any attempt to try to develop a marketing code within WHO would be opposed by the USA.

The message was repeated at the 1984 WHA. Caught by surprise over a resolution on infant feeding which called for WHO to look at the promotion of unsuitable weaning products, Boyer claimed the resolution would 'push WHO into more controversy and diminish international support for WHO.... WHO should not get involved in marketing practices across the world.'[83] The USA followed up its annoyance at the baby foods debate with a 'no' vote a few hours later on a resolution on drugs. According to *Business International* the negative vote by the USA was 'out of fear that any discussion on pharmaceutical selling and promotional practices would foment LDC sentiments for an easy multilateral solution to what it sees principally as an issue for domestic regulation'.[84] The resolution's main worry was the demand for WHO to arrange a special meeting to be held in 1985 with experts from governments, health workers, industry, and non-governmental organisations to discuss the 'means and methods to ensure rational use of drugs' and to discuss the 'role of marketing practices in this respect, especially in developing countries'.[85] The meeting sounded as if it would be similar to the one in 1979 which led to the development of the International Code of Marketing of Breast-milk Substitutes.

HAI put considerable effort into lobbying the 1984 WHA. A small team of journalists was recruited to work on the production of a newspaper, *Health Now*, during the two-week WHA – a strategy used by other NGOs at UNCTAD conferences and a few other UN international meetings. Five issues appeared which reported on some of the proceedings of the WHA, gave background information about the drugs problem (and other subjects), and provided a vehicle for getting HAI's message across to the delegates. *Health Now* proved to be popular reading with most of the delegates, and the lobby team found itself being sought out by delegates for copies, and inevitably a chat about the drugs problem. Also popular was an exhibition and a video presentation which called attention to the problems of drug marketing in developing countries. A pack for delegates included a leaflet,[86] *The Way Forward*, which called the WHO APED 'one of the most important initiatives ever taken' by WHO. HAI noted that while the policies of the APED offered considerable hope, there was still much to be done in terms of putting those policies into practice. HAI also said that the time had come for the expansion of the programme to cover the private as well as the public sector and that *all* drugs should:

- meet real medical need
- have significant therapeutic value
- be acceptably safe
- offer satisfactory value for money.

HAI said that these principles 'should be emphasised as an integral part of WHO's Action Programme on Essential Drugs'. Within a year, they were: the first issue of WHO's *Essential Drugs Monitor* highlighted the principles on its front page, and subsequent issues continued to do so.[87] The leaflet argued that WHO should take the lead in helping to develop 'acceptable international standards for drug marketing and promotional practices' and that governments should then use such standards as the basis for national legislation.

HAI's lobby effort was described as 'hard to beat' by *Business International*.[88] The industry too clearly recognised the effectiveness of the lobby.

As Richard Arnold, the new executive vice-president of the IFPMA, put it in October 1984, 'the vigorous campaign by the activists has had some discernible effect.... I am sorry to say we are an industry under attack.'[89]

## Towards Nairobi

If tension had been evident at the 1984 WHA, it became magnified as preparations got underway for the international conference of experts which WHO was supposed to hold. In November 1984, Dr Mahler consulted with the WHO Executive Board's ad hoc committee on drug policies about the organisation of the conference, which led to the development of an agenda and a list of working papers. The government of Kenya was asked whether it would be willing to host the conference, and agreed to hold it in Nairobi. The choice of Kenya was in part because it was one of the countries with a well-developed essential drugs programme, which would enable participants to see such a programme in action.[90] As the time for the conference, which was held at the end of November 1985, drew near, an incredible veil of secrecy[91] was wrapped around it. The 92 participants – drawn from governments, national drug regulatory authorities, the pharmaceutical industry, consumer and patient organisations, health care providers, academics and representatives from other UN agencies and from NGOs – were asked by WHO not to divulge the contents of the 10 background papers in advance of the conference. Even the list of participants was kept a closely guarded secret to avoid 'undue pressure' on them, according to one WHO official. An edition of WHO's *Essential Drugs Monitor* due out before the conference, which planned to give extensive coverage of the issues to be discussed, was scrapped. The way in which the conference was structured, totally in plenary sessions with no working groups, meant that the 92 participants would have an average of 10 minutes each to speak, hardly an encouragement for dialogue. And, rather than allow the participants to develop recommendations, the conference was to be summed up by Dr Mahler, and his summation would form the report of the conference to the 1986 WHA.[92] Two consultants who were asked to prepare one of the ten background papers – that on the distribution and use of pharmaceuticals in developing countries – noted after the conference that their original paper was 'skillfully augmented, rewritten and presented to participants in a format more compatible with WHO's need for an "objective" context rather than a provocative one', which led them subsequently to publish the paper in its near original form.[93] Several other papers were also 'modified' and one was not submitted to the conference at all, apparently because of 'its strong bias against the private pharmaceutical industry'.[94]

In September 1985, when WHO learned that HAI planned to hold a regional meeting about pharmaceuticals in Nairobi immediately before the WHO international conference, in order to be able to invite some of the participants at low or no cost, an attempt was made to persuade HAI to cancel the meeting, or at least postpone it until after the WHO event. When because of local arrangements this was not possible, WHO confirmed in writing that it understood that the HAI meeting was only 'concerned with the drug situation in East Africa and is not related to the WHO Conference' and that 'no press statement bearing on the WHO Conference will be issued after the HAI East African Drug Meeting'.[95]

One of HAI's international coordinators at the time, Virginia Beardshaw, said that there had been 'extraordinary industry pressure' to keep the WHO conference as 'low-key and uncontroversial as possible', and that she was concerned that some people within WHO were seeing the conference primarily as 'a damage limitation exercise' rather than an opportunity to take a stand and move forward.[96] Certainly the industry wanted to see the conference focus on the less controversial questions of quality and safety. According to Monique Caillat, head of communications for the IFPMA, the industry wanted to see some proposals emerging to strengthen the WHO quality certification scheme. 'We've always been in favour of this.'[97] Richard Arnold of the IFPMA suggested that adequate training of health workers and wiser procurement of only high-quality products were other issues that the industry would be prepared to agree with.[98]

One issue that the industry did not want to see discussed was an international code of marketing. HAI had earlier recognised the futility of arguing for a code and had already changed its strategy for the conference. An indication of this became apparent by June 1985 when Charles Medawar of Social Audit, an active participant in HAI, attended a seminar entitled 'Another Development in Pharmaceuticals' organised by the Dag Hammarskjöld Foundation in Uppsala, Sweden. He presented a paper on 'International regulation of the supply and use of pharmaceuticals' which noted that it would be unrealistic to expect WHO to develop and operate a full-scale code, but that it could and should develop a set of criteria for the approval and rejection of different types and classes of drugs – something which could be of major use to drug regulatory authorities – and should develop some basic standards relating to the supply, promotion and use of drugs.[99] HAI's major focus had shifted from the concept of a code to one of more general standards but, more importantly, it was working towards limitations on the numbers of drugs on the market. As Medawar put it, 'reducing the number of drugs must come first. There is no point in trying to control the promotion of, or provision of information about, drugs that aren't wanted in the first place. The first priority is to have these drugs removed.'[100]

## A 'serene' meeting

Dr Mahler said at the beginning of the WHO conference that he hoped it would 'create no sensations'.[101] He stressed that the participants were present in their individual capacities as 'experts' on the subject of drugs. Drawing attention to the experts from the pharmaceutical industry and the consumer groups, he said they were not in Nairobi 'to vent their particular positions and to create a battleground for different opinions between consumers and industry'.

Outside the meeting, both the pharmaceutical industry and HAI set up information offices and kept a steady stream of material pouring into the hands of Nairobi's journalists. One correspondent for a major news agency said he had never before received so much information on a single subject.

The conference itself was conducted in what Dr Mahler described in a final press conference as a 'serene atmosphere'. The experts present called for the development of national drug policies based on objective and unbiased information, and invited WHO to take a leadership role without becoming 'a supranational manipulator of governments'. Dr Mahler pointed out that the essential drugs concept was vital to the rational use of drugs and that WHO would 'make a very special effort to try to make this penetrate into governmental national drug policies. We can only be an international supporter of governments as they put their drug house in order.'

The pharmaceutical industry supported the conclusion that WHO could not function as a supranational regulatory body. According to the IFPMA, 'most of the major decisions involving the use of drugs must be taken by national governments'.[102]

WHO was asked to establish an expert committee to produce guidelines on ethical advertising by expanding and updating a 1968 WHA resolution. Dr Mahler emphasised that at no time during the meeting was the case made for the development of an international code. He said that if the 1986 WHA approved the recommendations of the Nairobi meeting, he would call in consumer groups, industry, drug regulatory agencies and others to develop the guidelines on advertising as part of an entire package supporting national drug policies.

The question of how to decide which drugs are 'essential' brought disagreement within the meeting. Although there was resounding support for WHO's essential drugs concept, Dr Mahler noted that the 'tactical variants' in implementing it brought differences of opinion. Some experts argued that concentrating on the supply of 30–50 essential drugs to the poorest sectors of the population was the right approach, while others called for reductions in the overall numbers of drugs first, so that the selection of essential drugs and the provision of information about them would be easier to handle. Dr Mahler noted that with a better flow of information about drugs, in many countries there would probably be fewer drugs on the market.

Dr Mahler said the conference agreed that no country could cope with the 'irrationalities without having very firm drug regulatory mechanisms', and recommended that WHO convene a working group to develop the minimum requirements for drug regulation, leaving it up to individual governments to implement and improve upon them. This was described by Dr E. L. Harris of the UK Department of Health as a key measure and he pledged UK government support for training programmes for such authorities.

As expected, improvements in WHO's certification scheme were called for, so that more information about how and why drugs are registered would be made available to importing countries. The meeting also recommended better information for both the prescribers and consumers of drugs. Dr Mahler said the question of how to provide better information to consumers permeated everything that was discussed about national drugs policies. Consumers should understand the drug regulatory authorities, the selection of drugs, and why they were being selected. 'Unless we succeed in communicating with the consumers we will fall very short on any rational use of drugs. Most of us, being representatives of gods on earth as doctors, are not very good at communicating through this kind of arrogance with our consumers and therefore there is a whole new ball game in training all of us in much better facilities for communicating.'

One of the disappointments of the meeting was expressed by Dr Elizabeth Quamina, chief medical officer from Trinidad and Tobago. Although she agreed that a firm strategy had been developed, she pointed out that there had been little identification of resources to sustain implementation of the strategy. Dr Mahler replied that because the meeting had been conducted in a serene atmosphere and arrived at broad consensus, he felt many governments at the 1986 WHA would declare their willingness to provide money and manpower.

## Controversy in the corridors

Serenity within the meeting was not matched outside. The opening day of the meeting saw an angry response from Dr Mahler at a preliminary press conference when he discovered that a six-page document prepared by the conservative US-based Heritage Foundation had been slipped into WHO's information pack for journalists.[103] The Heritage Foundation material urged the experts to oppose 'medical need' as a criteria for evaluating drugs. Dr Mahler called the incident a 'highly undesirable practice' and said he would take the matter up with the local authorities. The author of the document, Roger Brooks, was in Nairobi and claimed he had been given permission by the Kenyan government information service to distribute it. Subsequent investigation revealed that Brooks had spoken to a technician installing microphones in the press conference room. The technician said he told Brooks he was unable to give permission, but Brooks went ahead and put the document inside WHO's press kit. Later in the week, he said that because of his experience with other UN agencies where reports of the Heritage Foundation were 'routinely confiscated from UN premises' and thrown away, he wanted to make sure the paper got out. 'I didn't intend in any way to either disrupt the press conference or imply that WHO condoned the views in that paper.' He subsequently sent Dr Mahler a long letter of apology.

The Heritage Foundation paper drew heavily on a booklet prepared by the US PMA,[104] but a PMA spokesman said that Brooks had acted independently and that if the PMA had been aware of his action, it would have tried to stop him.

Before the shock waves of this incident had receded, a new controversy hit Nairobi. WHO and Radio Nederland TV had been working on a film about essential drugs, *The Pill Jungle*, which was to be screened at the meeting for press and participants. But two hours before the film's producer and Radio Nederland's director of public relations were due to fly to Nairobi, they received a telex from WHO cancelling the screening without explanation. When they arrived in Nairobi, they were told by WHO that they could go ahead with a showing of the film to the press, but not to the delegates.

Dr Mahler explained that the film 'was disturbing a very important group of experts' and it was his duty to 'try to recreate serenity'. He declined to identify this group, but diplomatic sources in Nairobi confirmed that the pharmaceutical industry had met with WHO staff the evening before the telex was sent. The same sources said that they had been told by WHO officials that if the film was shown the industry could not guarantee participation in the meeting. The film's producer, Willy Lindwer, said the industry had acquired a copy of the first draft of the script, which was later substantially altered, and used this as the basis of the complaint. 'The film is not controversial at all. It just shows the facts.'

Dr Mahler denied that WHO was under any pressure during the meeting. 'Nobody has come into my office to say "if you present it this way or that way we shall do this or that". Pressure in my opinion implies a threat and there has not been one of these groups ever implying a threat to me personally or, as far as I am concerned, to any other WHO staff.'

Despite the controversy, Dr Mahler was confident that the proposals from the meeting would be accepted by the 1986 WHA. 'They make eminently good sense within what the Assembly has already decided upon with Health for All and Primary Health Care.'

According to Dr Harris, from the UK Department of Health, 'the various conflicting groups got together in a sensible and educative way without polemics to discuss the subject in a rational manner'. Many other delegates described the meeting as 'productive' and 'constructive', and praised the consumers for their articulate and intelligent contributions.

Overall, the pharmaceutical industry described the meeting as 'constructive' and welcomed the 'low-key' discussion. Industry spokesmen declined to comment on the specific proposals outlined by the meeting 'since many of the points are subject to widely ranging interpretation'.

HAI consultant Dr Wilbert Bannenberg said, 'We got a lot of things done that would have been impossible a couple of years ago. We're making progress towards the reduction of numbers of drugs.' He added that the work would continue at the next and subsequent WHAs. Charles Medawar noted that a senior WHO official had told him that the conference 'couldn't have happened two years ago. The industry would simply have walked out.'[105] Ironically, the words echo almost exactly the comments made by Dr Mahler at the conclusion of the WHO/UNICEF meeting on infant and young child feeding in October 1979.[106]

## Preparing for the next round

In a final press release, WHO coined a phrase to describe the success of the Nairobi conference: the 'spirit of Nairobi'. The idea that WHO sought to convey was that the conference had inspired a sense of co-operation and collaboration. It was not necessary to look further than the brief report drafted by PMA president Gerry Mossinghoff within days of the end of the conference to see how fragile the Nairobi spirit was, and how much of a myth was the idea that the participants were simply 'experts' representing their own viewpoints.[107] Mossinghoff told his colleagues in the industry:

> We should all be deeply grateful for the strong support we received from the US Government at all levels in keeping Nairobi from getting out of control, particularly the very effective work of Frank Young [US FDA Commissioner] before and during the Conference.[108]

According to the International Organisations Monitoring Service (IOMS), Young went to Nairobi with a detailed series of 'briefing books' and a point-by-point reply to each of the over 50 discussion points raised by the conference background papers. The US State Department, the FDA, the President's Office of Science and Technology Policy and the US Surgeon-General's office were among those represented on an inter-agency group which prepared the documentation. In Nairobi, WHO was shown the briefing books to get the point across that the US Government 'took this exercise very seriously; was well prepared for it; had sent Commissioner Young not just to speak for himself, but for the united, coordinated voice of the US Government – including the White House'.[109]

The IOMS report left corporations with a sobering, although erroneous, prediction. IOMS concluded from its 'sources' that the Nordic bloc governments were working with HAI members to develop a resolution for the May 1986 WHA that would use the Nairobi Conference results as the excuse to pursue a pharmaceutical code. The PMA obviously took this piece of 'intelligence' to heart, as in April 1986 Mossinghoff told the PMA annual meeting that 'there may be a move at the WHA by some countries to go beyond the Nairobi results ... we are working hard with Dr Young and the State Department in preparing for the Geneva meeting'.[110]

Interestingly, the US administration had also clearly 'swallowed' the IOMS intelligence. Dr Otis Bowen, Secretary of the US Department of Health and Human Services, also told the PMA annual meeting that the government would not want to see 'an international drug marketing code under the auspices of the WHO'.

Mossinghoff's report in December 1985 noted that in order for the proposals from Nairobi to be put into effect, a series of expert committees would be necessary 'and we can expect the US Government and other Western nations to oppose additional funding for these committees'.

Indeed, by the beginning of 1986, funding was a major concern for WHO. Several US Congressional budgetary amendments adopted in 1985 were aimed at reducing the US contribution to the UN and its agencies unless they were prepared to introduce voting on financial matters in accordance to the proportion of the budget paid by each country and/or by the proportion of US funds used for the benefit of communist countries and by the proportionate share of the salaries of Soviet nationals in the UN agencies. WHO was clearly aware of some of the dangers it was facing.

## The controversy increases

The May 1986 WHA had three highly controversial issues on its agenda – infant and young child nutrition, tobacco, and the rational use of drugs. Dr Mahler had already told WHO's Executive Board, which met in January 1986:

> on many occasions over the past few years, the very survival of WHO has been at stake. Was it not a justifiable cause of anxiety when a president of

the Health Assembly was told at midnight by certain delegates that unless a highly sensitive political issue was resolved by the following morning there would be very serious consequences for the Organisation?[111]

In his usual fashion, Mahler referred to some real event in such an oblique manner that his listeners were able to interpret it in an endless series of ways. He could have been referring to the infant feeding debates, the drugs debates, the tobacco debates, the debates about the health consequences of nuclear war, the health circumstances of the Palestinians, the health consequences of the Iran–Iraq war or of the *contra* attacks and US economic blockade of Nicaragua. The 'certain delegates', like the 'important group of experts' in Nairobi, were equally unidentified, as were the 'serious consequences'. But he was able to convey a sense of crisis, and a need for caution.

When it was brought to Mahler's attention that HAI, this time in conjunction with IBFAN, was planning to produce another series of its successful newspaper *Health Now* at the WHA, he decided this was an unnecessary provocation and wrote to Lars Broch, the director of the International Organisation of Consumers Unions (IOCU), which was a founding member of both networks, and an NGO in official relations with WHO. Mahler pointed out that the privileges of official relations 'certainly do not entitle you to distribute newspapers to delegates in the course of the Health Assembly. I trust you will take the necessary measures to prevent action whose consequences for the relationships between the IOCU and WHO are obvious.'[112] Broch responded that IOCU had no intention of breaching any rules, nor of distributing the paper during sessions of the WHA.[113] (The distribution strategy which had been worked out in 1984 and which was repeated in 1986 was to deliver copies of the newspaper to the hotels where delegates were staying. HAI and IBFAN lobbyists and the journalists working on the paper also carried copies with them and, if asked, would give one to a delegate.) A report by IOMS noted that during the WHA IOCU's representatives 'behaved with seriousness and dignity, winning the sympathy and attention of a large number of delegations'.[114]

Before the WHA even began, WHO was under a much more real threat than anything which an NGO-produced newspaper could deliver. The Heritage Foundation had produced yet another document that was critical of WHO and which called on the US Government to get tough with WHO, even to the point of considering withdrawal from it.[115] As IOMS pointed out,[116] the Heritage report was likely to be associated with the viewpoint of US business and of the US administration. As a whole, IOMS noted that the report suffered from a 'poor quality of analysis' and that the section on company issues was particularly bad as it contained 'numerous factual errors, relies too heavily on hearsay and only provides quotes out of context as evidence'. Because the only sources cited in this section were from US industry associations and executives, IOMS said that it appeared that Heritage had the full co-operation of US industry in preparing the report and that therefore the faulty analysis might be erroneously seen by WHO and some of its member states as indicative of the perspective of US executives concerning WHO. Certainly this was the view taken by two major articles which later appeared in the *Times of India*.[117] Ironically, the Heritage report contrasted strikingly with a 1985 report from Heritage which said that WHO was an agency worthy of US support.[118]

It was little wonder then, that Dr Mahler's first major speech to the WHA contained yet another cryptic allusion. He told the delegates: 'when you are up to your neck fighting alligators, remember, you came to drain the swamp in the first instance'. In a wry comment, a *Lancet* report on the WHA noted that 'there was no shortage of alligators, in all shapes and sizes. Alligators are native only to America.'[119]

Certainly there was some interesting 'wildlife' in Geneva during that 1986 WHA. Daniel Nelson, the associate editor of the London-based Gemini News Service, related an incident that occurred as attempts were underway to work out the wording on a controversial resolution about infant feeding:[120]

> When a group of delegates at the Geneva Assembly met privately to work out a compromise resolution on the babyfood issue, the microphones which normally carry the simultaneous translations were left on, so that the conversation could be heard in the gallery upstairs. At least three people discovered the oversight, and decided to listen in. I was tipped off and found two senior infant formula company representatives crouched on the floor to avoid detection, listening to the confidential discussion and making notes.

One of them was a senior executive of an American company which also has sizeable pharmaceutical interests.

Once again, it was Neil Boyer from the US State Department who laid down the constraints within which WHO should be operating.[121] He said it was the USA's

> strong position that the World Health Organization should not be involved in efforts to regulate or control the commercial practices of private industry, even when the products may relate to concerns about health. This is our view regarding infant food products, and pharmaceuticals and tobacco and alcohol.

## Revised drug strategy

The USA again opposed a resolution on infant foods, but supported resolutions on pharmaceuticals and on tobacco. The resolution on pharmaceuticals was a bland one, simply endorsing Dr Mahler's summary of the Nairobi Conference and approving a 'revised drug strategy' based on the deliberations in Nairobi. Included in the strategy was a provision for six meetings of experts on: extending the WHO Certification Scheme; developing model drug information sheets and a model drug formulary and guidelines for rational prescribing; preparing guidelines for a simple drug regulatory authority; updating the ethical criteria for drug advertising approved in 1968; preparing guidelines on national drug policies; and preparing guidelines on communicating with patients.[122] Bland though it was, the resolution clearly confirmed WHO's mandate to continue work on the essential drugs programme.

In summarising the WHA, IOMS noted that groups such as HAI which 'were an insignificant political force just five years ago ... are here to stay and will be a much more serious international force in the future'.[123] In addition to the success and impact of *Health Now*, IOMS singled out a HAI publication, *Problem Drugs*,[124] released just before the WHA debate on pharmaceuticals, as an impressive document. The publication focused on nine categories of drugs, and pointed out that some 70–80 per cent of the products in most of those categories were ineffective, irrational, or harmful. According to IOMS:

> It is already seen by many as essential source material and will remain so for some time to come, since industry has no alternative package. Some industry representatives found the HAI package to be poorly researched and inadequate. Their claims carried no credibility, however, since they had no better-researched alternative information.

HAI's behaviour at Nairobi and at the WHA – low-key, professional, sensible – won considerable respect. With the industry still looking for HAI to push for a pharmaceuticals code, HAI had been able to focus on a different approach and develop the necessary information to reinforce its call for a reduction in the numbers of products on the market. Nearly three years earlier, HAI had heard from officials within WHO that it was totally unrealistic to expect WHO to act on moves for a code, but that it was a very useful strategy to push from time to time in order to keep the industry nervous. The strategy had succeeded.

Five years after its founding, HAI had reached an important stage in its development. To consider this and to plan for the future, after the 1986 WHA, HAI staged an international meeting involving 45 participants from 27 countries. From this there emerged a clear recognition that the expert committee meetings were an important focus, as was the need to hone in on some of the more obviously useless drugs.

In March 1987, *International Barometer* – a newsletter designed to inform business, government and other opinion leaders of the aims and activities of issue-oriented organisations – described HAI as a 'model international activist network' which had been able to stop the marketing of a number of drugs and 'successfully helped shape international and national debate on health care systems'. It noted that HAI's ability to transform the drugs market was due to its 'painstaking documentation' of how drugs are promoted and used, coupled with public education campaigns 'built on solid information and powerful emotional pleas'.[125] Another important strength was the ability of HAI to act as an international support system for efforts by groups at the national or regional level to work for changes in local health and drug policies. And, in several countries, changes were occurring which offered some real hope that people would begin to get the medicines they needed without having to put up with the jungle of ineffective or potentially harmful products.

# 6.   National experiences

*Yet another lesson is to be nervous when there is no opposition –
as in the passing of the National Drug Policy when all of the 200
Congressmen are sponsors of the bill and all of the 23 senators are
co-sponsors of it. The absence of overt opposition means that there
is a covert opposition (especially in this country).*

Dr Alfredo R.A. Bengzon, Secretary of Health of the Philippines[1]

If the development of health and drug policy at an international level is fraught
with difficulty, its development at the national level is often doubly so. By
mid-1989, more than 100 countries had at least started on the road to change.[2]
In Latin America, Africa, Asia and even in Europe, national governments have
had varying degrees of success in putting into practice the policies of rational
drug use. The case of Bangladesh is an interesting one.

## Bangladesh

At the Golden Drug Store in Dhaka, Mufazzal Huq handed over 10 diazepam
tablets made by the local company Square, without asking for a prescription or
even enquiring why such a powerful tranquilliser might be needed. He claimed
he was a licensed pharmacist but was unable to produce his certificate. When
asked about giving out drugs without a prescription, he said, 'I have made a
mistake. I won't do it again.'[3]

In Dhanmondi, Akhtar runs a small roadside stall selling cigarettes, sweets,
fruit and Glaxo's brand of paracetamol. He gets the paracetamol from the same
wholesaler who supplies the cigarettes. He knows it is a remedy for fever and
pain and sells about 60 tablets a day.

Near the riverfront in Dhaka, a vitamin salesman complete with a portable
tape recorder, 30-minute tape, and a profusion of anatomy charts, encourages a
crowd of onlookers to try his vitamins for everything from blood disorders to
sexual impotency. The capsules, a combination of vitamins A and D, are
imported from China. The label contains no information about dosage, which
company produced them, no batch number, no date of manufacture. He said he
sold about 30 bottles a day, and claimed to have a licence to sell medicines 'but
I left it at home'. The only sensible advice on the tape was the message, repeated
every few minutes, that people in the crowd should be careful of pickpockets.

Almost anybody can sell drugs in Bangladesh. There are 15,000 *licensed* drug shops and an uncountable number of small stalls selling medicines. The Drug Administration is now very strict about not giving out licences for new shops unless there is a pharmacist, preferably an owner pharmacist. But what has gone on in the past is very difficult to undo.

### A typical market
Until mid-1982, the Bangladesh pharmaceutical market was fairly typical of an underdeveloped country. Although some 160 companies produced drugs in Bangladesh, the market was dominated by just eight foreign transnationals, who controlled 70 per cent of local production.[4]

A 1940 Drugs Act, described by one government source as 'outdated and grossly inadequate', did little to regulate pharmaceutical supply. Promotional activities by the companies had created a demand for many non-essential drugs with no relevance to real health needs.[5] Many physicians prescribed drugs at random, preferring a 'shotgun' approach to therapy rather than careful selection. This was further complicated by extensive self-medication on the part of many consumers. Traditional Unani, Ayurvedic and homoeopathic products were completely exempt from any control under the drug legislation.

The country's unregulated marketplace also led to overpricing. Evidence of transfer pricing by some TNCs was strong. The cost and freight charges (C&F) for oxytetracycline raw materials paid by various companies in 1979, given in the table below, vary enormously. A 1979 World Bank report on the viability of local production described the very high costs of some medicines as 'striking.' The study team calculated that tetracycline capsules could be produced for only one-fifth of the average commercial prices if raw materials were purchased from the cheapest reliable sources. Overall, the team concluded that all but one of the 31 essential drugs selected for primary health care could be produced at significantly lower costs.[6]

### Early efforts to change
This situation existed despite attempts by successive governments to improve matters. In 1974 the former President, Sheikh Mujib, tried to introduce central-ised buying of drugs from the cheapest source – mainly within the Soviet bloc

---

**Table 6.1 C&F price of oxytetracycline charged by various drug companies in Bangladesh (1979)**

| *Company* | *Source of supply* | *Price: $/Kg* |
|---|---|---|
| ICI (TNC) | ICI, London | 164.17 |
| Pfizer (TNC) | Pfizer, Hong Kong | 80.36 |
| Glaxo (TNC) | Glaxo Group Ltd., Yugoslavia origin | 54.55 |
| Pharmadesh (local) | Yugoslavia origin | 42.00 |
| KDH Labs. (local) | Yugoslavia origin | 33.00 |

Source: Chowdhury, Z. and S. 'Essential drugs for the poor'

or China. The idea was scrapped when the USA suggested that due to the apparent Eastern or Communist bias developing in the country, it might have to reconsider whether continued US food aid to Bangladesh made sense. Similar threats in Sri Lanka and Pakistan also led to the dissolution of plans in those countries to rationalise drug procurement and supply.[7]

A fledgling Drug Administration, established in 1975, had been slowly chipping away at the number of drugs on the market, but had difficulty cancelling registrations on the basis of doubtful efficacy, lack of usefulness or irrational combinations.

A list of 182 essential drugs was drawn up in 1978, but its application was confined to government procurement of drugs by the Central Medical Stores. New drug legislation was drafted in 1978, but could not be enacted 'due to persistent opposition from interested quarters', according to one government source.

One encouraging aspect of the market situation was the high level of local formulation. Only some 20 per cent of the total drugs consumed were imported as finished drugs; the raw materials required for the local formulation were still, however, a considerable drain on the country's foreign exchange bill. In 1981, more than 600 million taka ($32 million) was spent on imports of raw materials,[8] some 1.7 times more than the entire 1979–80 health budget.

Sadly, much of that import bill was for raw materials for non-essential products. Dr Humayun Hye, Director of Drug Administration in Bangladesh, cited the case of Fisons where 'almost 40 per cent of the foreign exchange allocation' for the import of pharmaceutical raw materials was used for making 'non-essential, practically useless preparations'.[9]

In Bangladesh, in 1981, an estimated 1,750 million taka ($79 million) was spent on drugs.[10] According to an expert committee set up to develop a national drug policy, 'nearly one-third of this money was spent on unnecessary and useless medicines such as vitamin mixtures, tonics, alkalisers, cough mixtures, digestive enzymes, palliatives, gripe water, and hundreds of similar products'.[11]

The expert committee also noted that the excessive production of these non-essential products meant that the country, as well as individual families, suffered. 'Though the multinationals have all the technologies and know-how to produce sophisticated essential drugs ... in Bangladesh, these companies are engaged mostly in formulation of simple drugs, including many useless products.'[12] As a result, 90 of the 182 essential drugs needed for the public health services were not being produced in the country.

In a country where less than 20 per cent of the population were able to buy medicines[13] and the government health services were constantly without drugs, Dr Hye said, 'inadequate resources should not be wasted on drugs that are irrelevant or of marginal usefulness, while millions are dying without health care, deprived of live-saving drugs'.[14]

## Little access to health care

According to the Bangladesh Medical Association (BgMA), five out of every six people die in the country without being seen by a doctor.[15] But as Dr Halfdan

Mahler, Director General of WHO, commented in 1981, 'most of the world's medical schools prepare doctors not to care for the health of the people but to engage in a medical practice that is blind to anything but disease and the technology for dealing with it'.[16] Bangladesh is no exception. Doctors qualifying in 1980 after five years' training did not have even a single lecture on appropriate non-drug treatments for diarrhoea, although diarrhoeal diseases account for over half the country's illness.[17] Most doctors are ill-prepared for work in the rural areas, yet that is where some 85 per cent of the country's 100 million-plus population reside. While the national average is one doctor for every 8,200 people, in the rural areas the ratio is a staggering one for every 36,000.[18] One rural health programme had to interview more than 200 newly qualified doctors before it found three who could identify and treat the major diseases prevalent in the country.

Generally, health conditions in Bangladesh are poor. The infant mortality rate is estimated at around 120 per 1,000 live births, with life expectancy only 52 years.[19] The five main diseases which contribute to infant mortality are diarrhoea and dysentery, neonatal tetanus, measles, respiratory infections, and various fevers.[20]

For those who survive infancy, childhood is grim – 40 per cent of children under five suffer mild to moderate malnutrition, and one in every ten children suffer severe malnutrition.[21] Yet Bangladesh has the most fertile soil and the largest potential inland fish resources in the world and could produce enough to feed its total population properly. The main obstacle to increased agricultural production lies in the structure of landholding: one tenth of the population own half the agricultural land. More than half the households are landless and rarely get enough to eat. In Bangladesh, a child whose family has no land is three times more likely to die by the age of one than if his or her family owns land.[22]

Well under 10 per cent of the infant population are immunised against the major six killer diseases. While immunisation is important in helping prevent disease, so too is access to clean water. In Bangladesh, only 41 per cent of the population have access to clean drinking water.[23]

Bangladesh's population is over 100 million and growing at the rate of 2.6 per cent per year,[24] yet only 19 per cent of married women under 50 years of age use some form of contraception – the two most popular are sterilisation and the rhythm method[25] – despite a multitude of agencies, both Bangladeshi and foreign, running all sorts of family planning activities, and despite a separate family planning budget that is some 40 per cent more than the health care budget.

## Low expenditure on health

In Bangladesh, the health budget is approximately 3 per cent of the country's total budget – only $1 per capita – yet the military budget is some 15 per cent. Even in neighbouring countries the expenditure on health is higher: in Burma it is $2 per head, in India $3, while Sri Lanka manages $4.[26]

The BgMA says the overall health budget is far too low. Health Minister Salauddin Quader Chowdhury, agrees that $1 a head is 'absolutely nothing. We just haven't the resources for providing health care facilities for our population.'

As an editorial in the *New Nation* newspaper put it during August 1986: 'The year 2000 is around the bend – and a dollar per head is too meagre an amount to reach that bend.'[27]

## Ruling elite

There has been no real political stability in Bangladesh since the country won its independence from Pakistan in 1971 after a bloody war. The army has taken over several times and although a National Assembly was elected in early 1986 and presidential elections were held towards the end of the year, long periods of martial law are a common occurrence.

Successive governments have failed to control excessive accumulation of wealth by the urban and rural elite. A relatively few people or families control the country – there may be coups and counter coups but essentially power revolves among a small group of people. Parties lack policies, they buy support and depend on the personal appeal of a figurehead. This is important in terms of health (and everything else) because it means that political parties do not have to make plans for national, workable structures. Francis Rolt, who studied the economic and political situation in Bangladesh over several years, comments that:

> none of the major political parties have research cells – everything is done on an ad hoc basis. What planning there is, is done by a self-interested bureaucracy, by international organisations like the UN which have little understanding of the political realities and by non-governmental organisations which are small and relatively powerless.[28]

## National Drug Policy

Following a coup in March 1982, the new government set up an eight-person Expert Committee to draft a drug policy. In June 1982, the National Drug Policy and the Drug (Control) Ordinance was enacted. The drug policy was designed to encourage the availability of essential drugs, reduce prices of drugs and raw materials, eliminate useless, non-essential and harmful drugs from the market, promote local production of medicines, improve the quality of drugs and of manufacturing practices, ensure the proper use of drugs, improve the standard of hospital pharmacies and retail pharmacies, promote the standardisation and quality of traditional Ayurvedic and Unani medicines and homoeopathic medicines, and ensure co-ordination among the government's various administrative branches of drug supply and control.

Chairman of the Expert Committee Professor Nurul Islam, described the task as 'herculean'. The committee drew up a list of 16 criteria for evaluating drugs, based on the most up-to-date scientific information available. Professor Islam said: 'This is rare for a developing country. Usually the information available is years out of date – not just one or two years – but several.'

The 1982 policy identified 150 essential drugs necessary for most therapeutic purposes – 12 for the use of village health workers, another 33 to be used by district health facilities, and the rest for use at the tertiary level of health care – together with an additional 100 supplementary drugs that some specialists in hospitals might require. Professor Islam said that this list, regularly reviewed to keep up to date with latest developments, would be adequate for the therapeutic needs of the country and in line with its economic resources. 'There would be no need for any additional products. The best way to give good medicine to the people is to take bad medicine away.'

The drug policy's most controversial measure was the removal of some 1,700 drugs described as 'useless, non-essential and/or harmful'. This led to a wave of protest from TNCs and many local companies, including a massive advertising campaign against the drug policy. The main line of attack was that the policy would destroy the pharmaceutical industry in Bangladesh, which in turn would affect other industries such as packaging and glass bottle manufacturing. A 1¼-page advertisement in the national press from the industry association, Bangladesh Aushadh Shilpa Samity (BASS) – whose member companies produce some 70 per cent of the country's drugs – was titled 'Crisis in drug industry – conspiracy against nation's drug industry must be thwarted'.

A Pfizer executive said that strict implementation of the policy could mean 'little hope for the future viability of the manufacturing units such as ours, and as a consequence would require a reconsideration of continuing our operations in Bangladesh'. He said the drug policy 'does not benefit the Bangladesh people and it certainly does not benefit Pfizer'.[29]

The Association of the British Pharmaceutical Industry (ABPI) called the drug policy 'a self-inflicted wound' to Bangladesh's health prospects. 'We believe that the policy is not going to yield the improvement in the availability of medicines in Bangladesh which the government are seeking.'[30]

The BgMA voiced opposition to the policy, although according to its secretary-general, Dr Sawar Ali:

> The Association did agree to the objectives of the drug policy. The way the drug policy came in was objected to by the Medical Association. The BgMA was not consulted as a national organisation in the formulation of the drug policy. Every medicinal product does have both a risk and a benefit, and the people who can judge whether it is risky for a particular patient or not are the doctors.

## External pressure

Other sources of opposition included the governments of the USA and Western European countries. One after the other, the ambassadors to Bangladesh from the USA, West Germany, the UK and The Netherlands paid 'courtesy' visits on the Health Minister and the Chief Martial Law Administrator. The message they conveyed was virtually identical: rescind this policy, or run the risk of a loss of foreign investment.

The US State Department admitted that the US PMA had asked it to bring pressure on the Bangladesh government to delay implementation of policy pending discussions with the manufacturers. 'The US Government is concerned that these regulations may inhibit further investment in Bangladesh.' Its involvement was justified by saying that the State Department 'has a statutory responsibility for assisting American interests abroad'.[31] Part of that assistance included the US Ambassador to Bangladesh, Jane Coon, helping to arrange a series of meetings for a group of 'scientific experts' from the USA who arrived for a week-long visit at the end of July 1982. The 'experts' were from the PMA, Squibb, Wyeth and SmithKline.[32]

Douglas Hurd, Minister of State at the UK Foreign and Commonwealth Office, said that although the UK was keen for Bangladesh to use its scarce resources wisely, it was

> also keen that they should succeed in their policy of encouraging foreign investment to help with the development of an industrial economy. We, in common with other Western governments, have explained this to the Bangladesh Government through our High Commission in Dhaka. It is important that in trying to achieve the aims of the pharmaceutical policy they do not discriminate against foreign owned manufacturing companies in Bangladesh and do not frighten off prospective foreign investors.[33]

Amidst all the pressure, the Bangladesh government decided to establish a Review Committee comprised of six military doctors to take another look at the drug policy. The Review Committee submitted its report to the government on 12 August 1982, but it was never made public. Reliable sources in Bangladesh confirmed that the report was extremely unfavourable to the policy: if its suggestions had been followed, today there would be no drug policy. The government made a small concession in September 1982 by rescinding the ban on 41 drugs and extending the time limits for removal of the other banned products.

Between 1982 and 1985 a regular stream of articles appeared in the local press about the drug policy. It would be tempting to accept what is written in the press as having some objectivity and substance, but in a country like Bangladesh, the media is highly political with many publications controlled by the government or friends of the government. Opposition newspapers often face periods of closure for printing articles which are too critical of government policy. Thus of the 13 main newspapers and magazines in the country, seven consistently supported the policy, four were consistently against the policy, and two sat on the fence for most of the time. Many of the articles which appeared, even those in favour of the policy, were based on rumours, misinformation and speculation. The government itself failed to issue any hard information about the policy until the end of 1983, when the general in charge of information, who personally objected to the policy, was removed from office. One publication which was particularly virulent against the policy was a 12-page weekly called *Pulse*, which pretends to be a 'medical journal'. Between November 1983 and May 1984, half of the 25 issues had page-one attacks on the policy. *Pulse* survives on advertising and on the fact that most of its 10,000 copies a week are bought by the drug TNCs and distributed by their sales representatives. BPI, the May and Baker subsidiary, for example, buys about 2,000 copies a week.[34]

## An appropriate policy

In 1986, Salauddin Quader Chowdhury, Minister of Health and Family Planning, described the Bangladesh drug policy as:

a dynamic step that could be beneficial to the Third World at large. If there is anything for which this particular administration would be remembered nationally and internationally, it would be in bringing forward a revolutionary policy in drug administration which is suited to the limited financial resources of our country and the priorities of our people. It has hurt some companies, maybe even some multinationals, but it would be unfair of any foreign company or multinational to assume that the drug policy was aimed to hurt any of them. The government really had a hard battle in implementing its policies, even at the risk of being misunderstood by many friendly countries and many friendly governments, but I'm sure by now that most of our friends have realised that our decisions were based on our national priorities rather than any motivated attempt at victimisation.

The US PMA was not one of those bodies that could be considered friendly. In 1985, it published a report[35] which claimed that the drug policy had 'fallen short of its objectives and accomplished little toward making "essential drugs" more available to the population'.[36] One of the key 'findings' of the report was that more than 100 prospective foreign investors had decided to withdraw applications to invest in Bangladesh. According to the PMA report, 'the effects on foreign drug companies of the Drugs (Control) Ordinance have left indelible scars on the country's image as a base for an attractive, safe, and reliable business community'. Another key criticism was that there was a 'total absence of quality control facilities' and that more than 100 of the 163 manufacturers in Bangladesh have no quality control operations 'worthy of mention'. The report also claimed that the retail prices of 160 drugs had increased by an average of 23 per cent between June 1982 and June 1984. The report also drew attention to an increase in the smuggling of banned drugs from India and Pakistan and the manufacture of 'spurious drugs' – imitations of products of 'reputable manufacturers' which were no longer available.

'Fictitious', says Dr Zafrullah Chowdhury, a member of the Expert Committee which drew up the policy. 'One or two of the drugs, if you try hard, can be bought on the black market, but the number is few and far between.'[37] In 1986 one researcher was unable to find more than one banned drug, despite a two-day search in four areas of Dhaka. That drug was a cough mixture, which had been smuggled into the country from India.[38]

The PMA's claim that Bangladesh's drug policy has led to a loss of foreign investment is virtually impossible to verify. However, within the pharmaceutical industry itself, there have been clear signs since the enactment of the policy that foreign companies have no intention of pulling out. In 1983, SmithKline actually opened up operations in Bangladesh and Ciba-Geigy confirmed plans to start a factory in 1987.[39] Glaxo 'has made a substantial investment in a new plant' in recent years.[40]

As far as quality is concerned, Dr Chowdhury had pointed out that 80 per cent of the drugs made in Bangladesh are produced by 20 companies – 8 TNCs and 12 local companies – 'and their quality I think would be comparable to Europe'. A report by the Danish and Swedish governmental aid authorities indeed found that quality control in Bangladesh was a problem, but that it had been a problem for some time and there was no evidence of a decline since the drug policy. In fact, government statistics showed that between 1983 and 1985 there was a steady decline in the percentage of substandard drugs found on the Bangladesh market, despite an increase in the number of samples taken over the three years. By 1985, only some 11 per cent of samples tested were found to be substandard, in comparison with neighbouring India, where a 20 per cent figure is common.[41]

Nonetheless, there are big gaps where drug inspectors cannot reach. One inspector is used for more than one district, and the Drug Administration sometimes relies on health service personnel to do the inspection and give a report. For minimum control, there should be at least one inspector for each of the 64 districts in Bangladesh, instead of the 35 currently employed. One of the main difficulties is the long delay in getting results, particularly on samples collected outside Dhaka. If a drug inspector collects a sample and is doubtful about its quality, he has to send it to Dhaka where it falls in the queue behind 200 other samples. By the time he gets the report, it is difficult to take action. Another difficulty, widely hinted at, but never proven, is that money changes hands to ensure that tests are favourable to the manufacturers.

**Price control**
Under a 1958 law, the Ministry of Commerce had the power to fix prices of essential items, including medicines. The 1982 drug policy and ordinance trans-

**Table 6.2 Comparative price of some imported raw materials in Bangladesh (1981–7)**

| Raw material | Average price ($/kg) 1981 | 1987 | % reduction |
|---|---|---|---|
| Amoxycillin trihydrate | 130 | 84 | 35.4 |
| Cloxacillin sodium | 95 | 88 | 7.4 |
| Doxycycline | 1,500 | 175 | 88.3 |
| Frusemide | 703 | 70 | 90.0 |
| Glibenclamide | 2,350 | 282 | 88.0 |
| Hyoscine butylbromide | 1,358 | 650 | 52.1 |
| Ibuprofen | 32 | 25 | 21.9 |
| Levamisole | 128 | 66 | 48.4 |
| Metronidazole | 56 | 22 | 60.7 |
| Mebendazole | 287 | 52 | 81.9 |
| Oxytetracycline | 54 | 23 | 57.4 |
| Propranolol | 490 | 23 | 95.3 |
| Rifampicin | 473 | 230 | 51.4 |
| Sulphamethoxazole | 37 | 18 | 51.4 |
| Tetracycline HCl | 64 | 42 | 34.4 |
| Trimethoprim | 60 | 26 | 56.7 |
| Metoclopramide | 1,200 | 80 | 93.3 |

Source: Bangladesh Drug Administration, 1988

**Table 6.3 Comparison of maximum retail price of some essential drugs before and after National Drug Policy in Bangladesh**

| Drug | Unit price ($) | | % decrease |
|---|---|---|---|
| | Before | After | |
| Tetracycline capsule 250 mg | 0.03 | 0.02 | 33.3 |
| Cotrimoxazole tablet 480 mg | 0.06 | 0.03 | 50.0 |
| Cotrimoxazole syrup | 0.78 | 0.43 | 44.9 |
| Amoxicillin capsule 250 mg | 0.10 | 0.07 | 30.0 |
| Amoxicillin syrup 60 ml | 0.96 | 0.68 | 29.2 |
| Cloxacillin capsule 250 mg | 0.06 | 0.05 | 16.7 |
| Cloxacillin syrup 60 ml | 0.84 | 0.66 | 21.4 |
| Metronidazole tablet 400 mg | 0.04 | 0.01 | 75.0 |
| Metronidazole syrup 60 ml | 0.70 | 0.46 | 34.3 |
| Levamisole tablet | 0.04 | 0.02 | 50.0 |
| Levamisole syrup 40 ml | 0.41 | 0.22 | 46.3 |
| Antacid tablet | 0.015 | 0.01 | 40.0 |
| Antacid suspension 200 ml | 0.69 | 0.60 | 13.0 |
| Metoclopramide tablet | 0.03 | 0.01 | 66.7 |
| Hyoscine butylbromide tablet | 0.04 | 0.02 | 50.0 |

Source: Bangladesh Drug Administration, 1988

ferred the power to fix drug prices to the Ministry of Health and its Drug Administration. One of the most important mechanisms for this was the requirement of prior approval for the import of raw materials. Government figures show that raw material prices for some key medicines have dropped by as much as 90 per cent. Some of this saving has found its way to the consumer, as retail prices for some essential drugs have dropped by anywhere from 13 to 75 per cent.

**Major achievements**
Another important change has been the tremendous increase in the local production of the 45 drugs most essential for primary health care. In 1981, only 30 per cent of local production was devoted to these 45 drugs; by 1987, the figure had reached 75 per cent. Much of the capacity displaced by the banned products has been taken up by this more useful production. Dr Hye described this as 'the number one achievement of the drug policy. In most developing countries you will not see a picture like this.'

Although the government admits that the supply of drugs to health care facilities is still far below requirements, statistics from the Drug Administration show that there has been a considerable improvement in the situation between 1981 and 1984.

Francis Rolt claims the policy has led to an increase in competition, lower prices for the most important drugs, increased production of essential drugs, fewer wasteful imports and better control over dangerous drugs – all without companies being 'seriously affected'.[42]

**Table 6.4 Drugs market in Bangladesh, 1981–7 (prices in $ million)**

| Year | 1981 | 1982 | 1983 | 1984 | 1985 | 1986 | 1987 |
|---|---|---|---|---|---|---|---|
| Total value all drugs | 65.92 | 74.22 | 79.18 | 96.25 | 111.38 | 120.36 | 132.07 |
| **IMPORTS** | | | | | | | |
| Total value | 13.5 | 11.8 | 10.7 | 10.5 | 11.9 | 14.3 | 9.4 |
| % of all drugs | 20.5 | 15.9 | 13.5 | 10.9 | 10.7 | 11.9 | 7.1 |
| **LOCAL DRUG PRODUCTION** | | | | | | | |
| Total value | 52.42 | 62.42 | 68.48 | 85.75 | 99.48 | 106.06 | 122.67 |
| % of all drugs | 79.5 | 84.1 | 86.5 | 89.1 | 89.3 | 88.1 | 92.9 |
| **By** TNCs | | | | | | | |
| Value | 33.92 | 36.92 | 33.33 | 41.21 | 43.00 | 41.52 | 50.84 |
| % of local production | 64.7 | 59.1 | 48.7 | 48.1 | 43.2 | 39.1 | 41.4 |
| **By national companies** | | | | | | | |
| Value | 18.50 | 25.50 | 35.15 | 44.54 | 58.48 | 64.54 | 71.83 |
| % of local production | 35.3 | 40.9 | 51.3 | 51.9 | 58.8 | 60.9 | 58.6 |
| **ESSENTIAL DRUGS** | | | | | | | |
| Value of 45 drugs | 15.90 | 22.74 | 35.39 | 55.45 | 64.24 | 74.24 | 91.70 |
| % of local production | 30.0 | 36.4 | 51.7 | 64.7 | 64.6 | 70.0 | 74.8 |

Source: Bangladesh Drug Administration, 1988.

**Table 6.5 Increased production of selected essential drugs compared with primary health care needs in Bangladesh (1981–4)**

| Drug | Unit | Est. need | Production 1981 | Production 1984 | % Increase | % of requirement 1981 | % of requirement 1984 |
|---|---|---|---|---|---|---|---|
| | | | (Millions of units) | | | | |
| Aspirin | tablet | 360 | 44.0 | 93.3 | 112.0 | 12.2 | 25.9 |
| Chloroquine | tablet | 360 | 60.0 | 71.6 | 19.3 | 16.6 | 19.8 |
| Antacid | tablet | 600 | 91.0 | 146.4 | 60.9 | 15.1 | 24.4 |
| Levamisole | tablet | 360 | 2.5 | 9.6 | 284.0 | 0.6 | 2.6 |
| ORS powder | sachet | 28 | 2.4 | 12.5 | 420.8 | 8.5 | 44.6 |
| Penicillin V | tablet | 450 | 24.0 | 90.2 | 275.8 | 5.3 | 20.0 |
| Ergometrine | tablet | 30 | 0.0 | 3.0 | | 0.0 | 10.0 |
| Iron | tablet | 360 | 86.0 | 197.0 | 129.1 | 23.8 | 54.7 |
| Ephedrine | tablet | 90 | 4.4 | 11.5 | 161.4 | 4.8 | 12.7 |
| Paracetamol | tablet | 600 | 50.0 | 297.2 | 494.4 | 8.3 | 49.5 |
| Chlorpheniramine | tablet | 150 | 52.0 | 70.8 | 36.2 | 34.6 | 47.2 |
| Procaine Penicillin | vial | 90 | 19.0 | 23.0 | 21.1 | 21.1 | 25.5 |
| Streptomycin | vial | 25 | 3.4 | 5.1 | 50.0 | 13.6 | 20.4 |
| Metronidazole | tablet | 360 | 31.0 | 125.1 | 303.5 | 8.6 | 34.7 |
| Tetracycline/oxytet. | caps. | 360 | 83.1 | 138.8 | 67.0 | 23.0 | 38.5 |
| Phenobarbitone | tablet | 50 | 8.6 | 15.0 | 74.4 | 17.2 | 30.0 |
| Intravenous fluids | bags | 10 | 0.8 | 1.2 | 50.0 | 8.0 | 12.0 |
| Vitamin B-complex | tablet | 180 | 38.4 | 71.0 | 84.9 | 21.3 | 39.4 |
| Benzyl Benzoate | bottle | 5 | 0.5 | 0.6 | 20.0 | 11.0 | 12.4 |
| Water for injection | amps. | 90 | 3.0 | 10.5 | 250.0 | 3.3 | 11.6 |
| Cotrimoxazole | tablet | 360 | 14.9 | 108.0 | 624.8 | 4.1 | 30.0 |

Note: Estimated needs are based on a 1979 World Bank survey.
Source: Bangladesh Drug Administration, 1986.

Today, although some controversy still simmers, most companies have learned to live with the drug policy. M. R. Chowdhury, general manager of BPI – a May and Baker subsidiary – said, 'We take it as a *fait accompli*.' For many local companies, although the policy initially hit them hardest, it has been a boon. Government statistics show that although the sales by multinational companies have not been reduced in absolute terms, their share of the market has declined from 65 per cent in 1981 to only 41 per cent in 1987. Four local companies now figure in the top 10 producers.

One company which is a major success story is the government-owned Essential Drugs Company Limited (EDCL). It was floundering badly in the early 1980s and in 1983/4 could manage a turnover of only 25 million taka ($925,000). However with the help of a loan from the Asian Development Bank to improve machinery, and a second plant financed by Japanese foreign aid, turnover increased to $8 million in 1987.

Those turnover figures understate the importance of EDCL because the company's drug prices are fixed by the board of directors which has the Minister of Health, the Secretary of Health, and Director of Drug Administration as members. As the government buys the entire output of the company, the buyer is also the manufacturer, and the prices are very reasonable, among the lowest in Bangladesh. The low price is made easier to achieve by the lack of any promotional costs, as EDCL has no need to employ any sales staff. Government sources claim if they had to purchase the medicine on the open market, it would cost at least 2.5 times as much.

Although the drug policy has not solved all the problems, nor indeed, even yet met all of its objectives, it has laid the foundation for the development of a drug market which meets the health needs of the country. Slowly, too, the prescribing patterns of doctors are changing. Professor Islam has pointed out that 'some doctors used to make every prescription out for six or eight drugs –

---

**Table 6.6 Top ten drug companies in Bangladesh (1987)**

| Company | Origin | Value of production $ million | % share of local production |
|---|---|---|---|
| Square | Bangladesh | 18.1 | 14.8 |
| Fisons | UK | 11.8 | 9.6 |
| Glaxo | UK | 10.0 | 8.2 |
| Pfizer | USA | 9.7 | 7.9 |
| EDCL | Bangladesh | 8.0 | 6.5 |
| BPI* | France | 6.3 | 5.1 |
| Opsonin | Bangladesh | 5.8 | 4.7 |
| Beximco | Bangladesh | 5.2 | 4.2 |
| Hoechst | FRG | 4.4 | 3.6 |
| Squibb | USA | 4.4 | 3.6 |

\* Owned by May and Baker, which is in turned owned by Rhone-Poulenc
Source: Bangladesh Drug Administration, 1988

two antibiotics, two types of vitamins, two enzymes and other drugs. Now they are putting down fewer medicines.'[43] The dire warnings of the pharmaceutical industry have been shown to be empty rhetoric. The TNCs are still making a profit; local companies have begun to thrive. In fact by 1986, BASS was full of praise for the policy, saying:

> it represents a philosophy whose scope extends beyond the need of today into realms of future.... The ordinance has been applied, tested and has to its credit today, many examples of its beneficial aspects ... lower drug prices ... reduced dependance on the foreign imports ... better appreciation of the people's needs by the industries.... Drug Control Ordinance 1982 has benefited not only the Pharmaceutical Industry but more the public at large.[44]

## WHO's position

Interestingly, WHO was somewhat slow in making favourable comments about the drug policy, even though Bangladesh was the first country to act after the introduction of the essential drugs concept. The local WHO representative, Dr Z. Sestack, said in July 1982, 'It is not WHO's role to either applaud or condemn the policy.'[45] When *South* magazine asked Dr J. Cohen, WHO's senior international health policy adviser for a comment, he replied testily, 'How would you like WHO to ask the government of Bangladesh to make comments on your magazine?'[46] It was not until WHO's Director General, Dr Halfdan Mahler, attended WHO's South East Asia Regional meeting held in Dhaka in September 1982 that a positive comment emerged. At the meeting, Dr Mahler congratulated Bangladesh 'on its courage in starting to put its drug house in order'.[47] As *South* pointed out, the behaviour of WHO led to a suspicion that the organisation was 'unwilling to tread on the toes of the transnational drug companies'.

Such a position is all the more remarkable considering that at the time, WHO was involved with the Danish and Swedish official government aid authorities, DANIDA and SIDA, in drawing up a project to improve drug supply and use in Bangladesh. A key figure in the negotiations was Dr Ernst Lauridsen, who had just been named as the new director of WHO's APED. The project was designed to deal with the one problem which the PMA had managed to identify accurately: that there were still difficulties in ensuring that people in the rural areas had access to essential drugs. Following an exploratory period, the project was finally launched in two areas (*upazillas*, each with a population of approximately 300,000). In addition to providing sufficient drugs to meet the health needs of these areas, the project is training health workers and looking at ways in which the management of the health service can be improved. As with the drug policy, the likelihood of some resistance was predicted, and the project is moving at a slow pace to try to ensure that producers, prescribers and consumers all work together to improve the situation.[48]

## Meeting basic needs in Norway

Whilst Bangladesh was a pioneer in the 1980s in implementing rational drug policies, Norway had built the basis for such an approach in the 1930s. One consequence of Norway's approach is the small number of preparations on the local market – about 2,000.[49]

The starting point for Norway's drug policy was that it should be an integral part of the country's national health care policy and that it should ensure that effective, safe, good-quality drugs were available to cover the country's health needs.

A number of key criteria are used for the selection of drugs in Norway. These include the following:

1. Selection should be based on scientific documentation.
2. The efficacy/toxicity ratio must be weighed against the severity of the disease.
3. New drugs should be more effective than those already on the market.
4. Drug combinations should be avoided unless they show a clear advantage over the use of each ingredient separately.
5. There should be a clear-cut medical need for any new product.
6. The number of drugs should be limited.[50]

Other considerations include price and local therapeutic traditions. As well, some drugs may be allowed on a restricted-use basis for hospitals or specialists only. Drug approval is limited to five years, thus ensuring a regular review of products.

The most controversial of these criteria is the so-called 'needs' clause. Between 1981 and 1983, approximately 60 per cent of the drugs rejected by the Norwegian authorities were turned down on the grounds that they did not meet a medical need in the country.[51] The term 'need' is not tightly defined and its use has really been defined in practice. In some cases, although there may already be a drug on the market which is effective in treating a particular disease condition, similar drugs may be permitted in order to encourage price competition or to ensure adequate supply in the event that the production capacity of a single manufacturer is insufficient.

**Drug use**

Does such an approach work? A detailed analysis of drug use in Norway during the 1970s found that some drugs were underused, some were overused, some were both, depending on the area of the country, and some were used reasonably correctly. Sales of anti-ulcer drugs increased, for example, despite a reduced incidence of peptic ulcers. In the early part of the decade, sales of laxatives were generally increasing, but in the latter part of the decade the shape of the market changed in response to information about the correct use of laxatives; there was an overall decrease in consumption and more purchases of bulk-forming laxatives, which were the drugs of choice. Sales of products containing iron or vitamin $B_{12}$ were estimated to be about twice the amount that could be predicted on the basis of medical need, and the researchers suggested that within this overuse figure, it was also likely that some sectors of the population who actually needed the drugs were not receiving them. Sales of antihypertensives were thought to be out of line with requirements: it seemed that sales promotion, tradition and the influence of specialists were playing a larger role than rational selection. Antibiotics were found to be overused: sales were enough to treat every man, woman and child in the country for four days each year, despite the calculation worked of a US study that the average person in an industrialised country has an illness that requires antibiotic therapy about once every five to ten years. The Norwegian study suggested that the use of anti-coagulants was probably below the optimum level. Whether or not the use of cardiac glycosides (like digitalis, for treatment of heart attacks), NSAIDs and other antirheumatic drugs, and both major and minor tranquillisers was optimal was unclear, although there was some suggestion that there was both under- and overuse. Contraceptive use and the use of narcotic analgesics, anti-epileptic drugs and anti-cancer drugs were considered to be reasonably rational.[52] Overall, the conclusion was that a level of drug use 'on the low side of present practice' would probably be the best advice, and that the way to achieve this improvement was through better education of prescribers and patients.[53]

The pharmaceutical industry has another opinion. Citing the case of beta-blockers, the industry claims that although only six such products are registered for use, 40 per cent of Norwegian doctors prescribe medicines for their patients which have not been approved for general sale, but which are available for use on a special request basis.[54] The implication is obvious: limited lists of drugs do not work and patients may be deprived of valuable therapy. To reinforce this point, the US PMA circulated a letter to patient groups and some health and development organisations in the USA in 1986 urging them to write to WHO to point out that restricted drug lists would 'increase the cost and risk of pharmaceutical research, reduce the number of new medicines, hamper the improvement of existing therapies and raise the ultimate cost of health care'.[55] To reinforce the message, the PMA also hosted a conference in 1987 on 'restricted drug lists: bad medicine, bad economics'. The strategy clearly worked, as in 1988 the IFPMA published selected comments from letters written to WHO by organisations such as the American Academy of Dermatology, the US Cystic Fibrosis Association, the American Medical Association, the American Society of Internal Medicine, the National Organisation for Rare Disorders, and the American Academy of Allergy and Immunology.[56] The Norwegian government, however, has no doubts whatsoever about the benefits of its approach to rational drug use. It says that the policy in Norway 'demonstrates that it is possible to limit the number of drugs on the market significantly without detriment to the patient'.[57]

## Costa Rica

Another country where efforts to rationalise drug use pre-date the WHO essential drugs concept is Costa Rica. The consequence of these efforts, together with other initiatives to provide extensive primary health care, has been a marked improvement in health, particularly infant and young child health, as was noted in Chapter 1. Today, the infant mortality rate is only 13.7 per 1,000 live births,[58] not much different from that of Norway.

The extensive public health care system reaches virtually the entire population. A national system of health insurance ensures that treatment at public sector hospitals or through public sector general practitioners is 'free'. As a consequence, the private sector is relatively small. A national formulary of 362 drugs in 522 dosage forms was developed for use in the government facilities, and supplemented in 1985 with a therapeutic guide, based on the most up to date scientific information, to provide instruction on drug therapies to ensure 'the optimal efficacy in the application and economy in the administration' of the drugs listed.[59] Both the formulary and the guide are updated regularly by multidisciplinary committees.

The government is also sponsoring continuing education programmes for doctors and pharmacists and issues regular information bulletins about drugs, drawing on regulatory decisions in the USA and the UK and on clinical evaluation evidence from around the world. Since 1982, efforts have been underway to study consumption patterns of 160 drugs in order to identify whether further effort is required to correct inappropriate use. A rudimentary adverse drug reaction notification system was started in 1986, and doctors are beginning to respond to this.[60]

## Self-medication

Although the system works well in Costa Rica, a significant problem, and one that is very difficult to deal with, is self-medication. Although the World Federation of Proprietary Medicine Manufacturers (WFPMM) claims that study after study from around the globe show that 'consumers are responsible about the medicines they take for self-care',[61] some observations from Costa Rica suggest there is room for doubt.

In Costa Rica's winter season, the temperature drops a few degrees and it usually rains for a few hours each day. The dampness and the cooler weather help to create the conditions for mild respiratory infections – coughs, colds and various flu-like viral infections. Most, of course, are self-limiting and will disappear in a few days with some rest, fluids and perhaps the occasional analgesic such as paracetamol to minimise the effect of aches and fever. Nevertheless, the local pharmacies do a roaring trade in cough and cold mixtures, many of which are of dubious efficacy. A recent study found that of the 2,198 cough and cold preparations listed in prescribing guides from 12 regions of the world during late 1987 and 1988, a staggering 86 per cent contained ingredients deemed by independent sources to be ineffective in the treatment of coughs and colds. A total of 26 per cent contained ingredients about which little is known and which are likely to be of very doubtful value in treating coughs and colds. And, to add injury to insult, 54 per cent of the products contained ingredients liable to cause harmful adverse reactions.[62]

Perhaps even more problematic is the widespread dependence on antibiotics to treat such illness. According to the American Medical Association (AMA), 'routine administration of antimicrobial agents to patients with colds has been shown to be completely useless'.[63] In theory, antibiotics are prescription-only medicines in Costa Rica. In practice, the prescription is easy to get. In 1985 a local researcher with a respiratory infection (and no time to rest) went into a pharmacy in the centre of Costa Rica's capital, San José, and came out a few minutes later with a handful of antibiotics. She said she had explained to the pharmacist that she had forgotten the prescription and was given enough antibiotics to tide her over for a day. On a Sunday afternoon in 1989, when one child in a family came down with a cold, she was taken to a pharmacy where a doctor was on duty. After a quick examination, an antibiotic syrup was prescribed. Later, other members of the family who also had a sore throat and felt a cold coming on made use of the medicine from time to time.

Clearly, as in Norway, both prescribers and patients still require much more education about the appropriate use of drugs.

## Peru

Self-medication is also a problem in Peru. A major study in Chimbote in 1984 found that 59 per cent of treatments for digestive and respiratory illness and for various kinds of pain were self-prescribed.[64] It also found that 40 per cent of all antibiotics used were self-prescribed and that a further 15 per cent were given on the advice of untrained staff working in pharmacies.

Like Costa Rica, Peru began looking at ways to rationalise drug use long before the WHO essential drug concept. In 1971, the then military government instituted a Basic Medicines Programme designed to encourage the use of generic products and to contribute to better health care. In all public sector health facilities it became compulsory to prescribe only from a list of basic medicines. Nevertheless, the programme was far from successful. It foundered for several reasons, among them that the public sector was responsible for only about 20 per cent of Peru's pharmaceutical consumption and the private sector flourished with a large number of irrational, branded drugs. As in most countries, manufacturers were more interested in promoting their higher-priced branded drugs and the government failed to promote effectively the use of basic medicines. The medical profession failed to support the programme, preferring to use the more well-known branded drugs. Economic and administrative difficulties also meant that drugs were not always ordered or paid for on time by the government and the companies manufacturing the basic drugs became less interested in their production. A final problem was that the distribution of basic drugs depended on the national health service, which was not well enough developed to cover the entire population, and in particular neglected the people most in need of basic medicines.[65]

A new government in 1980 tried to continue the Basic Medicines Programme under a new name – Essential Drugs Programme – but with little success. The main success of the programme was the publication in 1983 of a handbook listing the 232 drugs considered to be the most important therapies in the country, together with information about indications, contraindications and adverse effects of many of them. But many of the problems of the earlier programme were still evident: a parallel private market, a lack of education of the public and prescribers, the poor coverage of the health care system, and the lack of funds. By the middle of 1985, in many of the hospitals in major cities outside the capital it was difficult to find more than 15 or 20 of the drugs listed in the handbook.[66]

## New hope?

The change of administration in mid-1985 brought new hope for a better drugs programme. Dr David Tejada, a former Assistant Director General of WHO and one of the architects of the Alma-Ata conference on primary health care, was made Minister of Health, an appointment which caused some concern within the pharmaceutical industry.[67] One of his first acts was the establishment of a national committee for food and drugs (CONAMAD) which had the task of taking charge of the application, regulation, co-ordination, control and evaluation of the health ministry's national policies and programmes on food and drugs, as well as the authorisation and control of companies or other organisations producing or buying drugs, either in the public or private sector. CONAMAD was composed of representatives from the health, economy and industry ministries, health organisations, medical and pharmacy schools, and from the pharmaceutical industry. Also established was a National Medicines Fund (FONAME) with the task of obtaining and channelling the necessary funds for the purchase of medicines, particularly for the most disadvantaged parts of the country.

In 1986, a list of 21 basic drugs and 47 essential drugs was published and in view of the lack of most of them in health care facilities, it was declared a priority national interest to increase their supply and distribution. Through a series of negotiations involving the pharmaceutical industry, a clear accord was reached for improving the situation in the public sector, including agreement on low prices for the drugs. Two likely reasons for the industry's co-operation have been suggested.[68] First, the basic and essential drugs were a 'captive' market whereby costs of production could be reduced because commercial promotion of the products was unnecessary. The sales were guaranteed, the profits were guaranteed. The second reason was that by co-operating, the industry would create a system whereby the entire programme was dependent upon its good will. This could serve as a useful bargaining chip should efforts be made at a later date to interfere with the private market. In 1987 the private market was worth about $200 million a year, compared to sales of only $20 million for the basic and essential drugs. Nevertheless, CONAMAD did manage to ban some of the more obsolete and dangerous products on the market.[69]

During the first three years of the programme, a total of 90 essential drugs was selected for inclusion and 35 manufacturers, both national and transnational, were offered contracts for their production. The drugs were then distributed through the government health posts. The programme, like its predecessors, had some problems of administration and finance, unremarkable in the face of the severe economic crisis plaguing Peru. In a second phase which got underway in February 1989, agreement was reached with private pharmacies to distribute the drugs. As a result, it has been claimed that 10 per cent of the country's drug production now reaches 'the very poorest and most geographically isolated members of the population'.[70]

Hardly a statistic to be proud of, and a dubious statement in any case. With the political unrest in Peru, it is known that the government has difficulty maintaining control over some areas of the country. It is therefore very likely that there are some 'geographically isolated' places and people who are without access to the drugs they need. Even health care posts in relatively accessible locations outside the capital in 1987 still lacked both the quantity and variety of basic and essential drugs they required.[71] And, even accepting the 'optimistic' view that 10 per cent of drug production is focused on essential products, what of the remainder?

The problems that have been plaguing Peru's various essential drugs programmes still exist. At the root of them, as two researchers pointed out, is the fact that 'the consumption of medicines has come to be considered as the *solution* to the problems of illness in our country'.[72] And, with more than 5,000 preparations on the market, many of which are still irrational, useless or dangerous,[73] there seems little hope for improvements in the health of people in Peru.

## Kenya: improving rural drug supply

A country which has had more success in improving the supply of essential drugs is Kenya, although problems still plague the private drug market, as the example of antidiarrhoeal products mentioned in Chapter 3 demonstrates. The efforts of the Kenyan government were described by WHO's Director General, Dr Mahler, as 'a shining example to many other countries'.[74]

Before an essential drug programme got underway in 1980, rural health centres were frequently short of essential drugs. An estimated 20 per cent of drugs sent from the Central Medical Stores never reached their destinations but were lost on the way. The training of the health workers was also a problem: many had not received any refresher courses since taking up their posts some years before. As a result, wasteful prescribing practices were in evidence, partly due to the lack of diagnostic skills of many health workers and partly due to patient pressure to have a drug prescribed whatever their illness.[75]

Kenya's solution was to design a basic 'ration kit' system. First of all, an attempt was made to identify the common diseases in the country, particularly in rural areas. On this basis, a selection was made of 38 drugs that were considered to be the most important therapies. Kenyan manufacturers supply 13 of the more basic and simple-to-produce drugs, while the rest are obtained from European companies on the basis of an annual international tender. The average cost to supply sufficient of these drugs for the entire rural population of Kenya is $0.29 per person per year. Each health centre receives a monthly pre-packaged kit with enough of the 38 drugs to cover 3,000 patients, while smaller dispensaries receive a slightly different kit with only 31 drugs and enough to cover 2,000 patients. Dr Wilfred Koinange, director of medical services, commented in 1985 that the system covered the entire rural area, about 85 per cent of the total population of Kenya. He pointed out that 'the more medicines are limited, the more people learn how to handle those medicines and the more efficient the drugs become'.[76]

Health workers in the field are delighted with the new system. According to Mrs Alice Miako, a community nurse at a dispensary in Kiambu District, there have been no drug shortages since the programme started. 'It really makes a difference, because before, people couldn't always get the drugs they needed and were forced to go many miles away for them. Now, we can treat most conditions here. The patients tell me how satisfied they are.'[77]

An additional benefit of the programme is that health staff now have more time and more opportunity to discuss preventive measures with patients in the local communities. According to Dr T. Timarwa, medical officer of health in Kiambu District, between 60 and 70 per cent of the illness in his district could be prevented by better health education.[78]

A training manual has been developed for rural health workers which explains how and when to use the drugs in the kit, and also points out how to prevent illness in the first place. One of its most important messages is that not all patients need drugs. The health workers also receive regular training courses and, wherever possible, treatment and dosages have been standardised for the common illnesses. Dr Koinange said this has helped to solve some of the difficulties with the overprescribing of drugs.[79]

## Philippines

The development of a national drug policy in the Philippines, like that of Bangladesh, was tied to the coming to power of a new government. Although the Ministry of Health drew up an essential drugs list of 170 products in late 1983 (partly in response to the economic crisis in the country) industry opposition meant that the list was not actually released.[80] Not until the Aquino government came into power in early 1986 did work start in earnest to transform the country's medicines situation.

As Dr Alfredo Bengzon, the Secretary of Health, points out, about 16–18 per cent of the Department of Health (DOH) budget was spent on pharmaceutical products, which amounted to approximately $45 million worth of drugs in 1988, and an estimated $60 million in 1989.[81] Yet, as in other countries, public sector spending on drugs pales into insignificance when compared to the private sector. As Table 6.7 shows, total pharmaceutical sales in 1987 amounted to at least $460 million.

And, as in other countries, the marketplace was filled with products of dubious utility. Several studies have demonstrated the irrationality of the situation.[82] For example, in 1981 one doctor pointed out that 45 per cent of the drugs in the Philippines 'only relieve symptoms but do not cure the disease itself'. In 1984, 77 per cent of the 241 antibiotics on the market were not on WHO's essential drugs list; 54 per cent of antidiarrhoeal products contained antibiotics and 98 per cent of cough and cold remedies contained ingredients with no proven efficacy.[83] In 1987, there were somewhere between 9,000 and 12,000 registered drugs in the Philippines.[84]

## Table 6.7 Leading pharmaceutical manufacturers in the Philippines (1984–7)

| Company | Origin | Pharmaceutical sales (millions of pesos) | | | |
|---|---|---|---|---|---|
| | | 1984 | 1985 | 1986 | 1987 |
| United Labs | Philippines | 794.5 | 1,471.3 | 1,719.9 | 2,293.8 |
| Wyeth-Suaco | USA | 117.6 | 489.6 | 626.2 | 820.1 |
| Johnson & Johnson | USA | | 540.8 | 555.3 | 674.0 |
| Abbott Labs | USA | 150.3 | 480.2 | 564.5 | 661.5 |
| Ciba-Geigy | Switzerland | 106.8 | 258.5 | 331.4 | 413.1 |
| Pfizer | USA | 115.9 | 213.4 | 246.7 | 298.6 |
| Astra | Sweden | 66.3 | 172.8 | 199.0 | 273.1 |
| Roche | Switzerland | 78.2 | 156.7 | 185.4 | 265.9 |
| Medichem | Philippines | | 187.3 | 187.3 | 259.6 |
| Interphil | Philippines | | 182.5 | 219.5 | 254.6 |
| Squibb | USA | 66.1 | 162.5 | 174.8 | 234.2 |
| Boehringer Ingelheim | FRG | 96.2 | 156.9 | 181.3 | 225.5 |
| Sterling | USA | 88.8 | 213.1 | 186.6 | 220.2 |
| International Pharma | Philippines | | 106.4 | 112.9 | 205.4 |
| Glaxo | UK | 63.3 | 99.0 | 140.9 | 188.6 |
| A H Robins | USA | 71.3 | 110.3 | 122.2 | 137.8 |
| Bristol | USA | 205.4 | 383.8 | 126.6 | 125.3 |
| Merrell Dow | USA | 63.5 | 64.5 | 88.0 | 95.0 |
| Richardson Vicks | USA | 105.0 | 120.3 | 122.8 | 77.6 |
| Warner Lambert | USA | 169.8 | 424.9 | 509.7 | |
| Others | | 2,640.8 | 1,089.4 | 1,333.2 | 1,794.1 |
| **Total sales** | | **5,000.0** | **7,084.2** | **7,934.2** | **9,518.0** |
| **Total sales ($)** | | **301.0** | **378.0** | **388.9** | **461.4** |

Source: IMS data (1984); IBON, *The Philippine Drug Industry*, p.26; Tan, *Dying for Drugs*, pp.202–3.

Rhais Gamboa, the Under Secretary of Health, described the situation in the Philippines as one of:

> gross imbalance – with a strong supply side, essentially controlled by trans-national drug corporations which are almost completely import-dependent for active ingredients and technology; and an extremely weak demand side, comprising an ill-informed public, more than half of whom fall below the poverty line, with the professional health providers who make the decisions and choices for them, overtly influenced by the aggressive and expensive marketing and promotional practices of the big pharmaceutical companies.[85]

### Developing a policy

In 1986 the government set up a small task force to look at what could be done. Between November 1986 and March 1987, there were consultations with health professionals, consumer groups and the drug industry, including two major conferences where 25 position papers were submitted. Out of this came a selection of seven issues that needed to be considered: a proposed essential drugs list; the use of generic not brand names; advertising and promotion; procurement and self-sufficiency; self-medication; the basis for the registration of pharmaceuticals; and pricing.

The first skirmishes over the proposed new drug policy actually occurred in September and October 1986, when it became clear that the Philippine Medical Association (PhMA) was not only in favour of an essential drug list but had set up a committee to help prepare, in co-operation with the Philippine Society on Experimental and Clinical Pharmacology (PSECP), such a list for the 10 most common illnesses encountered in medical practice. The Drug Association of the Philippines (DAP), which represents all the major drug companies operating in the country, both local and TNCs, argued that such a list was unnecessary, particularly for the private sector. In fact, the DAP argued, there was no need to do anything more in the Philippines: 'all the objectives set out by WHO have already been met in the Philippines, as far as legislation and essential drugs are concerned'.[86] In a letter to the president of the PhMA, president of the DAP Leo Wassmer said that the PhMA decision to prepare an essential drugs list (EDL) was 'extremely dangerous not only to our industry, but also to the medical profession at large'. Wassmer argued that the medical profession was in the process of surrendering its freedom of choice over drugs for its patients and that the impact on the industry could include lay-offs, the possible closure of companies, less competition and higher prices. He summed up by saying that the 'imposition of an EDL on an established free-market system ... would be ruinous'.[87] Dr Estrella Paje Villar, chairperson of the PSECP committee on medical education, pointed out that such a list or formulary was needed 'since there are too many drugs available in the market that only confuse doctors as well as medical students'.[88] The PhMA formulary was issued in early 1988.

Despite the resistance of the pharmaceutical industry, by April 1987 the basic elements of a national drug policy had been decided upon, and were announced by President Corazon Aquino on 30 April when she opened new laboratories of the Philippines Bureau of Food and Drugs (BFAD). The policy focused on four main areas: strengthening BFAD; the government becoming 'a more aggressive participant' in the procurement, production and distribution of drugs; improvements in information for patients and prescribers; and efforts to encourage national self-sufficiency in drugs. As President Aquino pointed out:

> Uncritical reliance on the free market system neglects the majority of our people whose low purchasing power has made them an uninteresting market for industry. Industry can afford this neglect. Government cannot countenance this situation. The poorest are also the most ill; they are the most in need of medicines, and the least able to buy them. A democracy cannot survive when its industry cannot respond to one of the most basic needs of man.[89]

Two days later, President Aquino issued two Executive Orders amending the Pharmacy Law and the Food, Drugs and Cosmetics Law as the first step towards greater controls over drug safety and efficacy. Over the next two years, other efforts began to transform the policy into concrete action.

Early in 1988, an administrative order on advertising restricted the promotion of prescription drugs to the medical professions and banned the use of raffles, gifts, promises of reward or any form of inducement to the prescribers. Another administrative order called for the generic name of the drug to be printed twice the size of the brand name on labels, while a third issued guidelines on the requirements that combination products would have to meet before they would be registered.[90] The DOH had also been working on identifying products, many of which had been banned in other countries, that could be deregistered. A possible 265 drugs were found and the DOH wrote to several drug companies giving them 30 days to provide any scientific evidence as to why the products should remain on the market. Failing this, the drugs were either to be 'voluntarily' withdrawn or would be delisted.[91] At least four companies – Takeda, Hoechst, Roche and Wellcome – responded with law suits against the DOH.[92]

## The opposition grows

In February 1988 President Aquino received a letter from two US senators, Alan Cranston (Democrat, California) and Richard Lugar (Republican, Indiana) which urged her 'to look carefully at plans announced by your Ministry *(sic)* of Health to implement a national drug policy' because 'if decisions are made which jeopardize or penalize US firms presently doing business in the Philippines, the task of stimulating new US investment may become more difficult'.[93] The two senators were among the primary sponsors of a proposed $10 billion aid package for the Philippines. This, coupled with a warning to Health Secretary Bengzon from US Ambassador Platt that the drug policy would 'discourage foreign investment', was reminiscent of the efforts to interfere with the Bangladesh drug policy.

By April 1988, industry opposition to the policy was in full swing. A media campaign from the DAP got underway, with a press release explaining how the pharmaceutical industry was being 'pilloried' by the drug policy.[94] The host of one TV programme refused to allow a spokesperson from the newly formed Philippine Drug Action Network (PDAN) – a coalition of health NGOs – to mention any brand names of problem drugs because 'we might face a boycott from the Drug Association of the Philippines'. A journalist reported that she had been threatened with legal action by a drug company over an article she had written for one of the newspapers, as was a Manila physician after she had publicly corrected misinformation being spread around by a company's sales representative.[95]

In May 1988, the American Chamber of Commerce of the Philippines (AMCHAM) – the 'First American Chamber of Commerce Abroad', as it proudly announces on its letterhead – joined the fray with a stinging letter to Health Secretary Bengzon. In it the president of AMCHAM, A. Gordon Westly, expressed 'deep concern' and 'some dismay' over 'proposals to use government power to closely control, widely prohibit, and minutely redirect private activities in the health sector that do not conform to a state sponsored master plan'. He also raised the by-now familiar cry that the drug policy would have 'a devastating effect on the possibilities for job generating investment by foreign concerns', and said that the pharmaceutical companies were 'part of the health care solution and not a part of the health care problem'.[96] If American companies were worried, Swiss and Swedish companies clearly saw no problems. Ciba-Geigy announced a 17.9 million peso ($890,000) investment in its local subsidiary in September 1988, and Swiss Pharma Research Laboratory announced a 151 million peso ($7.5 million) investment to manufacture antibiotics and other pharmaceuticals.[97] In January 1989, Astra opened a new 350 million peso ($17.5 million) factory, its second biggest manufacturing plant outside Sweden.[98]

In an equally hard-hitting reply to Westly, Health Secretary Bengzon pointed out that AMCHAM's members had 'no reason to complain' about too much regulation. He said a comparison between the policies and procedures of the US FDA and the BFAD would show that 'the Philippine market for pharmaceuticals is a playground compared to the stringent regulations in the US. We are only doing what we should have done long ago: adopt the basic rules necessary to protect our consumers and apply these rules strictly and equitably.' As for foreign investment, he pointed out that the contribution of foreign companies to the Philippine economy was secondary to companies' primary goal of ensuring profit. Therefore, the role of the government was

> to devise ways that would allow you to make your profit *only* when you respect our national interests, *only* when your activities serve the real needs of our people, and *only* when you truly contribute to our economy. Other-wise, you are only exploiting us and this should not continue.[99]

In June 1988, President Aquino reiterated government support for the drug policy in a determined manner. While praising drug companies who had voluntarily withdrawn questionable drugs from the market, she warned others 'who remain adamantly wedded to their profits' that 'they will have to learn. This government will have to teach them.' She also warned that they should avoid using 'technicalities and maneuverings to preserve pharmaceutical profit' in the face of disturbing questions about safety and efficacy. She described the national drug policy as 'promotive, not restrictive. It is not anti-foreign or anti-business; it is pro-Filipino.'[100]

## Generics Act
In the same month, as further confirmation of the determination of the government to proceed with its drugs policy, the Philippine Senate approved a Generics Bill, calling for the use of generic names in the import, manufacture, distribution, marketing, promotion, prescription and dispensing of drugs. The Generics Act was signed into law by President Aquino on 13 September, and went into effect in April 1989. In an interesting reversal of roles, the DAP – which had been campaigning against the Act – announced its support for it; while the PhMA – which had been so much in favour of the EDL, which was based on generic products – was strongly opposed to it, or at least to its immediate implementation.[101]

By January 1989 the battle lines were shifting. The PhMA had cooled down a bit and was somewhat resigned to the Generics Act, simply urging that the DOH should issue implementing guidelines 'in conformity with those in the rest of the civilized world'. Meanwhile the DAP, 'in a stormy meeting', decided to file a law suit against the Act. It was a far from unanimous decision: US-based companies were in favour of taking legal action; European companies were against such a move.[102] However, by May 1989, the PhMA was back in the firing line: it filed a law suit questioning the legality of some of the Act's provisions.[103] In August, the DAP announced that it had filed its own suit.[104]

Even before these developments, there were signs that the pressure was beginning to bite. Administrative orders began to appear in the early part of 1989 to implement the Act, but some commentators believed they compromised on the basic principles of the drug policy.[105] Another sign of the pressure was the difficulties affecting 12 bills related to drug patents that were pending in Congress. Senator Vincente Paterno, the head of the Senate Economic Affairs Committee, told a member of the West German Pharmaceutical Manufacturers' Association that there was 'no serious consideration' of these bills and 'no thinking about the alteration of intellectual property laws'.[106]

In September 1989, Senator Orlando Mercado, principal author of the Generics Act, delivered a privilege speech at the Senate claiming that he had in his possession a document sent from the US State Department to the Philippines' Department of Foreign Affairs which, he claimed, said that:

> to avoid serious damage to the Philippines' reputation as a good place to invest, we urge the executive department of the Government of the Philippines to implement the generics law in as non-discriminatory and non-compulsory manner as possible, and to make it clear to Congress its opposition to bills aimed at the pharmaceutical industry.[107]

President Aquino and Foreign Affairs officials denied knowledge of the document, while a spokesman for the US Embassy, Gerald Huchel, said that he could neither confirm nor deny the existence of the document. Whether such a document did exist, Health Secretary Bengzon told the Senate that the DOH had been visited by a group from the US Trade Representative to remind officials that the Philippines was on a watchlist for being 'anti US trade'. He also mentioned a March 1989 article by the Heritage Foundation which claimed that the Philippine economy would improve if the Generics Act was 'reversed'.[108]

In October 1989, some good news for the policy emerged when the DAP law suit was dismissed 'for lack of merit'.[109]

It took just over four years before resistance to the Bangladesh drug policy began to fade. It is unlikely to take less time in the Philippines. The experience of the Philippines demonstrates that, as Health Secretary Bengzon put it, 'you cannot leave anything to chance particularly when you craft a policy that seeks to change, in a fundamental way, structures, historical practices and the behaviour of people'.[110]

# 7.  By the year 2000

*Getting essential drugs to underprivileged people in developing countries is not at all simple. It has profound implications for international trade in drugs. It depends very much on having well-defined national drug policies, national drug regulations and provision of impartial information for health personnel, the public and policy makers. Making information of that kind freely available is crucial. Much of the polemic surrounding the use of drugs has arisen around the ethical principle of telling the truth, the whole truth and nothing but the truth and the all-too-often unethical practice of not doing that. Ethical promotional practices are no less important, as are adequate health infrastructures with efficient supply systems, trained health personnel and managerial man- power, and sufficient money to buy drugs as well as hard currency to buy them abroad.*

Dr Halfdan Mahler, WHO Director General, 1986[1]

Early one evening in April 1983 I was visiting at his home in Copenhagen a friend who had been working as a consultant for the Danish International Development Agency (DANIDA). He was helping to develop the joint WHO/ DANIDA/SIDA-supported essential drugs project in Bangladesh. He had gone into another room to get me some information about the project when his doorbell rang. He asked me to get the door. Standing outside, obviously excited, was his upstairs neighbour, Dr Ernst Lauridsen, who was the head of DANIDA's health division.

Dr Lauridsen had come to announce that shortly before he left his office that evening, a telex had come through from the Bangladesh government announc- ing approval of the project. It was good news, but even better news was to follow. For several weeks rumours had been flying about who was going to be appointed programme manager for WHO's Action Programme on Essential Drugs (APED). That evening, Dr Lauridsen told me he had accepted the job and that his appoint- ment would be announced a few days later at the World Health Assembly.

The following morning, I met Dr Lauridsen at his office and we talked about Bangladesh and about the APED. Although excited by the prospect of his new job, he was also realistic about the opposition he was likely to face, particularly from the pharmaceutical industry. He talked about the importance of HAI and other NGOs in helping to support progressive drug policies and said that he expected a time to come in the future when industry pressure would make it difficult for WHO and the APED to remain effective. Within five years, his fears were starting to come true.

## Putting action into the APED

Following the Nairobi meeting and the approval of the revised drug strategy (RDS) by the WHA in 1986, WHO organised a series of consultations to develop further the policies included in the RDS. Between May 1986 and the early part of 1988, the APED was perhaps at its most active and productive. By then, Dr Lauridsen had assembled a strong multidisciplinary team which worked well together and was achieving results. Some 109 countries had national essential drug lists, 37 had operational programmes, 24 were at the planning stage, and 19 were actively considering a national drug policy. Expert groups met to draft guiding principles for small national drug regulatory authorities, guidelines for the development of national drug policies,[2] and ethical criteria for drug promotion.[3] Following some written consultation, revisions were made to the Drug Certification Scheme to include raw materials and products for veterinary use, and to increase the amount of information to be supplied by exporting countries.[4] A revised edition of the Essential Drugs List was prepared,[5] as was a major report on the world drug situation.[6] Operational research projects, including epidemiological studies, a health survey, and socio-economic and socio-cultural studies on drugs, were also underway.[7]

The main difficulties lay in the improvements in information flow about essential drugs. Although the WHO *Drug Information Bulletin* – which reports on regulatory and therapeutic developments – had been revamped and was now appearing more regularly, with a paid subscription of more than 1,000, the long-awaited model prescribing information on the use of essential drugs had still not appeared. The root of the problem was that unlike the APED which had raised considerable extrabudgetary funds for its work, the unit responsible for drug information, the Pharmaceuticals Programme, was dependent upon the WHO regular budget. And the WHO regular budget was severely stretched.

## Financial constraints at WHO

One of the main causes of WHO's financial difficulties was the non-payment by the USA of its contribution for 1986. In January 1987, the USA paid $10 million of the $63 million it owed for 1986, but $3 million of that was to pay off arrears from 1985.[8] By January 1988, the situation had reached crisis proportion. Health programme activities were cut by some $44.5 million, another $11 million of working capital was used up, and only an internal reallocation of $10 million made it possible for the organisation to limp along.[9] An editorial in *Science* pointed out that the USA was by then in arrears to the amount of $118 million, representing nearly 25 per cent of WHO's annual budget, which had been held to zero growth for six years. The editorial noted that, ironically, one alone of WHO's achievements – the eradication of smallpox during the 1970s – was saving the USA $110 million a year in vaccination costs.[10]

Dr Mahler picked up on this theme in a speech to the 1988 WHA in which he told the member states that they had all received the equivalent of their 40 years' contribution to WHO with interest as a result of the smallpox programme.[11] The message seemed to work: a few days later the USA announced a payment of $20.5 million which erased the 1986 arrears and began to eat into the 1987 arrears. The US Ambassador in Geneva said that the USA was able to make this payment 'only by according more favourable treatment to WHO than to some of the other major organisations in the UN system' and that it was a recognition of 'the high regard in which the United States Government holds WHO'.[12]

The 1988 WHA was an emotional one for Dr Mahler and for most of the people attending. It marked the 40th anniversary of WHO and the 10th anniversary of the Alma-Ata Declaration on Primary Health Care. It was also the end of an era, as it marked the impending retirement of Dr Mahler. He had worked with WHO for 37 of its 40 years, serving 15 years as Director General. During his period of leadership, WHO was transformed from a low-key technical agency attempting to minimise the effects of individual diseases – such as yaws, malaria and smallpox – into a highly respected body treading the same difficult tightrope of balancing the need for social justice and equity without falling completely into the quagmires of political conflict that has plagued many of the other UN agencies. Yet he refused to run from controversy: vigorous action on essential drugs, infant feeding, and the health hazards of smoking were bound to anger vested interests. At the same time, Dr Mahler saw efforts to encourage better health transform children's immunisation rates from barely 5 per cent to over 50 per cent in just 10 years, with a subsequent saving of more than a million children's lives. The efforts of the diarrhoeal disease programme were estimated to be saving another million children a year.[13] It was a proud record, and one that would be difficult to follow. As Sir John Reid of the UK, a former chairman of WHO's Executive Board, put it, 'Mahler's departure is an event in medical history'.[14]

## A new Director General for WHO

Mahler's retirement was an event which neither the APED staff nor people involved in HAI were looking forward to. Mahler's early speeches about 'drug colonialism' and the rampant irrationality of drug supply in developing countries indicated his constant support for efforts to improve the situation. His successor, 60-year-old Japanese physician Dr Hiroshi Nakajima, was somewhat of an unknown quantity, even though he had been director of WHO's Western Pacific Region since 1979. After qualifying as a doctor in Japan, Dr Nakajima had continued his studies in France, and worked from 1958 to 1967 with the National Institute of Health and Medical Research at the French Ministry of Health, before returning to Japan to take up a post as director of R&D with the

Japanese subsidiary of Hoffmann-La Roche. He had begun his career with WHO in 1974 when he was appointed to the headquarters Pharmaceuticals Programme.

Dr Nakajima's approach to management was seen as more autocratic than the patient and consensus-building approach favoured by Dr Mahler.[15] Another worry was whether he would maintain the social equity policies that character- ised Dr Mahler's leadership, or instead spend more time promoting technology. When asked about his position on appropriate technology, he said that 'appropri- ating technology' is very important; everyone should have technology.[16]

His initial selection by WHO's Executive Board in January 1988 was some- what controversial. The 31 members of the board narrowly voted, on a third ballot, by 17 to 14 in favour of Dr Nakajima over Dr Carlyle Guerra de Macedo, a Brazilian who is the director of the Pan American Health Organisation (PAHO). The confirmation vote at the WHA was conducted by secret ballot and one country was reported to have voted against Dr Nakajima's election, in contrast to Dr Mahler's unanimous support on each of his three terms in office. However, in the two-hour public session that followed confirmation of the appointment, 87 member states took the floor to congratulate Dr Nakajima, as if to ensure that their country could not be identified as the dissenter. The USA was the first country to register its support for Dr Nakajima, despite having been solidly behind Dr Guerra de Macedo in January.[17]

## A nervous US industry

In the run-up to the WHA, the usual nervousness was evident once again at WHO and within the pharmaceutical industry. The major cause for concern was the report of the expert group on ethical criteria for drug promotion. The pharma- ceutical industry, despite having had an opportunity to make a presentation to the group as did HAI,[18] and despite having several representatives on the expert group, was less than happy with the result. Joe Williams, then president of the IFPMA, said that the RDS 'represents a shift away from meeting the real pharma- ceutical needs of developing countries' and that 'the supply of essential drugs to underserved citizens in developing countries has lost priority'. In particular, he said, the industry regarded the ethical criteria for drug promotion as 'un- necessary and inappropriate': WHO should instead concentrate its 'limited technical, financial and advisory resources' on paying greater regard to the structure of pharmaceutical procurement and distribution systems in developing countries.[19]

In many ways, though, despite Williams's claims, his position reflected the view of US companies rather than of the entire industry. Gunter Lewandowski, the head of Ciba-Geigy's Pharma Policy unit, said:

> We do not think that this would be a wise position. In associations like the IFPMA, there is a tendency of the association to have the speed of the slowest. Most of our American colleagues are over nervous against WHO. Our position

here is that co-operation with WHO makes sense, is necessary, and has brought quite a lot of progress and in this respect all the Swiss manufacturers hold the same view. And the other thing is, and I always repeat it, and this is a clear, clear credo and we try to consequently improve the implementation of it: a drug is a substance plus information. Absolutely. It is silly to deny or to try to overlook it.[20]

Barely a week before the WHA opened, the US PMA heard from its president, Gerry Mossinghoff, that consumer activists were 'believed to be planning a renewed effort to promote a binding code'.[21] A few days later, Harry Schwartz, generally accepted as the person who says the things the PMA wouldn't dare say for political reasons, wrote a blistering attack on the RDS in his column in *Scrip*.[22] He said that the ethical criteria, the progress report on the RDS and *The World Drug Situation* 'contribute little that is really useful to the WHO's central task in the field of drugs, helping the poor developing countries to get the pharmaceuticals they need and to make them available to their citizens'. He added that there was 'no need for a WHO presence in pharmaceuticals' in the industrialised countries.

### HAI's challenge to the world health community

HAI was also not particularly enthralled by the ethical criteria report but had no intention of pushing delegates at the WHA to make any changes. Rather, HAI prepared an analysis of the ethical criteria and the IFPMA code, offering suggestions on weak points, and encouraged national governments interested in doing so to implement stronger measures.[23] Overall, HAI had decided that the limits of changing international policy had virtually been reached, and that it was time to focus more on implementation at the national level. HAI's approach to lobbying at this WHA took on a new nature and had a new set of objectives. Discussions were held with national delegates to gather information and build contacts, and with several programmes within WHO to look at ways in which HAI could collaborate more extensively with them. The main aspect of 'traditional' lobbying was to encourage praise and support for the APED, an easy task given its results during the previous two years.

Dr K. Balasubramaniam, one of HAI's international co-ordinators, addressed the WHA as a spokesperson of the International Organisation of Consumers Unions (IOCU) and praised the work of the APED. He referred to the challenges to the world health community issued by Dr Mahler earlier in the WHA to eradicate polio and to subject health policies and practices to a kind of 'social audit', whereby efforts were judged by how much they contributed to social equity, and on behalf of IOCU and HAI he issued a few additional challenges:

1. By the 43rd WHA (1990), there should be no longer any antidiarrhoeal preparations containing unnecessary antibiotics on the market, and the amount spent on promoting the rational use of drugs should have at least doubled.

2. By the 45th WHA (1992), the majority of member states should have implemented regulations to control unethical drug promotion.
3. By the 47th WHA (1994), all member states should have national drug policies in place as an integral part of primary health care and national health policies.
4. By the 49th WHA (1996), the majority of member states should have established continuing medical education programmes for health workers which were free from undue commercial influence.[24]

Dr Balasubramaniam concluded by pointing out that both IOCU and HAI were committed to face up to these and the other challenges on the road to better health and the more rational use of drugs, and to play their part 'in the continuing social audit of the world health community now, in the year 2000, and well, well beyond'. It was a strong message that HAI had no intention of fading away.

## The decline of the essential drugs programme

The WHA unanimously adopted four resolutions on drugs – one confirming support for the RDS and calling for its continued implementation; one adopting the ethical criteria; one incorporating amendments to the WHO Certification Scheme; and one on the use of traditional medicines and medicinal plants, which called for the conservation of medicinal plants and their sensible use.

Thus, yet another green light had been given for continued work on the rational use of drugs; however, within months, things had changed. When Dr Nakajima took over as Director General in July, he began to reorganise the APED. The first change was a new command structure; whereas previously Dr Lauridsen had reported directly to Dr Mahler, now he was required to report via an assistant director general. The APED, the Pharmaceuticals Programme and the divisions on biologicals, traditional medicines, psychotropics and narcotics and health laboratory technology were linked together in a Drug Management and Policies division, under Assistant Director General Dr Hu Ching-li, who had previously worked with Dr Nakajima in the Western Pacific office. Dr Vittorio Fattorusso, who had retired from WHO as the director of the drug division which preceded the introduction of the APED, and who was a former colleague of Dr Nakajima's when he worked for WHO in Geneva, was brought in as a consultant to Dr Hu, and subsequently became the acting director of the division. The new structure meant stringent bureaucratic and financial controls on the APED.

In October 1988, Dr Nakajima looked as if he was rewriting the RDS to fall in line with industry desires when he told the IFPMA's assembly in Washington that no one could reasonably take issue with the concept of essential drugs if applied 'as was originally intended, "to extending the accessibility of the most necessary drugs to those populations whose basic health needs cannot be met by the existing supply system" ' on the understanding that the decisions involved were a matter of individual national policy.[25] He pointed out that it was WHO's responsibility, because of its commitment to social equity, to pay particular attention to the health needs of the less affluent countries, and that WHO looked to the pharmaceutical industry for support in these basic objectives. In particular, he said, WHO expects the industry 'never to exploit, through abuse of trust, the communities that it has the prerogative to serve'. Richard Arnold, the Executive Vice-President of the IFPMA, said that the industry was encouraged by the speech and that 'the prospects for fruitful collaboration between the industry and WHO have never looked so promising'.[26]

At the end of 1988, another shock hit the APED when the Swedish government asked Barbro Westerholm – a Swedish Liberal MP, who was a close friend of Dr Mahler, a strong campaigner for women's rights in health and chairperson of the WHO Executive Board's ad hoc committee on drugs – to resign from the WHO Executive Board, which she was due to chair in 1989. There was considerable speculation that Dr Nakajima had played a hand in this decision in an attempt to achieve a 'clean sweep' of some of the people who had been advocating the more radical approaches to rational drug use.[27]

By January 1989, the changes had become too much for Dr Lauridsen. He resigned in protest at the way the aims of the RDS were being 'watered down'. He talked about increasing bureaucratic 'harassment' and said the message that had been made clear to him was that, under the new regime, 'he need not feel obliged to stay on at the WHO'. One of the final straws was the refusal to give him permission to go to the Philippines at the request of Health Secretary Bengzon to help in drawing up the country's national drug policy.[28] Ironically, Dr Nakajima, in April 1988, while still serving as the Western Pacific regional director, had congratulated Bengzon 'for his firm determination in pursuing a new national drug policy for the Philippines'.[29]

In May 1989, R. J. Samsom, the Deputy Director General of Health in The Netherlands, told the WHA that his government was concerned about what was happening to the APED. The Netherlands government had paid $5.6 million towards the APED's work in 1986 and 1987 (nearly 46 per cent of the extra-budgetary funds raised for the programme) and with another $4.6 million pledged to be paid between 1988 and 1991, its opinion carried some weight. Samsom pointed out that 'the existing effective leadership in the Drug Action Programme has disappeared. This has an immediate adverse impact on the continuity and dynamism of that Programme.'[30] A progress report published by the APED in May 1989 confirmed the problems that the departure of Dr Lauridsen and two other key members of the staff had caused both to the implementation of planned and ongoing activities and to the further development of the programme.[31]

During 1989, Dr F. S. Antezana, another former colleague of Dr Nakajima's from his time at Geneva, was brought in to replace Dr Lauridsen as programme manager for the APED. Nonetheless, in October 1989, several members of a management advisory committee which had been established to help review the work of the programme expressed concern about whether the staffing levels of the programme were sufficiently high for it to meet its objectives.[32]

While Dr Antezana is a capable official, he lacks the dynamism of Dr Lauridsen. As the Dutch Deputy Director General of Health said in his speech in May 1989, the qualifications of the new manager of the APED would 'be indicative of the direction and dynamism which the present WHO administration intends to give to the programme'.[33]

The justification for the changes in the organisational structure of the APED were described by Dr Nakajima as purely administrative, rather than being indicative of any change of policy.[34] At one level this could be accepted as a valid argument, as clearly the style of management of the APED was somewhat unorthodox when compared to most other WHO programmes or divisions. In part this was due to the style of leadership and the energetic enthusiasm of the staff of the programme. In part, too, it was because of the nature of the work and the basic objectives the programme sought to achieve. Among those objectives, in addition to the more technical issues of helping to advise on national essential drug programmes, was the need to play an advocacy and communications role to ensure a high profile for the essential drugs concept itself. This inevitably led to a certain degree of opportunistic response to situations, with less emphasis on long-term planning. Although some broad long-term targets were established, much more emphasis was placed on responding to perceived needs rapidly and flexibly and to establishing a 'critical mass' of reasonably successful initiatives which could serve as the political base from which to continue working. In some ways, the APED resembled much more an action research oriented NGO than a unit within a cautious bureaucracy.

Such an approach as APED's engenders inherent political tensions, and was also an isolating factor. Other divisions within WHO were often slower to respond to initiatives, having to take time to clear the usual bureaucratic hurdles before proceeding and, as a consequence, the APED was not particularly well integrated into other programme activities. As long as the command chain was the straightforward link from the APED, via Dr Lauridsen, direct to Dr Mahler as Director General, the programme was reasonably secure. With Dr Mahler's departure and subsequently that of Dr Lauridsen, the programme became more vulnerable, as an evaluation of the APED pointed out in late 1989.[35] Even so, the evaluation, which was proposed and financed by the major donor countries to the APED, concluded that the programme had been reasonably successful in achieving its broad objectives and deserved further support. It noted, however, that in the immediate future it was likely that the current leadership of the APED would probably focus more on technical aspects than on advocacy, and that other organisations would probably have to take on that role.[36]

## Financing health care through drug sales: the Bamako Initiative

While the fortunes of the APED appeared to be on the wane, a new initiative by UNICEF was beginning to gather momentum. In September 1987, UNICEF's Executive Director, James Grant, in an address to a meeting of the member states of WHO's Africa region held in Bamako, Mali, proposed a radical plan for financing primary health care (PHC) through a cost recovery scheme, using essential drugs as the mechanism. The Bamako Initiative, as it came to be called, was outlined by Grant as a visionary scheme to expand PHC throughout Africa within five years. In summary, the idea was that UNICEF and other donor agencies would initially supply essential drugs, which would then be sold at a little above their cost to the patients receiving them. This money would then be used to both finance the future purchase of necessary drugs and to cover the costs of expanding health coverage. Through decentralised management and community involvement in decisions about local health priorities, the scheme would mobilise new resources for health care. By late 1988, more than 20 countries in sub-Saharan Africa were drawing up plans to implement the scheme.[37]

The Bamako Initiative was based on the results of two small pilot projects, one in Benin (involving 12,000 people) and the other in Ghana (30,000 people). But, as an editorial in the *Lancet* pointed out, the scheme had some fundamental flaws.[38] First, any cost recovery scheme based on charging for drugs, no matter how low the price, would discriminate against the poorest members of society – generally those most susceptible to ill health. Second, if one exempts the poorest from such charges, then the price charged to the rest in order to ensure adequate income for basic PHC services could well be prohibitively high, perhaps four to six times the cost price of the drugs. Third, the concept of health care staff being dependent upon the sale of drugs to finance their own salaries or to maintain the facility in which they work is likely to lead to overprescribing of drugs. Fourth, even if sufficient local currency is generated by such a scheme to pay for improvements in health care and to purchase new supplies of drugs, the purchase will almost inevitably require foreign currency, something which most African countries lack. Finally, the management capability of the rural poor is in doubt; without a well-integrated programme to develop their skills and understanding about managing such a revolving fund, decision-making power over what to do with the money is liable to pass back to more centralised levels, and there is then no guarantee that the desired objective of community participation will be achieved.

Both the World Bank and WHO expressed grave concerns about the Bamako Initiative. The World Bank noted that the initiative failed to address the much broader and complex question of health financing in Africa and said that the assumption that drugs will generate sufficient revenue was 'too ambitious'.[39] WHO listed 15 points of concern including the lack of incentive to develop capabilites to fulfil national responsibility in drug supply and to contribute to the development of national drug policies. It also noted that decentralisation was a long-term process which could take some years before sufficient local capacity existed for maintaining the process.[40]

In looking at a much less ambitious plan – using drugs sales simply to finance the resupply of drugs – four researchers from the US-based Management Sciences for Health concluded after examining programmes in a variety of countries that while these types of revolving drug funds offered great potential, they were prone to seven common pitfalls:

1.  underestimation of capitalisation costs;

2. prices set below true replacement cost, frequent failure to collect payment;
3. delays in cash flow which make funds unavailable for replenishment of drug stocks;
4. too rapid programme expansion without sufficient funds;
5. losses due to theft and deterioration;
6. unanticipated price increases due to inflation or changes in exchange rates;
7. foreign exchange purchase restrictions.[41]

Two WHO staff reached similar conclusions and pointed out that a drug sales scheme needs price-setting, accounting, and stock management skills which may be lacking in rural communities. It is also dependent on good prescribing and consumption habits. They concluded that the complexity of setting up such schemes was not always appreciated, with the result that avoidable errors were made. 'Careful planning is therefore vital.'[42]

In late 1988, HAI began to take an interest in the developments around Bamako and realised that little or no public discussion was occurring about the scheme. Of particular concern to HAI was the fact that many local non-governmental groups who were involved in PHC programmes were largely unaware of the planning going on among the international agencies. A further concern was that traditional donors to UNICEF lacked the expertise to evaluate effectively some of the sketchy ideas being put forward. In most cases, UNICEF's good name was usually sufficient to ensure initial financing for the scheme. HAI launched a research and discussion programme at the beginning of 1989, drawing in all the interested parties, and in September 1989 co-sponsored a meeting in Sierra Leone to elaborate better approaches to the cost recovery idea. The discussion at the meeting, which involved UNICEF, WHO, representatives from several African governments and from African NGOs active in health care, and donor agencies, led to a series of guidelines which stressed the necessity for basing any such cost recovery schemes firmly in the context of national health and drug policies, particularly emphasising the need to ensure a rational use of drugs.

The work on Bamako served to reinforce HAI's growing stature as an important partner in drug policy development. The change of emphasis in HAI's approach, which began in January 1988 as the result of an international meeting held in Penang, Malaysia, which outlined a four-year work programme, and which was seen in action at the 1988 WHA, confirmed HAI's ability to do more than simply criticise the pharmaceutical industry: HAI and its participating groups had been doing more than that for years, but the most obvious manifestation of its work had been its clashes with the industry. By the end of the 1980s it was clear that it was time to move forward from that stereotype, although the industry still needed watching.

## Changes in the industry

WHO has set an ambitious target – 'health for all' – by the year 2000. The target does not mean the abolition of illness; rather, it offers the hope that everyone will have the means at his or her disposal to attain a reasonable standard of health. In its constitution, WHO defines health as 'a state of complete physical, mental and social well-being and not merely the absence of disease or infirmity'.[43] That definition is also useful in examining the 'health' of the pharmaceutical industry to determine if it, too, can be 'healthy' by the year 2000.

The underlying assumption is, of course, as Graham Dukes, Professor of Drug Policy Science at Groningen University in The Netherlands, puts it, 'that we *want* a healthy drug industry'. Further than that, Dukes notes that we *need* a healthy drug industry: to produce innovative products, to contribute to the economy, and most of all, 'because a healthy industry is one way to ensure healthy people'.[44]

In terms of 'physical' health – measured by the yardsticks provided by economics – the pharmaceutical industry is positively glowing. But what of the 'mental and social well-being' of the industry?

## The industry's 'mental' health

Two factors are important in considering the industry's 'mental health': first its creative functioning – its R&D efforts and the choices that it makes about what type of products to research and bring onto the market; and second its self-image – the way it perceives its functioning, the way that perception is communicated to others, which in turn leads to its 'social well-being' – the way in which it interacts with others in society.

The criticisms levelled at the pharmaceutical industry for developing imitative rather than innovative products is at the core of the current debate, and an important matter to be resolved if the products of the future are to avoid similar criticisms. In its defence, the pharmaceutical industry argues that while 'me-too' products may not offer significant therapeutic gain across an entire community of patients, they may be of benefit for a minority who do not respond to existing products. A second line of defence is the 'quantum leap' argument which suggests that the incremental improvement of therapy provides added knowledge about how the human system behaves, thus opening pathways for truly innovative discoveries. A third defence uses the 'serendipity' argument, that in the course of imitative research, a chance discovery can lead to a major breakthrough in therapy in quite unexpected ways, or that a drug originally marketed for one indication may be found to be effective in a quite separate disease.[45]

The arguments contain some compelling logic, at least at a theoretical level. However, when examined in practical terms, the logic begins to vaporise. The questions of limiting the number of drugs on the market and directing research more precisely towards real innovation must be resolved if a healthy pharmaceutical industry is to be achieved. The answer is not to claim, as Jay Kingham of the PMA has done, that the critics of the industry hold the view that the WHO list of some 200 essential drugs is a 'ceiling' on the market;[46] this false claim enables him to dismiss entirely any negotiation on which drugs could be removed without appreciable discomfort to the industry and without loss of adequate therapy.

At the moment, research choices are made with at least one eye on the 'bottom line' – the potential return on the investment in sales and profits. As the spectre of AIDS looms larger, company after company is transferring at least some research capacity towards finding a cure, or a vaccine to prevent transmission of the disease, or diagnostic aids to identify it more readily. Great honours will undoubtedly flow to the scientist who discovers either a cure or a vaccine for AIDS. Great wealth will flow to the company marketing such a product. That is not necessarily a bad scenario. AIDS is a major threat to world health. However, it is worth putting it in some proportion. Currently, the total number of people who have died from AIDS is approximately equal to the number who die every month from malaria, every week from diarrhoeal diseases, or every 11 days from the six vaccine-preventable diseases – measles, whooping cough, diphtheria, tetanus, tuberculosis and polio – that have been targeted by WHO and UNICEF's immunisation programmes.[47] In Africa, generally considered to be a continent where the spread of AIDS is a particular problem, only two out of the 1,600 annual deaths per 100,000 people can be attributed to AIDS.[48]

It is particularly disturbing to see the threat of AIDS being used as a justification to halt the progress being made on rationalising the use of drugs. Harry Schwartz, for example, called on WHO to end 'the anti-pharmaceutical industry atmosphere' of much of its activity and said that the industry could only conduct the needed research if it had very large economic resources to pay for this expensive effort. 'The least the WHO can do is to stop trying to reduce pharmaceutical industry revenues on the basis of concocted conspiracy fantasies which see our industry as the enemy.'[49]

Schwartz's interpretation had at least four flaws:

1. WHO's activities are not 'anti-pharmaceutical industry'.
2. The opportunity for a 'new relationship' has been there for years.
3. WHO has recognised for years the need for 'effective research' on many disease conditions, and the support it has been able to generate from the pharmaceutical industry for the Special Programme for Research and Training in Tropical Diseases (TDR) demonstrates that the industry, too, appreciates this.
4. The resources to pay for such research do not necessarily have to come only from the industry.

Ironically, in another article,[50] Schwartz himself makes the point that everyone in the pharmaceutical industry, from the smallest to the largest company, knows that 'the future will belong to those who come up with tomorrow's important and innovative drugs. Those who plan to survive with the 65th beta-blocker and the 33rd ACE-inhibitor simply won't.'

**Tropical disease research**

Creative solutions to research problems are possible – not simply the solution of finding a new drug – but the whole approach to how research is organised, what resources can be mobilised, and how the benefits of that research can be equitably shared. If the efforts of the international agencies such as WHO and

UNICEF to tackle primary health care problems over the past decade have demonstrated anything, it is that extraordinary levels of resources – both in economic and social terms – can be brought together in new relationships in the search for solutions. This type of 'innovation' is not impossible for the pharmaceutical industry. Several companies have already demonstrated that it is both possible and rewarding. As the Dag Hammarskjöld Foundation (DHF) has noted, 'It may be that the companies which cultivate the growth markets of the Third World with research and development on pathologies which exist in massive numbers among the poor will be the companies more likely to be around 20 years from now.'[51]

Indeed, in talking about tropical disease research, John Vane and Win Gutteridge of Wellcome suggest that one possibility could be the creation of an Institute for Tropical Medicine, funded by a once-and-for-all capital investment. The capital funding could come from charitable trusts, international agencies or:

> perhaps best of all, the pharmaceutical industry itself. Kudos and profit (if any) would be shared equitably between contributors. A capital sum of the order of $100 million could well fund such an Institute in perpetuity, and thereby guarantee a realistic and enlarged search for the new medicines so desperately needed for the tropics.[52]

Despite the generally low level of research on tropical disease within the industry, WHO has been reasonably successful in developing co-operative ventures in this field. In 1976, the Special Programme for Research and Training in Tropical Diseases (TDR) was created, sponsored by UNDP, the World Bank and WHO. The TDR programme has two main objectives: to harness all available technology to develop new tools and methods to improve disease control, and to strengthen research in tropical diseases in the countries where these diseases are endemic. Specifically, the programme is focused on six diseases: malaria, schistosomiasis, trypanosomiases (both sleeping sickness and Chagas' disease), filariasis (including onchocerciasis or river blindness), and leprosy. In all, more than 3,000 scientists in some 125 countries are working together to combat these diseases. Included in that figure are some 80 scientists from 41 pharmaceutical companies.[53]

## Tackling malaria

One of the most encouraging successes of the programme has been the development of mefloquine as a treatment against malaria. Both the development and utilisation of the drug are liable to become classic examples of rational drug use. After initial euphoria in the late 1950s at the joint impact of chloroquine, as both therapy and prophylaxis in malaria, and DDT to eradicate the mosquitos which spread the disease, it soon became apparent that resistance to both the pesticide and the drug was developing. By the 1970s, strains of *Plasmodium falciparum* – the protozoa which causes malaria – that were resistant to the standard anti-malarials were spreading. But in 1971, following a massive screening programme, the Walter Reed Army Institute of Research (WRAIR) in the USA discovered mefloquine – a quinoline-methanol derivative related to quinine. After a meeting between the TDR's scientific working group for the chemo-therapy of malaria, WRAIR, and Hoffmann-La Roche, it was agreed that meflo-quine would be developed jointly by the three bodies. Roche had already isolated compounds similar to mefloquine, though its research work was at least a year behind that of WRAIR and because Roche's compounds were more closely related to quinine, they would be more difficult to synthesise and more expens-ive to produce. After careful testing, when it was discovered that mefloquine was effective and well tolerated, the drug was brought onto the market in 1984.[54]

As both animal studies and clinical trials demonstrated, the malaria parasites were capable of developing resistance to mefloquine. WHO therefore decided that in order to preserve the usefulness of the drug, it was important for its introduction to be undertaken in a rational and deliberate manner. One of the approaches used was the development of a three-drug synergistic compound, combining mefloquine with two other anti-malarials. In order further to prevent resistance from developing, the drug is not being distributed through pharma-cies, but through national health authorities, such as hospitals, malaria clinics or bodies responsible for malaria control programmes. Roche accepted these unusual conditions in order to protect this anti-malarial compound, which is considered an essential weapon against malaria for many tropical countries.[55]

Work is also proceeding to test several other drugs with anti-malarial proper-ties, as well as to identify an effective malaria vaccine. At the same time, research is continuing into effective control of the mosquitos which transmit the disease. As the IFPMA points out:

> If the exciting potential of the new anti-malarial drugs and vaccines is not to be wasted, their use must be fully integrated into comprehensive and sus-tained programmes of malaria control alongside education, training, surveil-lance, vector control, and within the larger framework of primary health care.[56]

**River blindness and hepatitis**
River blindness (onchocerciasis) is a parasitic disease that affects an estimated 18 million people and threatens some 85 million more in West and Central Africa, the Middle East and parts of Central and South America. The disease is caused by parasitic worms that produce millions of tiny embryos which circulate in the bloodstream of infected individuals, and the result is severe itching, disfiguring skin changes and a variety of eye lesions which eventually lead to blindness. Merck Sharp and Dohme began investigating the possibilities of an antiparasitic drug used in animals, ivermectin, and found that it showed some promise. It co-operated with WHO in the clinical development of the drug, beginning in 1980. The drug eliminates the tiny embryos from the skin after a single oral dose, after which they gradually disappear from the eye. As a result, the drug is useful in both treating infecting patients and in helping to prevent the spread of the disease.[57] In 1988, Merck agreed to supply quantities of the drug free of charge to qualified onchocerciasis programmes in 11 African countries as part of large-scale investigations into the drug's potential.[58]

In a similar development, SmithKline has donated 1 million doses of hepatitis B vaccine to WHO. Hepatitis B is more infectious and more deadly than AIDS and kills more people each day than AIDS kills in a year.[59] An incurable disease, it can lead to cirrhosis of the liver and is the cause of 80 per cent of all cases of primary liver cancer. Prevention is the only hope, but the previously high cost of vaccines made their use in immunisation programmes difficult. The Smith-Kline vaccine is the first genetically engineered hepatitis B vaccine. According to SmithKline's William Packer, 'its development made it possible for the first time to produce hepatitis B vaccine at a competitive cost and on a scale large enough to permit eradication of the disease'.

At face value, both these offers suggest a new altruism emerging within the pharmaceutical industry. However, they are in essence little different from the everyday behaviour of the industry to ensure that new drugs are adequately tested and introduced to the market. A loss leader of 250,000 doses of ivermectin for use in large-scale trials is a small price to pay for access to a potential market of some 85 million people. Similarly, SmithKline is actively lobbying for the inclusion of hepatitis B vaccine in the WHO Expanded Programme on Immunisation so that all new-born and young children would be automatically vaccinated. The estimated market by the year 2000 is more than 300 million doses. Offers of free drugs are standard business practice for the industry. The only difference between these offers and, for example, Richardson-Merrell's distribution of 2.5 million thalidomide tablets in the USA in the 1960s, or Roche's 141 million Valium capsules to hospitals in Canada, was that instead of handing out the drugs to several hundred physicians or health care facilities scattered around a country for them to try out with their patients, the drugs are being channelled through a single source – the WHO.

## Other industry-financed initiatives

Over the past few years, the pharmaceutical industry has been pursuing other avenues of co-operation with governments, international agencies and NGOs to bring about improvements in drug supply and distribution.

In the Gambia, for example, 13 PMA member companies financed a two-year project to improve the management and distribution of pharmaceuticals. In 1984, the Gambia's Permanent Secretary of Health, Labour and Social Welfare told the WHA:

> The Gambia now had a system which, in the foreseeable future, could be managed within the limits of national resources, since there had not been an injection of any supplies over and above what the country could absorb. The system developed in this country should, all things being equal, ensure access by every member of the community to essential drugs.

Following on from this, 14 PMA member companies have financed another project in nearby Sierra Leone. While the Gambia project concentrated on making an existing primary health care drug delivery system more efficient, the

Sierra Leone project aimed to help build a delivery system in a single district where the infrastructure was weak or virtually non-existent. It also included a revolving drug fund scheme. Sierra Leone's national primary health care pharmaceutical programme is now building on the basis of this project.[60]

Six member companies of the ABPI are providing finances for two projects – in the Maldives and in Kenya – to help with the supply of medicines. The Kenyan project, operated in conjunction with the African Medical and Research Foundation (AMREF), aims to improve a Flying Doctor service by the incorporation of proper laboratory facilities to provide clinical diagnoses to serve as an accurate base for the rational use of medicines.[61] In the Maldives, the ABPI is collaborating with UNICEF to provide a custom-designed central medical store, a specially designed mobile health boat, and improved 'cold chain' equipment for the country's immunisation programme. In co-operation with Voluntary Services Overseas, ABPI is also sponsoring a pharmacist to review existing procedures and train local pharmacists.[62]

Dozens of other examples abound where initiatives have been taken by the industry to improve drug distribution, assist in training programmes, or participate in collaborative research ventures.[63] A cynic might wonder how much of this is window-dressing, a sign that good public relations is now recognised as important by the industry. For example, a common factor in most of the drug supply projects that the industry has supported in developing countries is the relatively small market size of the countries concerned. In other words, they are in markets that are relatively unimportant for short-term profits.

At its 1986 assembly, the IFPMA's president, Joe Williams, argued that the decision in 1984 to adopt a 'more proactive and open' communications policy was beginning to pay off, and should be intensified to 'persuade the world outside our own circles that the industry is a significant part of the solution for better health care, and not part of the problem'.[64] In order to improve the image of the industry in the UK, the ABPI agreed a public relations budget of some $2.4 million (£1.488 million) for 1987.[65] Similarly, in the USA, the PMA launched a 'communications programme' at the beginning of 1987 to explain the contributions the drug industry has made to health, the cost-effectiveness of drugs, the current levels of research and the kind of advances that can be expected over the next 10–20 years. The budget was in the region of $1–2 million for the first 18 months,[66] and it was so successful that a second phase started in mid-1988 with a $2.5 million budget. Eugene Step, the PMA chairman, described the first phase as a time when 'the industry learnt how to apply its experience in selling products to the task of selling ideas'.[67] The programme aimed to identify 10 local campaigners in each of 15 key Congressional districts represented by politicians with particular interests in health care, in order to establish a permanent lobby network. In addition to advocacy materials for these campaigners and the PMA's member companies, the programme also aims to reach 85 newspapers and 25 top TV markets with video news releases and monthly features. In West Germany, the BPI launched a three-year campaign to improve its public image in 1989, with a total budget of $13 million.[68]

## Ciba-Geigy opens new ground

In contrast, Ciba-Geigy has taken a different approach. Ciba was a much criticised company in the 1970s and early 1980s. The main source of its notoriety centred on an antidiarrhoeal preparation called Entero-Vioform which contained clioquinol. At the beginning of the 1970s an illness in Japan which had been puzzling investigators for more than 15 years was finally linked to the use of drugs containing clioquinol or similar oxyquinoline derivatives. The illness, sub-acute myelo-optic neuropathy (SMON), causes degenerative damage to the spinal cord, and the optic and peripheral nerves. It can lead to paralysis and blindness. Nearly 200 products containing oxyquinolines were banned in Japan in 1970; more than 11,000 SMON cases had occurred by that time. Ciba was the major world manufacturer of clioquinol products, having introduced the drug in 1934 as a treatment for diarrhoea. Despite two reports from Argentina in 1935 which first described symptoms resembling SMON, and the horror of the Japanese situation, Ciba's clioquinol-containing products were not withdrawn by the company worldwide until 1985. The 15 years between the Japanese ban and Ciba's final climbdown were traumatic for the company.[69]

Gunter Lewandowski, head of Ciba's Pharma Policy unit which was established in the late 1970s, said that the company fell back on a 'typical' argument to defend itself over the SMON case: causality was not proven. He said that what people in the company had failed to realise at the time was that scientific development had moved on and that such an argument was no longer valid. Instead, it was necessary 'to live with probability both in terms of efficacy and on the risk side'.[70]

Before the problems with clioquinol were resolved, another shock was brewing for Ciba. The beginning of the 1980s saw the triumphal launch and hasty withdrawal of a handful of non-steroidal anti-inflammatory drugs (NSAIDs) for the treatment of arthritis. The major difficulty with these powerful pain killers was their side effects, which were all too frequently fatal. As more and more research emerged on this class of drugs, it became clearer that all the NSAIDs had similar patterns of side effects. For Ciba, this was a cause of considerable concern: by the end of 1983 nearly one-quarter of its pharmaceutical sales came from NSAIDs and pain killers.[71]

Its leadership in this market sector goes back to the years immediately after the Second World War. In 1952 Ciba introduced a phenylbutazone product, Butazolidin, and followed this up in 1960 with a close derivative, Tanderil (oxyphenbutazone). During the first year that Butazolidin was on the market, the first reports of fatalities due to agranulocytosis (a blood disease characterised by loss of white blood cells) appeared in the UK. By the end of 1981, an internal Ciba review found that Butazolidin was linked to at least 777 deaths. Another 405 deaths related to Tanderil were also revealed. At the same time, large numbers of serious side effect reports were on file. A confidential memo analysing the situation in February 1983 concluded that the risk and benefit ratio of the two drugs should be 'carefully reassessed' to see whether the continued promotion of the drug for the treatment of arthritis was warranted. But sales staff were advised to provide physicians with only 'selected' comments 'accompanied by appropriate comments' about the products. Not until a copy of the internal memos fell into the hands of Swedish paediatric neurologist Olle Hansson – who had been a leading campaigner in the SMON scandal – did the world begin to hear about the problems with these drugs. Hansson released the documents to the media in late 1983 and in little more than a year, Ciba agreed to withdraw Tanderil and restrict Butazolidin to a second-choice drug in the treatment of four specific conditions.[72]

According to Lewandowski, these drug scandals played a major role in changing Ciba's approach. In the late 1970s, when the Pharma Policy unit was created, the company began to try to become more open to criticism and less reactive. 'There was a brochure published at that time which was significantly called *To be different*. It was a systematic attempt at being open, but at that time it was less open than it is today and some of the people did not know which direction to go.' The SMON and Tanderil issues helped to clarify what needed to be done. Lewandowski says that a key event in this learning process was a meeting in 1984 between the company's president at the time, Louis von Planta, and Olle Hansson. Klaus von Grember, who was the head of Ciba's public affairs division at the time, took part in a preliminary meeting with Hansson. Both men were impressed with each other. Hansson said that although von Grember 'was a Ciba-Geigy man, he was quite different from the old gangsters there. He had some new ideas'.[73] Von Grember reported to von Planta that 'in hindsight, it is evident that it was a mistake not to have talked to Hansson for all those years, not to have had at least an exchange of views and opinion. I felt he, also, was interested in constructive dialogue. He's not out to destroy the company.'[74]

A tough but productive meeting in London with consumer representatives on Butazolidin and Tanderil helped to move the debate on, as did the eventual meeting between Hansson and von Planta. But as Lewandowski recalls:

> there was still a certain amount of uncertainty as to the professional direction. But then, due to some changes in top management both in the pharma division and within the corporation, in the years 1985 to 1987 the critical mass for major change was present and I think finally, the Sandoz fire and the subsequent Rhine pollution [in November 1986] diminished the opposition to change, because with this event and the public atmosphere, suddenly all the more progressive elements in the company were proven right beyond expectation.[75]

Lewandowski described the Rhine incident as typical for the learning process of individuals and of organisations. 'We only learn in periods of crisis. Think of thalidomide.' He said that within the pharmaceutical industry there now appeared to be a relationship between openness to new ideas and the extent to which a particular company had undergone a major drug issue.

**RAD-AR**

Ciba had established several measures to help manage potential or emerging product issues, including the Medical Product Committee (which monitors and constantly reassesses the safety of marketed products), the Product Information Policy and Product Communication Audit (which codifies and controls all drug information), and the Product Issue Management and Early Warning Systems (which address drug issues from a pharma-political perspective).[76] Nonetheless, the company wanted to do more about drug safety and at the end of 1986, Ciba began developing an ambitious programme on the Risk Assessment of Drugs – Analysis and Response (RAD-AR) whose aims were to improve understanding of the various factors involved in assessing drug risk in today's complex society, and to ensure that the company's methods of informing about and promoting its drugs did not contribute to that risk. As Lewandowski points out, 'one major risk factor, is the lack of knowledge of the prescribing physician. I think that in many, if not most, countries, the education of the medical profession on proper drug usage and drug evaluation is certainly not sufficiently developed.'

Since drug manufacturers provide the bulk of the information about drugs to health workers, clearly part of the responsibility for this situation rests with them. As Lewandowski puts it:

> it is clear that a good manufacturer has the greatest amount of knowledge of his drug and on the therapeutic class that the drug is in, and if we would only learn to change our promotional and even informational language to the most advanced rules of the art and would inform and promote the drug accordingly, we would make a very valuable contribution, because then it would be the medical science related to the problems of the practical treatment. And that is in fact our ambition which is behind RAD-AR. Our assumption is that it is absolutely necessary for a leading manufacturer that the development, production, and promotion of the drug is in line with leading internationally recognised state of the art requirements.

Like most pharmaceutical companies, Ciba was faced with a situation where the staff from different disciplines often failed to talk with each other or to understand the implications of their respective decisions and actions. RAD-AR is attempting to establish a multidisciplinary approach to drug evaluation. 'What we try to achieve with RAD-AR is to create a greater awareness and to teach and train our people to apply this in their everyday work on our product range, both present and future.' This includes taking into consideration a whole range of often subjective value judgements, not only the scientific evidence, when deciding whether a drug should remain on the market. 'Some drugs which were once accepted, no longer are,' says Lewandowski.

> Because political value judgments are involved we have to allow for transparency of decision making procedures and wherever possible for participation. For the RAD-AR project that means that our effort to improve the whole organisation is meant to take place more or less publicly with seminars where we bring in external people, not only supporters but neutrals and critics and we try to expose the organisation permanently to a sort of public challenge. One of our assumptions is that just as political power since the age of the Renaissance at least has had to learn to be exposed to public debate, criticism,

and challenge and has had to accept that balance of power, social control is needed as well in private business organisation. So RAD-AR is the simple catchword for a systematic effort, professional drug handling, in transparent procedures, so to speak, with particular emphasis on correct information, both in the gathering and the evaluation of data but also in the translation of appropriate messages. I think it fits quite well into the WHO revised drug strategy. It fits if it is appropriately implemented. Our company is by no means opposed to the WHO revised drug strategy and the way it has emerged in recent years is a very good political and professional basis for improvement.

An early ally in the RAD-AR programme was the small US-based company, Alza, which for some time had been re-evaluating its own approach to the safety of medicines and the type of information it provided to prescribers and patients. As Alza's president, Peter Carpenter, notes, it is in the industry's own interest to communicate information on both the benefits and risks of drugs. 'The less well that we balance information, the more likely it is that users of our products will be unpleasantly surprised. And regulators, physicians, pharmacists and the public do not like unpleasant surprises.'[77]

In what was perhaps a surprising move in April 1988, Ciba invited representatives from other companies and a few people known to be critical of the industry to a meeting to discuss broadening the RAD-AR approach. The objective was to encourage industry-wide collaboration in three key areas: pharmacoepidemiology, risk perception analysis, and pharmaceutical risk/benefit communication.[78] Lewandowski explained that Ciba was convinced that data on safety and efficacy of drugs on the market cannot be considered as confidential.

We hold the view for example that if we have a drug and our competitors have drugs in the same therapeutical area, a meaningful benefit/risk evaluation can only be made if you have access to all data. So, if Pfizer wants to have our data on Voltaren (diclofenac), for example, they get it; it's clear. And we expect other companies to share their data with us. That means a slight change in behaviour, not denigrating other drugs.

The response to the meeting was certainly a surprise, and according to Lewandowski, better than Ciba had expected. *Scrip* reported that reactions from other companies who attended ranged from 'the cautious to the enthusiastic'.[79] A report in the IFPMA's *Health Horizons* said that the consensus of the meeting was that an industry-wide effort which could draw on and integrate the specific strengths and areas of expertise of individual companies was 'the logical way' to tackle the issue of drug safety more effectively.[80]

Lewandowski sees Ciba's RAD-AR programme, together with the company's other efforts to open up, as a way to reduce controversy and to deal with controversies in a more professional manner. Within Ciba, he says that the majority of people now think this is good for business. Since he started working for the company in 1985, he says he has 'already been witness to remarkable changes'.

One of the changes has been Ciba's introduction in 1985 of its own code of marketing practice which is 'even more stringent' than the IFPMA code.[81] In order to check that subsidiary companies follow the Ciba code, the company employs Dr Franz Gubser as Marketing Communications Auditor. He travels worldwide to spend the better part of three days each year in each of at least 20 countries where the company has a major operation, to review any locally produced promotional material. In addition, other marketing campaigns are checked at random and a full annual audit is performed on the marketing practices of four subsidiaries each year. The benefits of this approach are two-fold: first over time, the quality of information produced by Ciba improves and second, as a result, health workers may see the company in a better light and tend to select Ciba's products over a competitor's. As Dr Gubser puts it:

> There is an inherent danger in the industry that sales can become all-important at the expense of ethical standards. In our case, the effect of constant auditing is that medical practitioners perceive that they can place a greater deal of reliance on what we are saying to them.[82]

## Searle's programme for patient information

The US-based G. D. Searle company introduced in 1989 what it calls 'the first comprehensive programme by a pharmaceutical company to provide easy-to-understand information about its prescription drugs to patients worldwide'. Following research in the USA which found that approximately half the 1.6 million prescriptions dispensed each year are used incorrectly by patients, Searle's chief executive officer, Dr Sheldon Gilgore, said there was an 'obvious need' to improve patients' understanding about prescription medicines. The programme will ultimately provide patient information on all future Searle products. It follows two earlier programmes launched in 1987, the first of which provided several Searle products free of charge to patients in need in the USA, and the second which offered an unconditional refund to patients in the USA if a prescribed Searle product does not achieve the desired therapeutic effect.[83]

Coinciding with the announcement of the new information programme was the news that, for the first time in nearly four years, Searle had been able to show a profit on its pharmaceutical trading.[84]

Both Ciba and Searle are finding that putting ethics before sales can ultimately mean even better sales figures.

## Towards a healthy industry

The transformation of the pharmaceutical industry into a 'health care industry' is possible, but it is not simply a question of changing image or applying a new name-tag to old ways of thinking and working. It requires some fundamental changes. In the short term, it may be economically advantageous for the industry to encourage the 'pill for every ill' mentality in prescribers and patients alike, but in the long term that may prove to be counter-productive. As the DHF points out:

paradoxically, the pharmaceutical industry's health depends in the long run on its willingness to state when consumption of its products is a bad idea.... The pharmaceutical industry could become a genuine health care industry by promoting non-drug approaches to the maintenance of health and the treatment of illness.[85]

Demonstrating that this is possible, Ciba-Geigy has recently published an exceptionally good kit about diarrhoea control, stressing the importance of oral rehydration therapy. Recently too, the ABPI has joined with the British government's health education campaign on heart disease by publishing a series of advertisements which point out that preventing heart attacks through better diet and more exercise is much more effective than relying on drug therapy.

There are literally thousands of pharmaceutical companies around the world, but only a handful are engaged in innovative research. Dr Vernon Coleman suggested more than 10 years ago that steps should be taken to reduce the number of companies making ethical pharmaceuticals. 'With fewer companies there would be fewer "me too" drugs and less research effort would be wasted.'[86] More recently, Graham Dukes has postulated a similar proposal, noting the need for the major part of the industry to be organised in sufficiently large units

> to be able to undertake sophisticated basic and applied research in order to develop truly innovative products, large enough to survive comfortably between innovations without the need to introduce the third-rate or maintain the outdated, and large enough to provide its goods and services worldwide and not merely to the most lucrative sectors of the market.

Alongside these companies, there would be room for smaller units 'studying and exploiting traditional knowledge',[87] and also, one could add, perhaps focused on some specific disease conditions or particular aspects of health care technology.

A part of this change involves the industry's self-image and its relationships with others outside the industry. In the words of Richard Arnold, Executive Vice-President of the IFPMA, 'we are an industry under attack'.[88] The psychology behind such a statement is one of defensiveness, in which a siege mentality takes over. The question that needs to be asked (and which this book has outlined) is: 'why are we under attack?' In broad terms, the criticisms levelled at the industry have validity. The fine details may be open for debate, but unquestionably there have been and continue to be numerous practices of the industry that are not in the best interests of public health.

A siege mentality, bordering on paranoia at times, refuses to confront the issues. It sees things in terms of battles. Joe Williams of the PMA, for example, claims that the industry is 'too timid' in its responses to critics, while Walter von Wartburg of Ciba-Geigy, despite the new openness of the company, warns of 'career critics' who seem impossible to placate.[89]

The DHF notes that companies that 'scoff at their critics, or even attempt to suppress honest criticism or render it suspect' may ultimately be the least successful in the future, whereas the companies most likely to maintain a prominent place in the world industry may be those

> which negotiate with their critics in the consumer movements and in the health care professions. This is because it is the companies who listen and respond to the increasing assaults on their reputations who will find the capacity to build a new industrial base out of their responsiveness.[90]

Charles Medawar of Social Audit thinks that part of the problem is that the criticism has yet to sink in.

> The industry is so intent on shouting back in response to criticism, just in order to save face, that it never actually listens and, therefore, never actually understands. And, therefore, the criticism increases.... Because of the energy the industry puts into denouncing the motives of its critics, the industry gets caught in a vicious downward spiral. If the industry cannot behave in such a way as to take seriously the criticism made of it, then any witness to the confrontation, who in any way agrees with the criticisms made, is likely to be turned against the industry, even more than before. Quite frankly, unless the industry does something to improve this, it is going to get into far more trouble than it is in now.[91]

Ciba-Geigy is one company which appears to have recognised the sense of this approach. When the company thinks that it is time to review a product's risk/benefit, it brings together a group of scientists, consumers, and media representatives under a neutral chairperson to discuss the product. 'That's what we call transparency', says Lewandowski. 'This is a political attitude and it makes sense. It's like everyday political life. You increase intelligence and decrease lack of professionalism if you provide public exposure.' Even when the company is developing internal guidelines, it is now beginning to send draft copies to reliable critics to ask for their comments. 'I think this is good for both sides, because both sides can learn from each other.' Lewandowski compares the existence of industry critics to an opposition party in a democracy.

> It's legitimate, it's necessary, and it would be a major error to try to remove it. You know where you end up if you eliminate the opposition. So you have to allow for transparency of your own procedures through creating a sub-stantive dialogue. Dialogue means prepared for change, but it also means being prepared to defend a position when you are convinced that it is justified and you have valid acceptable reasons.

Until other companies follow this approach, the industry's 'mental' state – both in terms of its creative impulses and its self-conception – will not be as healthy as it could be.

## Social well-being
Aside from the questions already raised about the types of products being made and the types of research being carried out, one of the major indicators of social well-being is the degree to which the industry is sincere and honest in its

dealings, or, as the IFPMA code puts it, uses 'complete candour in dealings with public health officials, health care professionals and the public'.

Harry Schwartz, generally a strong supporter of the industry, recently expressed surprise that 'the two most important pharmaceutical industry meetings in 1986' – the IFPMA assembly and the PMA's annual meeting –

> were completely devoid of scientific content. No biologist, chemist, pharmacologist or other similar scientist engaged in industry drug research was invited to address either meeting.... Yet the major theme of both gatherings was that drug research by pharmaceutical companies is their most important activity.... [A] hypothetical outsider ... might well have wondered if there was not a contradiction between the vows of undying fidelity to pharmaceutical research heard at both meetings, and the conspicuous absence on the programmes of people actually engaged in that research.[92]

Generally, as has been noted earlier, the quality of information provided by the industry about products still has room for improvement, despite the claim by the IFPMA that information from the manufacturers 'provides prompt, detailed and accurate information for the benefit of both doctor and patient'.[93] In a ruling on the inappropriate promotion of anabolic steroids by the Dutch company Organon, the Dutch industry association NEFARMA, pointed out that:

> generally speaking a pharmaceutical company putting medicines on the market in another country should pay attention to the infrastructure of this country and should take into consideration the circumstances under which the sale of these medicines can reasonably be expected to take place, and ... the pharmaceutical company should act with greater responsibility and with more care, as the infrastructure offers less safeguards for a sound use of medicines concerned.[94]

As Dukes has pointed out:

> If we want the pharmaceutical industry to be not only physically healthy but also socially healthy by the year 2000 a lot has to change. Part of that process of change has started; part has as yet hardly been contemplated. It is in the interests of everyone that this should happen.... Sections of the industry should be seen to be trying harder than they have been so far. At the very least, people working in this industry should be as open as possible about their motives, activities and faults.[95]

It may be that the influence of companies like Ciba-Geigy is beginning to have some impact on the rest of the industry. In 1989, the IFPMA published a report by Klaus Leisinger,[96] Ciba's head of international relations, in which the pharmaceutical industry is advised to shoulder responsibilities above and beyond those laid down by laws and regulations. Leisinger argues that if companies want to maintain the degree of freedom which they currently enjoy, they will have to offer constructive solutions to key social issues. And, he says, it makes good business sense. 'The short-term costs of responsible action and the sacrifice of potential – and perhaps ethically dubious – turnover and profit are thus, in effect, long-term investments in greater market share, turnover and profit.'

Even so, there is a strong residue of resistance to change within the industry. In 1988, Richard Arnold told his colleagues attending the IFPMA assembly that the debate over the previous five years or so around the WHO RDS had not really benefited the sick. 'We can reasonably ask the question how many lives would have been saved or how much suffering avoided if the money and resources devoted to the largely sterile debate had been channelled into supplying medicines and care to those who needed it.'[97]

One could equally, and perhaps more legitimately, argue that had the money and resources that the industry has wasted over the past 25 years or so propping up ineffective or unimportant medicines been devoted to meeting real health needs, the dream of health for all would now be a little closer to reality.

## Co-operation or confrontation?

Speaking at the IFPMA assembly held in Madrid in October 1980, Patrick Jenkin, then UK Secretary of State for Social Services, said there was a need for a satisfactory accommodation between the interests of the industry on the one hand and the aspirations of developing countries on the other.

> There is only one way that it will be reached – through understanding, consultation and negotiations.... The way forward is not, surely, confrontation but a sympathetic search for a middle way that makes sense for both sides and in particular helps to identify the real needs of developing countries.[98]

It is likely that the pharmaceutical industry will face a continuing period of both confrontation and opportunities for co-operation. The degree to which one or the other will prevail is difficult to predict. In part, it depends on the willingness of the industry to ask itself some serious questions about its future directions.

The issues that have been raised over the past 25 years in relation to pharmaceuticals are, for the most part, still on the table. Drug safety has improved, at least in most industrialised countries, although there are still some concerns about potentially risky products being sold in developing countries. Drug prices, particularly in today's economic climate, will continue to be a major issue, as governments and consumers try to get the best possible value for their health expenditures. Better training and better information about drugs and their proper roles in health care will be the topic of continuing debate and, it is to be hoped, further action. Methods to improve the distribution of essential drugs, particularly in the rural areas of developing countries, will be an ongoing concern. Some of these topics are less contentious than others, although there is more scope for co-operation than for confrontation in most of them. However, the major sticking points are liable to be the questions of which drugs and how many, both in terms of products currently on the market and the research choices that set the future market.

Above all, the debate until the end of this century and perhaps well into the next is liable to focus upon the rational use of drugs. A 'good' drug used badly is as much of a problem as a 'bad' drug. Discussions going on within HAI at the moment indicate that many of its participating groups intend to concentrate on improving drug utilisation and making sure that more openness and honesty about drugs emerges. The quality of drug information is liable to be under scrutiny for some time to come.

In a resource-limited world, pressure will increase on companies that continue to follow the 'me too' path of research and marketing. The concept of improving information on some 50,000 or more different brand-name drugs defies rationality. The logistics of organising comparative clinical trials to assess objectively their relative effectiveness and safety, and of monitoring their adverse effects after marketing is beyond the capability of any country, company or international body.

Underlying this issue is the whole question of a challenging restructuring of the pharmaceutical industry. The possibility exists for this to happen. Analysts outside the industry, and a few brave souls within it, have been offering the most tentative of rough sketches as to what a redesigned industry might look like. To turn these sketches into full-scale models requires the full and honest participation of the industry in wide-ranging debates and negotiations. Some companies will lose in the process. But for most, certainly for the truly research-based enterprises, the process can only be beneficial.

Better patent protection and secure and profitable rewards for real innovation are amongst the 'carrots' on offer. So too is the opportunity to shed the image of the pharmaceutical industry as an industry bulging with economic muscle on the exterior, but possessing a paranoid psychology and the sense of being a social outcast, and replace it with an industry that has a healthy glow both inside and out and is welcomed as a beneficial partner in society's development.

There is no dispute between the industry and its critics that the latter picture is the most desirable. 'We've got to have a flourishing industry,' says Charles Medawar of Social Audit. 'If the industry were producing drugs which people needed, and if the industry were promoting them responsibly, I wouldn't for a moment argue that it shouldn't make money out of that.'[99]

The other side of the equation – the 'stick' – is that pressure will increase on those companies that are not prepared to shed their defensive attitude and their old ways of working. In that sense, the attitude of the PMA, which has made it clear that it will defend strongly the industry's right and duty to its shareholders to make profits and will resist over-zealous government interference in the way in which it conducts its business in both the developing and developed world,[100] does not augur well for the path of co-operation. As the DHF has noted:

> the critics of the present situation should not aspire to convert the entire pharmaceutical industry to their cause. They will accelerate change by concentrating their energies on dialogue with the new managers of the health-centred companies whom they would like to see grow while bringing increased public pressure on the drug-centred companies.[101]

The opportunities are there. The 'middle way' is a possibility, although at the moment, it is overgrown with the tangle of past conflicts. The map charting its course has long been lost and the only way through now is with the spirit of exploration – a step at a time. It is a challenging, but exciting prospect, and there will be deviations along the path on all sides. However, the benefits of the changes that could occur offer hope that, if not by the year 2000, then at least sometime in the not-too-distant future, there can be a healthy pharmaceutical industry happily co-existing with a world population that has access to health for all. Despite the industry's protests, in the long run the pharmaceutical industry may well be the ultimate winner.

# Notes

## Introduction

1. Muller, M., *The Health of Nations*, Faber and Faber, London, 1982, p.227
2. Ibid., p.226
3. See for example: Lappe, M., *When Antibiotics Fail*, North Atlantic Books, Berkeley, Calif., 1986; Curry, P., 'Society tomorrow', *Guardian*, 1 Jul 1987, p.11 (quoting homoeopathic physician George Vithoulkas)
4. Medawar, C., *The Wrong Kind of Medicine?*, Consumers' Association and Hodder and Stoughton, London, 1984, p.40
5. Baistow, T., 'Point of departure', *Guardian*, 30 Apr 1985 (quoting from James Cameron's autobiograpy, *Point of Departure*)
6. Laurence, D. R. and Bennett, P. N., *Clinical Pharmacology* (6th edn), Churchill Livingstone, London, 1987, p.6

## Chapter 1

1. Muller, *Health of Nations*, p.158
2. UNICEF, *The State of the World's Children 1987*, Oxford University Press, Oxford, 1986, pp.5, 9, 45, 111
3. Ibid., pp.27, 34, 111
4. Ibid., p.57
5. UNICEF, *The State of the World's Children 1986*, Oxford University Press, Oxford, 1985, pp.22, 76
6. Brandt, W., et al., *North-South: a programme for survival*, Pan, London, 1980, p.90
7. Rabeneck, S. and Stone, T., *Strategies for Nutrition in CIDA*, CIDA, Ottawa, 1982, p.4
8. IOCU, 'Food first, never anabolic steroids', *Consumer Interpol Focus*, No. 6, Dec 1983, p.1
9. Ebrahim, G. J., *Child Care in the Tropics*, Macmillan, London, 1978, p.39
10. Cameron, M. and Hofvander, Y., *Manual on Feeding Infants and Young Children* (2nd edn), FAO, Rome, 1980, p.31
11. UNICEF, *The State of the World's Children 198*  Oxford University Press, Oxford, 1983, p.11
12. Chetley, A., 'Health for all', *Bernard van Leer Foundation Newsletter*, No. 48, Oct 1987, p.2
13. Helsing, E., 'Malnutrition in an affluent society', *World Health*, Oct 1984, p.14
14. Mass, B., *Population Target*, Women's Press, Toronto, 1976, p.160
15. White, A., *British Official Aid in the Health Sector*, IDS Discussion Paper No. 107, University of Sussex, Brighton, 1977, p.12
16. Thomas, H., 'When family planning is necessary', *Guardian*, 18 Jul 1984
17. Harrison, P., *Inside the Third World*, Penguin, London, 1979, p.273

18. Bronstein, A., *The Triple Struggle*, War on Want, London, 1982, p.220
19. Banerji, D., 'Population planning in India: national and foreign priorities', *International Journal of Health Services*, Vol. 3, No. 4, 1973, p.774
20. UNFPA, *1984 Report*, New York, 1985, p.8
21. Doyal, L. and Pennell, I., *The Political Economy of Health*, Pluto Press, London, 1979, p.285
22. Bekele, M., 'Social and economic factors affecting women's health', *Assignment Children*, 49/50, Spring 1980, pp.77–8
23. Ratcliffe, J., 'Social justice and the demographic transition: lessons from India's Kerala State', in Morley, D., Rohde, J. and Williams, G. (eds.), *Practising Health for All*, Oxford University Press, Oxford, 1983, p.65
24. Ratcliffe, 'Social justice', p.79
25. UNICEF, *The State of the World's Children 1989*, Oxford University Press, Oxford, 1988, p.10
26. Rabeneck and Stone, *Strategies for Nutrition*, p.1
27. Rohde, J. E., 'Why the other half dies: the science and politics of child mortality in the Third World', *Assignment Children*, 61/62, 1983, p.39
28. UNICEF, *State of the World's Children 1987*, p.81
29. Mahler, H., *World Health – 2000 and Beyond*, address to the 41st World Health Assembly (Doc. No. WHA41/DIV/4), WHO, Geneva, 3 May 1988, p.3
30. Doyal and Pennell, *Political Economy of Health*, p.28
31. Sterky, G., 'Towards another development in health', *Development Dialogue*, No. 1, 1978, p.9
32. Illich, I., *Limits to Medicine*, Penguin, London, 1977, p.56
33. Collier, J., *The Health Conspiracy*, Century Hutchinson, London, 1989, pp.3–14
34. Banerji, D., 'The political economy of Western medicine in Third World countries', in McKinlay, J. B., (ed.), *Issues in the Political Economy of Health*, Tavistock Publications, New York, 1982, pp.258–9
35. UNICEF, *State of the World's Children 1984*, p.7
36. Ibid., pp.9, 33
37. Harrison, *Inside the Third World*, p.294
38. Morley, D., *Paediatric Priorities in the Developing World*, Butterworth, London, 1977, p.4
39. World Bank, *World Development Report 1980*, Oxford University Press, New York, 1980
40. Kennedy, I., *The Unmasking of Medicine*, Paladin, London, 1983, p.34
41. Rohde, 'Why the other half dies', p.60
42. Banerji, 'The political economy of Western medicine', pp.269–70
43. Djukanovic, V. and Mach, E.P. (eds.), *Alternative Approaches to Meeting Basic Health Needs in Developing Countries*, WHO, Geneva, 1975
44. Rohde, J., 'Health for all in China: principles and relevance for other countries', in Morley, D., Rohde, J. and Williams, G. (eds.) *Practising Health for All*, p.13
45. See for example: Mohs, E., 'Infectious diseases and health in Costa Rica: the development of a new paradigm', *Pediatric Infectious Disease*, Vol. 1, No. 3, 1982, pp.212–16; Weller, T. H., 'Too few and too little: barricades to the pursuit of health', *Reviews of Infectious Diseases*, Vol. 5, No. 6, Nov-Dec 1983, pp.994-1,002
46. WHO, *Handbook of Resolutions and Decisions, Vol. II, 1973–1984*, WHO, Geneva, 1985, resolution WHA30.43, p.1
47. WHO, *Primary Health Care. Report of the International Conference on Primary Health Care, Alma-Ata, USSR, 6-12 September 1978*, WHO, Geneva, 1978
48. *Daily Telegraph*, 30 Sep 1983

49. Williams, G., 'WHO: reaching out to all', *World Health Forum*, Vol. 9, No. 2, 1988, p.194
50. Cunliffe, P.W., 'Pharmaceuticals in the Third World', *Pharma Topics*, No. 4, Mar 1982, p.1
51. Pfizer, *Pfizer and Third World Health Issues*, New York, 1983, p.3
52. Wood, M., *Pharmaceuticals in the Third World*, AMREF, Nairobi, Jun 1982, text of a speech delivered at the International Federation of Pharmaceutical Manufacturers Associations assembly in Washington, DC, in Jun 1982
53. Rohde, 'Why the other half dies', p.41
54. Muller, *Health of Nations*, p.21
55. See for example: McKeown, T., *The Role of Medicine*, Blackwell, Oxford, 1979; Doyal and Pennell, *Political Economy of Health*, pp.56–7; Burkitt, D., *Don't Forget Fibre In Your Diet*, (4th edn), Martin Dunitz, London, 1983, pp.18–19; Sanders, D. and Carver, R., *The Struggle for Health*, Macmillan, London, 1986, pp.25–37; Lappe, *When Antibiotics Fail*, pp.17–19.
56. Sanders and Carver, *Struggle for Health*; Lappe, *When Antibiotics Fail*
57. Lappe, *When Antibiotics Fail*
58. Cited in Wood, *Pharmaceuticals in the Third World*

## Chapter 2

1. Gould, D., *The Medical Mafia*, Sphere, London, 1985, p.157
2. Mossinghoff, G., report to the PMA Board of Directors, PMA, Washington, 1 Dec 1985
3. *Scrip*, No. 1,062, Dec 1985, cited in: Dag Hammarskjöld Foundation, 'Editorial: the rational use of drugs and WHO', *Development Dialogue*, No. 2, 1985, p.3
4. Hailey, A., *Strong Medicine*, Pan, London, 1985
5. Redwood, H., *The Pharmaceutical Industry: trends, problems and achievements*, Oldwicks Press, Felixstowe, 1988, p.25
6. Ibid., p.26
7. Ibid., pp.27–30
8. UNCTC, *Transnational Corporations and the Pharmaceutical Industry*, (ST/CTC/9), UN, New York, 1979, p.15
9. Ibid., p.16
10. Braithwaite, J., *Corporate Crime in the Pharmaceutical Industry*, Routledge and Kegan Paul, London, 1984, p.164
11. Ibid., p.206
12. Ibid.
13. Ibid., p.207
14. Ibid.
15. Muller, *Health of Nations*, p.80
16. Braithwaite, *Corporate Crime*, pp.4-5. (The company also provided the extermination gas used at the camp: p.389.)
17. Ibid., p.5
18. Redwood, *Pharmaceutical Industry*, pp.43–4
19. PAHO, *Policies for the Production and Marketing of Essential Drugs*, (CD29/DT/1), Washington, 18 Apr 1983, p.12
20. Braithwaite, *Corporate Crime*, p.68
21. Ibid.
22. Although thalidomide was withdrawn, it has been used experimentally in controlled circumstances and was subsequently found to be of value in treating leprosy and Behcet's disease. See Taylor, D. and Griffin, J. P., *Orphan Diseases, Orphan*

*Medicines and Orphan Patients*, ABPI, London, 1985. Alşo, research with animals at Johns Hopkins University in Baltimore suggests that thalidomide could be useful in improving the survival rates in organ and tissue transplants. The researchers suggest that it could replace cyclosporin, an immunodepressant currently used in transplant cases, which has a fairly high incidence of adverse effects. The researchers noted, however, that 'there is a public relations problem with the use of thalidomide' (from a news item on *America Today* programme, Worldnet, broadcast 19 Apr 1987).

23. Braithwaite, *Corporate Crime*, p.65
24. Ibid., pp.68–72
25. Lumbroso, A., 'The introduction of new drugs', in Blum, R., et al (eds.), *Pharmaceuticals and Health Policy*, Social Audit/IOCU/HAI, London/Penang/The Hague, 1983, pp.73–4
26. Lesser, F., 'Drugs monitor needs sharper teeth', *New Scientist*, 17 Mar 1983, p.731
27. UNCTC, *Transnational Corporations*, 1979, p.69
28. See WHO, *The Rational Use of Drugs*, Geneva, 1987, pp.137–41, for a reproduction of most resolutions concerning pharmaceuticals from 1948 to 1975.
29. Haslemere Group, *Who Needs the Drug Companies?*, Haslemere Group/War on Want/Third World First, London/Oxford, 1976, p.1
30. Ibid.
31. Coleman, V., *The Medicine Men*, Arrow Books, London, 1977, p.166
32. Ledogar, R.J., *Hungry for Profits*, IDOC, New York, 1975, pp.54–5
33. UNCTC, *Transnational Corporations in the Pharmaceutical Industry of Developing Countries*, UN, New York, 1984, p.17
34. Ledogar, *Hungry for Profits*, pp.57–9
35. Heller, T., *Poor Health, Rich Profits*, Spokesman Books, Nottingham, 1977, p.43
36. UNCTC, *Transnational Corporations*, 1984, p.33
37. Muller, *Health of Nations*, pp.193–4
38. In 1989, as many as 32 pharmaceutical companies in Venezuela were reported to be under investigation for allegedly making illicit profits on imports of pharmaceuticals and other products. Authorities discovered discrepancies between the quanties of foreign exchange requested and the actual prices paid for individual imports. In some cases the prices quoted by importers for the same product were reported to have varied over a thousand-fold. Along with national companies, Pfizer, Upjohn, Warner-Lambert, Glaxo, Schering AG, Ciba-Geigy, Merrell Dow and Bristol-Myers were under investigation. See *Scrip*, 'Profit probe in Venezuela', No. 1,440, 23 Aug 1989, p.19.
39. Braithwaite, *Corporate Crime*, pp.184–6
40. Ibid., pp.176–7
41. Ibid., pp.182–3
42. Adams, S., *Roche versus Adams*, Jonathan Cape, London, 1984, pp.27–40
43. Ibid., p.35
44. Ibid., pp.14–26, 41–2, 76–81
45. Muller, *Health of Nations*, p.179
46. Agarwal, A., *Drugs and the Third World*, Earthscan, London, 1978, p.1
47. From a speech delivered on 18 Feb 1988 at a retreat for American private voluntary organisations in Vermont, reproduced as Appendix C in *The Grafton Compact*, InterAction, New York, 1988
48. Speech delivered 17 Feb 1988 at a retreat for American private voluntary organisations, reproduced as Appendix B in *The Grafton Compact*, InterAction, New York, 1988
49. Doyal and Pennell, *Political Economy of Health*, p.220
50. Ibid., p.226

51. Haddon, C., *Women and Tranquillisers*, Sheldon Press, London, 1984, p.15
52. Doyal and Pennell, *Political Economy of Health*, p.227
53. Toynbee, P., 'The patients who get hooked on tranquillisers', *Guardian*, 25 Nov 1985
54. Querubin, M. P. and Tan, M. L., 'Old roles, new roles: women, primary health care, and pharmaceuticals in the Philippines' in McDonnell, K. (ed.), *Adverse Effects: women and the pharmaceutical industry*, IOCU, Penang, 1986, pp.180–3
55. McDonnell, *Adverse Effects*, pp.3–4
56. Cary LaCheen, 'Population control and the pharmaceutical industry', in McDonnell, *Adverse Effects*, p.109
57. Ibid., p.108
58. Cooper, W. and Smith, T., *Everything You Need to Know about the Pill*, Sheldon Press, London, 1984, p.35; see also Grant, E., *The Bitter Pill*, Corgi, London, 1986, and Guillebaud, J., *The Pill* (3rd edn), Oxford University Press, Oxford, 1984.
59. Pappert, A., 'The rise and fall of the IUD', in McDonnell, *Adverse Effects*, pp.167–71
60. Liskin, L.S. and Quillin, W. F., 'Long-acting progestins – promise and prospects', *Population Reports*, Series K, No. 2, May 1983, pp.K19–K21
61. Tudiver, S., 'The strength of links: international women's health networks in the eighties', in McDonnell, *Adverse Effects*, pp.187–210
62. Melrose, D., *Bitter Pills*, Oxfam, Oxford, 1982, pp.184–5
63. UN, *Towards a World Economy That Works*, UN, New York, 1980, p.14
64. George, S., *A Fate Worse Than Debt*, Penguin, London, 1988, p.12
65. Tucker, D., *The World Health Market*, Euromonitor Publications, London, 1984, p.183
66. WHO, *Prophylactic and Therapeutic Substances* (report by the Director General, Doc. No. A28/11), WHO, Geneva, 3 Apr 1975

**Chapter 3**

1. WGBH Educational Foundation, 'Prescriptions for profit', *Frontline*,, WGBH Transcripts, Boston, 1989. Transcript of television documentary broadcast 28 Mar 1989, p.5.
2. WHO, *A Manual for the Treatment of Acute Diarrhoea* (Doc. No.: WHO/CDD/SER/80.2) WHO, Geneva, 1980, p.13
3. *Martindale: The Extra Pharmacopoeia* (28th edn), Pharmaceutical Press, London, 1982, p.81
4. AMA, *Drug Evaluations* (4th edn), AMA, Chicago, 1980, p.972
5. *Martindale*, p.1,011
6. Rohde, J. E., 'Selective primary health care: strategies for control of disease in the developing world. XV. Acute diarrhoea', *Reviews of Infectious Diseases*, Vol. 6, No. 6, Nov–Dec 1984, p.846
7. Chetley, A. and Gilbert, D., *Problem Drugs*, HAI, The Hague/Penang, 1986, p.5 of 'Antidiarrhoeals' section
8. HAI, 'The Pharmaceutical Industry – "Continued Research in Pursuit of Excellence"?', press release, 22 Nov 1985
9. From IMS data, 1985.
10. Report of the Workshop on Diarrhoea: current concepts, held in Frankfurt, 23 Sep 1983, p.63
11. Cited in Chetley and Gilbert, *Problem Drugs*, p.2 of 'Antidiarrhoeals' section
12. Elarabi, I. I., 'Where drugs don't help', *World Health*, Apr 1986, p.10
13. UNICEF, *State of The World's Children 1986*, p.20
14. Ibid., p.91

15. *Lancet*, Vol. II, 5 Aug 1978, p.300
16. Bevan, J. A. (ed.), *Essentials of Pharmacology*, Harper and Row, New York, 1976, p.301
17. UNICEF, *State of the World's Children 1984*, pp.18-22
18. Bradshaw, C., 'Treating children with diarrhoea and vomiting', *The Practitioner*, Vol. 228, Sep 1984, pp.834–5
19. Rohde, 'Selective primary health care', p.850
20. In 1989, following a critical UK television documentary by *World in Action*, Wellcome agreed to suspend worldwide distribution of ADM, 'pending an internal investigation into the appropriateness of the product'. The company said that it had already been reviewing the labelling and appropriateness of the the product before the documentary had been screened. The worldwide suspension came almost exactly four years to the day after HAI first drew Wellcome's attention to the misleading labelling in Kenya. For further details, see: 'Wellcome suspends ADM distribution', *Scrip*, No. 1,468, 29 Nov 1989, p.13; 'Misuse of antidiarrhoeal medicines', *Lancet*, 21 Oct 1989 and 'Wellcome to withdraw ADM from sale', *Lancet*, 25 Nov 1989
21. 'New NZPMA name stresses research', *Scrip*, No. 1,406, 26 Apr 1989, p.20
22. Burstall, M. L. with Senior, I., *The Community's Pharmaceutical Industry*, EC, Brussels, 1985, pp.23–4
23. 'Dollar fall hits US company rankings', *Scrip*, No. 1,270/1, 1/6 Jan 1988, p.6
24. *Scrip Yearbook 1987*, PJB Publications, Richmond, UK, Dec 1986
25. PAHO, *Policies*, p.10
26. *Fortune*, 'The Fortune 500', 24 Apr 1989; 25 Apr 1988; 27 Apr 1987
27. Redwood, *Pharmaceutical Industry*, p.216
28. Ibid., p.217
29. Ibid., p.219
30. 'Glaxo heading for number one?', *Scrip*, review issue, 1989, p.8
31. *Scrip Changes and Trends: an analysis of four years of Scrip's League Tables*, PJB Publications, Richmond, UK, Jul 1986, p.45
32. WHO, *The World Drug Situation*, Geneva, 1988, p.36
33. 'US pharma R&D spending up 12.3%', *Scrip*, No. 1,483, 26 Jan 1990, p.15
34. 'Worldwide pharma R&D trends', *Scrip*, No. 1,471, 8 Dec 1989, p.25
35. WHO, *World Drug Situation*, pp.35–7
36. Burstall, M. L. and Michon-Savarit, C., *The Pharmaceutical Industry: trade related issues*, OECD, Paris, 1985, p.26
37. The PMA data are reproduced in WHO, *World Drug Situation*, p.36
38. The calculation of 424 is based on 316 NCEs introduced by US companies between 1961 and 1977, and 69 between 1981 and 1985 (both figures cited by Redwood, *Pharmaceutical Industry*, pp.186 and 189) plus an estimate of 13 NCEs a year for 1978–80 (based on an average world introduction of 55 NCEs a year during that period, cited by WHO, *World Drug Situation*, p.37 and the assumption that US firms maintained the 25 per cent share of total NCE introductions cited by Redwood, during the period).
39. Bowers, A., 'Managing the multinational pharma company in the 1990s', *Scrip*, No. 1,372/3, 23/28 Dec 1988, pp.16–19
40. PAHO, *Policies*, p.12
41. Ibid., p.13
42. Burstall, M. L., Dunning, J. H. and Lake, A., 'Multinational enterprises, governments and technology; pharmaceutical industry', OECD, Paris, 1981; summary published as: *An Industry like no Other*, Pharma Information, Basle, 1982, p.11
43. For example Dr Joseph Zammit-Lucia of Cambridge Pharma Consultancy, in 'The secret of pharma success?', *Scrip*, No. 1,411, 12 May 1989, p.18; Sir James Black, the inventor of two of the world's best-selling drugs, in 'Prof Sir James Black on

"precept and prejudice" in R&D', *Scrip*, No. 1,309, 18 May 1989, pp.24–5; Professor Sir John Vane, a Nobel Prize winner and leading researcher in the prostaglandin field, in Chustecka, Z., 'Professor Sir John Vane on research and drug discovery', *Scrip*, No. 1,300, 15 Apr 1988, pp.20–2.

44. WHO, *World Drug Situation*, p.40
45. Melrose, *Bitter Pills*, p.53
46. Muller, *Health of Nations*, p.66
47. Ibid., p.62
48. Melrose, *Bitter Pills*, p.54
49. UNCTC, *Transnational Corporations*, 1984, p.30
50. Redwood, *Pharmaceutical Industry*, p.194
51. Sonenclar, R., 'Prescription for profits: be selective, be careful', *Financial World*, 17–30 Oct 1984, p.14
52. Girolami, P., 'A European view', *World Link*, Dec 1988, p.70
53. Collier, *Health Conspiracy*, p.32
54. Levi, J., 'Patent side-effects hit Wellcome', *Business*, Jan 1988, p.32
55. 'Zovirax spurs Wellcome growth', *Scrip*, No 1,362, 18 Nov 1988, pp.8–10
56. Medawar, C., talk given at a HAI training seminar, Sweden, Aug 1987
57. Collier, *Health Conspiracy*, pp.48–9
58. Gwinner, E., 'Nobel Prize for Medicine goes to three pharmaceutical industry research scientists', *Health Horizons*, No. 6, Jan 1989, pp.18–19
59. Chustecka, 'Professor Sir John Vane', p.21
60. *Scrip*, review issue 1989, p.12
61. Teeling-Smith, G., 'The golden triangle', *Times Health Supplement*, 29 Jan 1982; also cited in PMA, *The Health Consequences of Restricted Drug Lists*, Washington, DC, 1985
62. Cited in: IBON, *The Philippine Drug Industry*, Manila, 1986, p.38
63. Management Sciences for Health, *Managing Drug Supply*, Boston, 1981
64. Sepulveda, C. and Meneses, E. (eds.), *The Pharmaceutical Industry in ASEAN Countries*, UN Asian and Pacific Development Institute, Bangkok, 1980, p.330
65. UNCTC, *Transnational Corporations*, 1984
66. Temple, R. J., 'The DESI Programme', in *Proceedings of the Third International Conference of Drug Regulatory Authorities*, Swedish National Board of Health and Welfare/WHO, Uppsala, 1984, pp.13–18
67. Marsh, P., 'Prescribing all the way to the bank', *New Scientist*, 18 Nov 1989, p.55
68. Barral, E., *Prospective et santé*, No. 36, Winter 1985/86, pp.89–95, cited in WHO, *World Drug Situation*, pp.38–9. See also: '10 years of NCE discovery analysed', *Scrip*, No. 1,062, 23 Dec 1985, pp.20–1.
69. Marsh, 'Prescribing all the way', p.55
70. Chetley, A., *Towards Rational Drug Use*, HAI, The Hague, 1988, pp.2, 17
71. Medawar, *Wrong Kind of Medicine?*, pp.45–6
72. 'ABPI "to fight tooth and nail"', *Pharmaceutical Journal*, 17 Nov 1984, p.599
73. Medawar, talk at HAI training workshop, 1987
74. PMA, *Health Consequences*
75. WHO, *The Rational Use of Drugs*, 1987, p.113
76. Clark, E., *The Want Makers*, Coronet Books, London, 1989, p.290

## Chapter 4

1. IFPMA, *IFPMA Code of Pharmaceutical Marketing Practices* (rev. edn), Geneva, March 1987

2. IFPMA, 'The international industry discusses marketing standards', *Health Horizons*, No. 4, May 1988, p.18

3. For a discussion on voluntary codes, see Hamilton, R. and Whinnett, D., 'A comparison of the WHO and UK codes of practice for the marketing of breastmilk substitutes', *Journal of Consumer Policy*, Vol. 10, 1987, pp.167–92.

4. Medawar, C., *Insult or Injury?*, Social Audit, London, 1979, pp.69–70

5. Personal correspondence with Dr R. B. Arnold, Executive Vice-President of the IFPMA, 12 Apr 1984 (Boehringer Ingelheim did, however, agree to delete the phrase 'remarkably safe' from future advertising).

6. Forty-nine companies were involved: ACP International, Alembic, Ayerst, Beecham, Behrin, Biochemie, Blue Cross, Boehringer Ingelheim, Chinoin/Medimpex, Chugai, Ciba-Geigy, Cilag, Daiichi, Delalande, East India Pharma., Ethico, Fisons, Franco-Indian, Geofman Pharma, Glaxo, High Noon Labs, Al-Hikma, Hoechst, IPCA, Janssen, Jean-Marie, Kali-Chemie, Leo, May and Baker, Medichem, Nicholas, Organon, Parke-Davis, Pfizer, PPP, Praffa Labs, Rotta, Sandoz, Searle, Servier, SG Pharma., Syntex, Tanabe, Therapharma, Torrent, United American, Wellcome, Wockhardt, Wyeth.

7. Clark, *Want Makers*, p.289

8. Waldholz, M., 'Pill promoters: marketing often is the key to success of prescription drugs', *Wall Street Journal*, 28 Dec 1981

9. WHO, *World Drug Situation*, p.43

10. IBON, *Philippine Drug Industry*, p.7

11. PMA, *Health Consequences*

12. Lall, S., 'Economic considerations in the provision and use of medicines', in Blum, *Pharmaceuticals and Health Policy*, p.199

13. Ledogar, *Hungry for Profits*, p.25

14. IFPMA, *The Need to Inform: the role of promotion in marketing medicines for the Third World*, Geneva, 1985

15. WHO, *World Drug Situation*, p.44

16. UNCTC, *Transnational Corporations*, 1984, pp.88, 94, 111

17. See for example: 'Is there a need for state medical reps?', *Scrip*, No. 1,343, 14 Sep 1989, pp.4–5; Lexchin, J., 'Doctors and detailers: therapeutic education or pharmaceutical promotion?', *International Journal of Health Services*, Vol. 19, No. 4, 1989, pp.663–79; Lexchin, J., 'Pharmaceutical promotion in Canada: convince them or confuse them', *International Journal of Health Services*, Vol. 17, No. 1, 1987, pp.77–89; Gould, *Medical Mafia*, pp.172–3; Avorn, J., Chen, M. and Hartley, R., 'Scientific versus commercial sources of influence on the prescribing behavior of physicians', *American Journal of Medicine*, Vol. 73, July 1982, pp.4–8; Hayer, F., 'Rational prescribing and sources of information', *Social Science and Medicine*, Vol. 16, 1982, pp.2,017–23; Walton, H., 'Ad recognition and prescribing by physicians', *Journal of Advertising Research*, Vol. 20, No. 3, Jun 1980, pp.39–48.

18. Lexchin, 'Pharmaceutical promotion in Canada', p.86

19. Round, I. R., 'Marketing and advertising trends', *BIRA Journal*, Vol. 5, No. 2, Jul 1986, pp.9–10

20. *British National Formulary*, British Medical Association and the Royal Pharmaceutical Society of Great Britain, London, No. 13, 1987, p.129

21. IFPMA, *Making the Most of Medicines*, Geneva, 1985, p.13

22. 'MaLAM's open letter to industry', *Scrip*, No. 1,457, 20 Oct 1989, p.22

23. Wade, V. A., Mansfield, P. R. and McDonald, P. J., 'Drug companies' evidence to justify advertising', *Lancet*, 25 Nov 1989, pp.1261–63

24. Anon., 'International drug marketing code', *Lancet*, 30 Apr 1988

25. Moulds, R. F. W., Bochner, F. and Wing, L. M. H., 'Drug advertising', *Medical Journal of Australia*, Vol. 145, 4–18 Aug 1986, pp.178–9

26. 'SK&F resigns from APMA', *Scrip*, No. 1,460, 1 Nov 1989, p.8; and 'SK&F and APMA resolve differences', *Scrip*, No. 1,465, 17 Nov 1989, p.10

27. Stimson, G. V., 'Information contained in drug advertisements', *British Medical Journal*, 29 Nov 1975, pp.508–9

28. Collier, *Health Conspiracy*, p.76

29. Collier, J. and New, L., 'Illegibility of drug advertisements', *Lancet*, 11 Feb 1984, pp.341–2

30. Veitch, A., 'BMA wants action against misleading drug adverts', *Guardian*, 30 Nov 1984

31. Herxheimer, A. and Collier, J., 'Self-regulation of promotion by the British pharmaceutical industry, 1983–1988: a critical analysis', *British Medical Journal*, 3 Feb 1990, pp.307–11; 'UK ad code more honoured in breach than observance?', *Scrip*, No. 1,488, 14 Feb 1990, p.7

32. Collier, *Health Conspiracy*, pp.81–2

33. 'FDA's drug promotion problems', *Scrip*, No. 1,389, 24 Feb 1989, p.14

34. 'FDA hits at Wyeth-Ayerst promotion', *Scrip*, No. 1,480, 17 Jan 1990, p.13

35. McComas, M., *Europe's Consumer Movement: key issues and corporate responses*, Business International, Geneva, 1980, p.II-86

36. Collier, *Health Conspiracy*, p.76

37. Clark, *Want Makers*, p.14

38. Bennett, C., 'The remedy for drugs', *Marketing Week*, 8 Jun 1984, p.42

39. Rolt, F., *Pills, Policies and Profits*, War on Want, London, 1985, p.21

40. Bennett, 'Remedy for drugs', p.42

41. Lexchin, 'Pharmaceutical promotion in Canada'

42. Harvey, K., 'The influence of advertising over prescribing', *Australian Journal of Hospital Pharmacy* (supplement to Vol. 18, No. 3, Jun 1988), p.25

43. Margo, J., 'A gift for persuasion', *Sydney Morning Herald*, 14 Jan 1989

44. Lexchin, J., 'The pharmaceutical industry in Canada', *HAI News*, No. 46, Apr 1989, p.2

45. WGBH Educational Foundation, 'Prescriptions for profit', p.15

46. 'Computers for Ciba-Geigy's US reps', *Scrip*, No. 1,277, 27 Jan 1988, p.8

47. Kathe, H., Laschet, H. and Schuler, G. (eds.), *Drugs and the Third World: facts, figures and the future*, BPI, Frankfurt, 1982, p.11

48. Blum, R. and Kreitman, K., 'Factors affecting individual use of medicines' in Blum, *Pharmaceuticals and Health Policy*, pp.158–9

49. Braithwaite, *Corporate Crime*, p.224

50. Lexchin, 'Doctors and detailers', p.665

51. Braithwaite, *Corporate Crime*, p.225

52. Murphy, P. A., 'One drug company's sales techniques', *New England Journal of Medicine*, Vol. 313, 25 Jul 1985, p.270

53. WGBH Educational Foundation, 'Prescriptions for profit', p.18

54. Ferriman, A., 'Exposed: drug giant's hard sell to doctors', *Observer* (London), 9 Jun 1985

55. Chadially, Z. H. and Telang, G. L., note to drug representatives, 3 Jun 1985

56. Lexchin, J., 'Doctors and detailers', pp.667–8

57. IFPMA, *The Need to Inform*, p.12

58. WHO, Resolution WHA21.41, May 1968

59. IFPMA, *IFPMA Code*, p.5

60. Tan, M., *Dying for Drugs*, HAIN, Manila, 1988, p.115

61. Ibid., p.117

62. Ibid., p.116
63. Picture and caption in the Thai newspaper *Matichon*, 22 Jan 1987
64. Hay, D. R., letter to the editor, *New Zealand Medical Journal*, Vol. 100, 8 Apr 1987, p.223
65. Anon., 'Paediatricians get their skates on', *Lancet*, 26 Sep 1987
66. Letter from Dr R. B. Arnold, Executive Vice-President IFPMA, 20 May 1988
67. Advertisements in *Australian Doctor* (12 Feb 1988) and *Medical Observer* (17 Mar 1988). See also: Totaro, P., 'Row as drug firm offers doctors prize', *Daily Telegraph* (Australia), 29 Apr 1988; McDonnell, D., 'Drug company in offer uproar', *Sun* (Australia), 30 Apr 1988; 'Doctors enticed to prescribe anti-diarrhoea pill' (press release), Australian Consumers' Association, Sydney, Apr 1988
68. Totaro, 'Row as drug firm offers doctors prize'
69. Margo, J., 'Medicine men bewitch doctors', *Sydney Morning Herald*, 14 Jan 1989
70. 'Bayer suspended from UK ABPI', *Scrip*, No. 1,166/7, 25 Dec 1986/1 Jan 1987, p.14. See also Erlichman, J., 'Drug firm suspended over gifts', *Guardian*, 18 Dec 1986 [the company was readmitted into the ABPI at the beginning of 1988; see 'Bayer allowed back into UK ABPI', *Scrip*, No. 1,277, 27 Jan 1988, p.3]
71. Graves, J., 'Frequent-flyer programs for drug prescribing', *New England Journal of Medicine*, Vol. 317, 23 Jul 1987, p.252
72. 'Ayerst US promotion under fire again', *Scrip*, No. 1,419, 9 Jun 1989, p.16
73. Article in Toronto *Globe and Mail*, 15 Dec 1988, cited in 'Squibb offers computers to MDs', *HAI News*, No. 46, Apr 1989, pp.9–10
74. 'Canadian drs warned on computers', *Scrip*, No. 1,390, 1 Mar 1989, p.23
75. Margo, 'Medicine men bewitch doctors'
76. 'French HM to take action against Squibb', *Scrip*, No. 1,481, 19 Jan 1990, p.5
77. Margo, 'Medicine men bewitch doctors'
78. 'RCP reports on doctor/industry relationship', *Scrip*, No. 1,145, 13 Oct 1986, p.1
79. Veitch, A., 'Criticism of tests on new drug by doctors' and 'Arthritis drug Suprol withdrawn', *Guardian*, 5 Nov 1984 and 24 Oct 1986
80. Margo, 'Medicine men bewitch doctors'
81. 'FDA hits at Wyeth-Ayerst promotion' *Scrip*, No. 1,480, 17 Jan 1990, p.13
82. Personal correspondence from Dr Richard Arnold, Executive Vice-President, IFPMA, 22 Jun 1987
83. *Fortune*, 9 Jun 1986, cited in Tan, *Dying for Drugs*, pp.129–30
84. Bowman, M. A., 'The impact of drug company funding on the content of continuing medical education', *Mobius*, Vol. 6, No. 1, Jan 1986, pp.66–9
85. Goldfinger, S. E., 'A matter of influence', *New England Journal of Medicine*, Vol. 316, No. 22, 28 May 1987, pp.1,408–9, and follow-up letters to the editor, Vol. 318, No. 1, 7 Jan 1988, pp.52–4; Health and Public Policy Committee, American College of Physicians, 'Improving Medical Education in Therapeutics', *Annals of Internal Medicine*, Vol. 108, 1988, pp.145–7
86. Rawlins, M. D., 'Doctors and the drug makers', *Lancet*, 4 Aug 1984, pp.276–8
87. Lexchin, 'Pharmaceutical promotion in Canada', pp.79–80
88. 'US FDA moves on PR breaches', *Scrip*, No. 1,389, 24 Feb 1989, p.15
89. Herxheimer, A. (ed.), 'Manufacturer-sponsored symposia', *Drug and Therapeutics Bulletin*, 21:6, 25 Mar 1983, p.24
90. 'FDA criticises S-Plough promotion again', *Scrip*, No. 1,447, 15 Sep 1989, p.19
91. 'RCP reports on doctor/industry relationship', *Scrip*, p.3
92. Nelkin, D., 'How to doctor the media', *New Scientist*, 20 Nov 1986, pp.51–6
93. Coney, S., 'Pharmaceutical advertising', *Lancet*, 20 May 1989, pp.1,128–9
94. Ferriman, 'Exposed: drug giant's hard sell'

95. Adams, *Roche versus Adams*, pp.215–16. Even before the programme was screened, it was subjected to considerable legal delays, and some parts were deleted at the last minute, including a piece on Roche's tranquilliser dealings in Canada. Ironically, I also appeared on the programme and was critical of the marketing of powdered baby milks by the Swiss multinational Nestlé. I showed a press clipping from a Guatemalan newspaper from January 1981 which reported that Nestlé had donated free baby milk to the mother of the first baby born in Guatemala that year. She was a teenage mother who lived in extreme poverty and a member of the hospital staff who had attended the birth had commented in a separate interview that it was unlikely that the baby would do well on the milk powder. Within a month, Nestlé had presented the BBC with signed affidavits from the editor of the newspaper, the mother's own doctor, and the head of the team which delivered the baby denying the incident had ever occurred, and pointing out that the baby was thriving.

96. ABPI, Minutes of the Half-Yearly General Meeting of the Association held at the Gleneagles Hotel, Auchterarder, on Thursday 14 October 1982, Ref. No. 1267/82, 20 Dec 1982

97. Veitch, A., 'Company objected to report critical of drug', *Guardian*, 14 Mar 1986

98. Weitz, M., *Health Shock* (rev. edn), Hamlyn Paperbacks, London, 1982, p.307

99. Ibid.

100. Mahler, H., 'Essential drugs for all', paper presented at the 11th IFPMA Assembly, Washington, 7–8 Jun 1982

101. IFPMA, *The Need to Inform*, p.13

102. Herxheimer, A., 'Problem drugs', *World Health Forum*, Vol. 4, 1983, p.245

103. Many of the publications listed in the bibliography refer to this problem. Most of the titles are self-evident in that they contain a reference to the Third World or a particular developing country, or to promotional practices.

104. Silverman, M., *The Drugging of the Americas*, University of California Press, Berkeley, 1976; Silverman, M., Lee, P. R. and Lydecker, M., *Prescriptions for Death: The Drugging of the Third World*, University of California Press, Berkeley, 1982; Silverman, M., Lee, P. R. and Lydecker, M., 'Drug promotion: the Third World revisited', *International Journal of Health Services*, Vol. 16, No. 4, 1986

105. IFPMA, *The Need to Inform*, p.14

106. Silverman, Lee and Lydecker, 'Drug promotion', p.660

107. Ibid., p.667

108. Ibid.

109. BUKO, *Hoechst: a cause of illness?*, Bielefeld, 1987, p.2

110. Personal communication with BUKO

111. 'Swiss firms under attack', *Scrip*, No. 1,455, 13 Oct 1989, p.1; '"Misleading promotion" in Africa attacked', *Scrip*, No. 1,483, 26 Jan 1990, pp.22–3

112. Richards, T., editorial, *British Medical Journal*, 24 May 1986

**Chapter 5**

1. Medawar, C., 'International regulation of the supply and use of pharmaceuticals', *Development Dialogue*, No. 2, 1985, p.36

2. Muller, *Health of Nations*, p.179

3. WHO, *International Code of Marketing of Breast-milk Substitutes*, Geneva, 1981

4. See for example: Chetley, A., *The Baby Killer Scandal*, War on Want, London, 1979; UNICEF/WHO/UNESCO, *Facts for Life*, New York, 1989; IBFAN, *Fighting for Infant Survival*, Geneva/Penang/Minneapolis, 1989

5. Muller, *Health of Nations*, p.212

6. Internal memo from E. Saunders to A. Furer (then Nestlé's chief executive officer), Aug 1980, reprinted with commentary as *Nestlegate: secret memo reveals corporate cover-up*, Baby Milk Action Coalition, Cambridge, UK, 1981
7. HAI press release, 29 May 1981, reprinted in UNCTAD, *Guidelines on Technology Issues in the Pharmaceutical Sector in the Developing Countries* (UNCTAD/TT/49), Geneva, 1982, p.60. See also 'Infant Formula Critics Now Planning Big Offensive Against Drug and Health Firms', *Business International*, 26 Jun 1981; Washington Business Information, *The Food and Drug Letter*, 17 Jul 1981
8. Among the organisations involved in both networks are: Oxfam, War on Want, IOCU, Consumers Association of Penang, Voluntary Health Association of India, CEFEMINA (women's organisation, Costa Rica), Freres des Hommes, Berne Declaration Group, Interfaith Center on Corporate Responsibility, Australian Consumers Association, New Zealand Coalition on Trade and Development.
9. *Food and Drug Letter*, pp.2–3
10. Radolf, A., 'UN has bitter pill in mind for international drug firms', *Examiner* (San Francisco), 16 Sep 1981, p.3
11. Kathe, Laschet and Schuler, *Drugs and the Third World*, p.2
12. Roepnack, C. G., 'Criticizing the critique: the international campaign against the pharmaceutical industry', *Drugs Made in Germany*, Vol. XXVIII, 1985, pp.64–7
13. Janviroj, P., 'The politics of drugs', *The Nation* (Thailand), 8 Dec 1987
14. Edwards, B. and Newens, S., *The Multinationals*, Liberation, London, 1979, p.24
15. UNCTAD, *Guidelines on Technology Issues*, p.3
16. UNCTAD publications included: Lall, S., *Major Issues in Transfer of Technology to Developing Countries: a case study of the pharmaceutical industry* (TD/B/C.6/4), United Nations, New York, 1975; *Case Studies in the Transfer of Technology: the pharmaceutical industry in India* (TD/B/C.6/20), United Nations, New York, 1977
    UNIDO publications included: *Lima Declaration and Plan of Action on Industrial Development and Cooperation*, Second General Conference of UNIDO, 1975; *Summary of the World-wide Study of the Pharmaceutical Industry, Preliminary Draft*, 1978; *The Steps Involved in Establishing a Pharmaceutical Industry in Developing Countries* (ID/WG.267/3) , 1978; *The Development of the Pharmaceutical Industry in Six Countries in Latin America*, 1978; *The Growth of the Pharmaceutical Industry in Developing Countries: problems and prospects*, 1978; *Assessment of the Pharmaceutical Industry in Developing Countries, its Potential, and the National and International Action Required to Promote its Development* (ID/WG.292/2), 1978; *Report of the Inter-regional Meeting to Prepare for Consultations on the Pharmaceutical Industry*, Cairo, (ID/WG.293/3/Rev.1), 1979.
17. UNCTC, *Transnational Corporations*, 1979
18. UNCTC, *Transnational Corporations*, 1984
19. UNCTAD, *Guidelines on Technology Issues*, pp.3, 50–2
20. Tape recording of a talk given by Surendra Patel at a HAI international meeting held in Penang, Malaysia, in January 1988
21. WHO, 'Certification scheme on the quality of pharmaceutical products moving in international commerce', *WHO Chronicle*, Vol. 31, No. 12, 1977
22. UNCTC, *Transnational Corporations*, 1984, p.79
23. WHO, *The rational use of drugs*, 1987, p.291
24. 'Export labelling harmonisation', *Scrip*, No. 1,392, 8 Mar 1989, p.20
25. Agarwal, *Drugs and the Third World*, pp.5–6
26. WHO, *The Selection of Essential Drugs*, Technical Report Series No. 615, Geneva, 1977. The most recent revision is *The Use of Essential Drugs – Model List of Essential Drugs (Fifth List)*, Technical Report Series No. 770, 1988.

27. von Wartensleben, A., 'Major issues concerning pharmaceutical policies in the Third World', *World Development*, Vol. 11, No. 3, Mar 1983, p.171
28. Reich, M., *Essential Drugs: who, how and why?* (mimeo), paper presented at the Notre Dame Program on Multinational Corporations and Third World Development, Conference on Third World Health Problems and the Role of Pharmaceuticals, 11–13 Dec 1985, p.2
29. Lauridsen, E., 'But some are more essential than others!', *World Health*, Jul 1984, pp.3–5
30. IFPMA, *Statement as adopted by the IFPMA Council on the Report of a WHO Expert Committee on the Selection of Essential Drugs*, Zurich, Apr 1978, p.1
31. Muller, *Health of Nations*, p.209
32. Radolf, 'UN has bitter pill in mind'
33. PMA, *Health Consequences*, p.3
34. See for example: 'ABPI "to fight tooth and nail"', *Pharmaceutical Journal*, 17 Nov 1984; 'ABPI begins campaign against "stupid and dangerous" proposal', *Pharmaceutical Journal*, 8 Dec 1984
35. WHO, 'IFPMA', *Essential Drugs Monitor*, No. 3, 1986, p.4
36. For more details see the press reports cited below.:

*Argentina: Scrip*, 'Argentina underestimated?', No. 1,144, 8 Oct 1986, p.20; 'Essential drug policy proposals', No. 1,149, 27 Oct 1986, p.19; 'Argentinian pharma spending questioned', No. 1,289, 9 Mar 1988, p.20; 'Limited lists in Argentina?', No. 1,309, 18 May 1988, p.20; 'Opposition to Argentinian pharma plan', No. 1,384, 8 Feb 1989, p.26; 'Argentinian pharma plan to go ahead?', No. 1,406, 26 Apr 1989, p.19

*Australia: Scrip*, 'Hoechst runs Australian protest ad', No. 1,392, 8 Mar 1989, p.19; 'Australian gvt policy threat to PBS?', No. 1,394, 15 Mar 1989, p.27; 'APMA's objections to fee proposals', No. 1,404, 19 Apr 1989, p.24; 'Australian price concerns intensify', No. 1,436, 9 Aug 1989, p.20

*Bolivia: Scrip*, 'Illegal importing in Bolivia', No. 1,258, 18 Nov 1987, p.18

*Brazil: Scrip*, '15% price increase in Brazil', No. 1,295, 30 Mar 1988, p.22; 'Brazil's summer plan', No. 1,384, 8 Feb 1989, p.26

*Denmark: Scrip*, 'Resistance to Danish savings proposals', No. 1,371, 21 Dec 1988, p.1

*Finland: Scrip*, 'FAIPI pricing initiative in Finland', No. 1,317, 15 Jun 1988, p.1

*France: Scrip*, 'New French pricing proposals', No. 1,288, 4 Mar 1988, p.1; 'French report on industry a "compromise"?', No. 1,396, 22 Mar 1989, p.11

*FRG: Scrip*, 'US moves on FRG reform proposals', No. 1,348, 30 Sep 1988, p.3; 'BPI on Health Reform Act', No. 1,361, 16 Nov 1988, p.1; 'BPI reacts to West German reforms', No. 1,367, 7 Dec 1988, p.1; 'FRG reference price wrangles continue', No. 1,377, 13 Jan 1989, p.1; 'FRG criticism of draft 4th amendment', No. 1,405, 21 Apr 1989, p.6

*India:* Organisation of Pharmaceutical Producers of India, 'Too many drugs – the number game', advertisement in *Hindustan Times*, 20 Nov 1986

*Ireland: Scrip*, 'FICI details Irish concerns', No. 1,437, 11 Aug 1989, p.8

*Italy: Scrip*, 'Essential drugs list in Italy?', No. 1,256, 11 Nov 1987, p.1; 'Italian EDL idea rejected', No. 1277, 27 Jan 1988; 'Italian HM on "useless" drugs', No. 1,314/5,

3/8 Jun 1988, p.2; 'Italian "nonsense preparations" claim', No. 1,321, 29 Jun 1988, p.6

*Japan: Scrip*, 'PMA, EBC step up price pressure in Japan', No. 1,437, 11 Aug 1989, p.20

*The Netherlands: Scrip*, 'Nefarma challenges sickfund lists', No. 1,152, 5 Nov 1986, p.6

*New Zealand: Scrip*, 'NZ cost-cutting moves criticised', No. 1,259, 20 Nov 1987, p.18; 'NZ PMA concerns on generics', No. 1,353; 19 Oct 1988, p.19; 'NZ generic substitution debate hots up,', No. 1,366, 2 Dec 1988, p.17; 'NZ PMA's substitution opposition', No. 1,378, 18 Jan 1989, p.21; 'NZ generic substitution in March?', No. 1,390, 1 Mar 1989, p.22

*Nigeria: Scrip*, 'Essential drug list in Nigeria?', No. 1,146, 15 Oct 1986, p.21

*Pakistan: Scrip*, 'Pakistani pharma industry defends itself', No. 1,292, 18 Mar 1988, p.18; 'MNC's health proposals in Pakistan', No. 1,401, 7 Apr 1989, p.20

*The Philippines:* Tan, M. L., 'A short primer on rational drug policy', *Drug Monitor* (Philippines), No. 9, 15 Oct 1986; Anon., 'DAP cites position on drugs list', *Manila Times*, 29 Sep 1986, p.1; *Scrip*, 'Philippine Generics Act signed', No. 1,346, 23 Sep 1988, p.23; 'Philippine generic impact assessed', No. 1,348, 30 Sep 1988, p.16; 'DAP on Philippines labels deadline', No. 1,449, 22 Sep 1989, p.19

*Portugal: Scrip*, 'Reimbursement changes in Portugal', No. 1,293, 23 Mar 1988, p.1; 'Portuguese draft decree on generics' and 'Portuguese health policies attacked', No. 1,394, 15 Mar 1989, p.1; 'Apifarma resorts to open letters in Portuguese press', No. 1,396, 22 Mar 1989, p.9

*Spain: Scrip*, 'Bonal outlines pharma aims for Spain', No. 1,322, 1 Jul 1988, p.5

*Sweden: Scrip*, 'Changes ahead in Sweden?', No. 1,291, 16 Mar 1988, p.6

*Thailand: Scrip*, 'Drug Act amended in Thailand', No. 1,293, 23 Mar 1988, p.22

*UK: Scrip*, 'Schering AG challenges UK lists', No. 1,114, 25 Jun 1986, p.3; 'Industry White Paper concerns stressed', No. 1,405, 21 Apr 1989, p.5; 'US PMA submission on UK White Paper', No. 1,425, 30 Jun 1989, p.5; 'ABPI keeps up pressure on NHS reform', No. 1,434, 2 Aug 1989, p.6

37. 'JPMA collaboration policy in 3rd World', *Scrip*, No. 1,406, 26 Apr 1989, p.19
38. Kingham, J., speech given at the National Council for International Health (NCIH) Open Forum on Pharmaceuticals and Developing Countries, held in Washington, DC, in February 1982; reproduced in NCIH, *Pharmaceuticals and Developing Countries: a dialogue for constructive action*, Washington, Aug 1982, pp.22–6
39. Melrose, D., 'Double deprivation: public and private drug distribution from the perspective of the Third World poor', *World Development*, Vol. 11, No. 3, 1983, pp.181–6
40. In 1984, Dr John Griffin of the ABPI said of the British government's proposals: 'It is almost as if Norman Fowler [then Social Services Secretary] and his Conservative colleagues are determined to make Britain a Third World country too.' (See 'ABPI to fight', *Pharmaceutical Journal*.) In 1987, Claudio Cavazza, president of the Italian pharmaceutical industry association, Farmindustria, said of the Italian Senate's attempts to introduce an essential drugs list, 'if they want to turn Italy into a third-world country, this is the way to go about it' (see: *Scrip*, No. 1,256).

41. See for example: Sidahmed, A., 'Medicine: a healthy business?', *Sudanow*, Jun 1981, pp.52–3; Cassels, A., 'Drug supply in rural Nepal', *Tropical Doctor*, Vol. 13, Jan 1983, pp.14–17; Kagimba, J., *The problems of drug supply in primary health care in developing countries* (mimeo), Nairobi, AMREF, Aug 1983; Anon., 'No money – no drugs', *Far East Health*, Nov 1986, pp.20–1.

42. Moore, G., 'Developing drug distribution', *Africa Health*, Dec 85/Jan 86, pp.24–5

43. Glucksberg, H. and Singer, J., 'The multinational drug companies in Zaire: their adverse effect on cost and availability of essential drugs', *International Journal of Health Services*, Vol. 12, No. 3, 1982, pp.381–7

44. WHO, *WHO's Revised Drug Strategy: report by the Director General* (EB81/25 Annex 1), Geneva, 22 Dec 1987, p.4

45. The pharmaceutical industry spends some $100 million on research and development of one new product, and with an average of some 50 new chemical entities coming onto the market each year, that makes a rough expenditure of some $5,000 million. It is generally accepted that the amount spent on research and development by most companies is approximately half that spent on promotion and marketing. Thus, promotion costs are likely to be in the region of at least $10,000 million, or 20 times the amount spent on essential drugs programmes.

46. Alliance for the Prudent Use of Antibiotics, *Statement Regarding Worldwide Antibiotic Misuse*, 4 Feb 1982

47. WHO, *Surveillance for the Prevention and Control of Health Hazards due to Antibiotic-resistant Enterobacteria* (Technical Report Series No. 624), Geneva 1978, p.8

48. Willard, N., 'Antibiotics: the resistance problem', *WHO Features*, No. 89, Oct 1984

49. Blum and Krietman, 'Factors affecting individual use of medicines', p.150

50. Ibid.

51. See for example: Amidi, S., et al., 'Antibiotic use and abuse among physicians in private practice in Shiraz, Iran', *Medical Care*, Vol. 18, No. 4, 1975, pp.341–5; Victora, C. G., Facchini, L. A. and Filho, M. G., 'Drug usage in Southern Brazilian hospitals', *Tropical Doctor*, Vol. 12, Oct 1982, pp.231–5; Group for Defense of Consumers on Pharmaceuticals, *Antibiotics, Analgesics and Vitamins: use and abuse in Recife, Brazil*, 1984; Hossain, M. M., et al, 'Antibiotic use in a rural community in Bangladesh', *International Journal of Epidemiology*, Vol. 11, No. 4, 1982, pp.402–5; Farrar, W. E., 'Antibiotic resistance in developing countries', *Journal of Infectious Disease*, Vol. 152, No. 6, Dec 1985, p.1,105; Harvey, K., et al, 'Use of antibiotics in a large teaching hospital', *Medical Journal of Australia*, Vol. 2, 1983, pp.217–21; Harvey, K., 'Antibiotic use in Australia', *Australian Prescriber*, Vol. 2 No. 4, 1988, pp.74–7

52. WHO, *A Manual for the Treatment of Acute Diarrhoea*, p.13

53. Tomson, G. and Sterky, G., 'Self-prescribing by way of pharmacies in three Asian developing countries', *Lancet*, 13 Sep 1986, pp.620–1

54. WHO, *A Manual for the Treatment of Acute Diarrhoea*, p.13

55. Willard, 'Antibiotics: the resistance problem'; 'Antibiotic usage in Uruguay', *Scrip*, No. 1,276, 22 Jan 1988, p.24

56. Fefer, E., speech given at the National Council for International Health (NCIH) Open Forum on Pharmaceuticals and Developing Countries, held in Washington, DC, in February 1982; reproduced in NCIH, *Pharmaceuticals and Developing Countries*, pp.10–13

57. Harvey, 'Use of antibiotics'

58. Lappe, *When Antibiotics Fail*, p.96

59. 'Drug promotional problems', *Medical Journal of Australia*, Vol. 150, 17 Apr 1989, p.463

60. Midtvedt, T., 'Increasing worldwide microbial resistance: a worldwide responsibility – for whom?', in Dukes, M. N. G. (ed.), *Side Effects of Drugs Annual 11*, Amsterdam, Elsevier, 1987, pp.223–4

61. Ibid.

62. Midtvedt, T., 'Increasing worldwide microbial resistance: a worldwide responsibility for all, including the pharmaceutical industry and the World Health Organisation', in Dukes, M. N. G. and Beeley, L. (eds.), *Side Effects of Drugs Annual 12*, Elsevier, Amsterdam, 1988, pp.206–8

63. See *Scrip*, 'Antibiotic usage in Uruguay', No. 1,276, 22 Jan 1988, p.24; 'Importance of training in EDP', No. 1,355, 26 Oct 1988, p.20; 'Kuwait's antibiotic consumption', No. 1,335, 17 Aug 1988, p.21; 'Misuse of antibiotics in Pakistan', No. 1,339, 31 Aug 1988, p.21; 'Inappropriate use of antibiotics in New Zealand', No. 1,313, 1 Jun 1988, p.20; 'Combination antibiotics questioned in Brazil', No. 1,296, 1 Apr 1988, p.18; 'WHO/ATH on the misuse of antibiotics', No. 1,272/3, 8/13 Jan 1988, p.26; 'WHO on multiresistant bacteria', No. 1,290, 11 Mar 1988, p.20.

64. 'WHO on multiresistant bacteria', *Scrip*, No. 1,290, 11 Mar 1988, p.20

65. Kotulak, R. and Van, J., 'They write, patients suffer: many doctors suffer "Rx fever"', *Chicago Tribune*, 9 Oct 1980, p.1

66. HAI, *Not To Be Taken: at least, not to be taken seriously*, The Hague/Penang, 1981

67. HAI, *A Draft International Code on Pharmaceuticals* (2nd edn), The Hague/Penang, 1981, May 1982

68. 'Pharmaceutical industry, police thyself, say HAI leaders', *International Barometer*, Supplement to Vol. 2, No. 10, Mar 1987, p.S-4

69. UNCTAD, *Guidelines on Technology Issues*, p.67

70. Fazal, A., 'The right pharmaceuticals at the right prices: consumer perspectives', *World Development*, Vol. 11, No. 3, 1983, p.268

71. 'HAI draft code on pharmaceuticals presented at UNCTAD', *HAI News*, No. 8, 8 Dec 1982, p.2; Schwartz, H., 'A war on drugs, "new order" style', *Wall Street Journal*, 24 Mar 1983

72. 'UNCTAD's wane', *HAI News*, No. 13, Oct 1983, p.5

73. 'Strong resolution on WHO drug action programme', *HAI News*, No. 5, Jun 1982, p.1

74. See: Muller, *Health of Nations*, p.187; 'Pharmaceutical industry takes varied approaches to threat to LDC sales', *Business International*, 9 Feb 1979, pp.43, 46; Cunliffe, 'Pharmaceuticals in the Third World', p.6.

75. Peretz, M., 'Pharmaceuticals in the Third World: the problem from the suppliers' point of view', *World Development*, Vol. 11, No. 3, 1983, pp.259–64

76. Muller, *Health of Nations*, p.187

77. Guest, I., 'Which comes first – the purity of American capitalism or curing the sick?', *Guardian*, 23 Jan 1984

78. Guest, I., 'America attacks drug code plan', *Guardian*, 21 Jan 1984

79. Muller, *Health of Nations*, pp.187–8

80. Reproduced in: Kingham, speech, p.24

81. Guest, 'Which comes first'

82. Guest, 'America attacks' and 'Which comes first'

83. Chetley, A., *The Politics of Baby Foods*, Frances Pinter, London, 1986, p.153

84. 'WHO moves closer to code for drug industry: who will be next?', *Business International*, 25 May 1984, pp.164–5

85. WHO, *Rational Use of Drugs*, Resolution WHA37.33, 17 May 1984

86. HAI, *The Way Forward: the World Health Organisation's action programme on essential drugs and vaccines*, The Hague/Penang, 1984

87. WHO, *Essential Drugs Monitor*, No. 1, 1985, p.1. (In 1986, following the adoption of a 'Revised Drug Strategy' by the WHA, the wording of the first principle was

changed to read: 'meet people's common health needs', probably as a concession to the pharmaceutical industry which, at the time, was arguing strongly against the exclusion of any drugs from the market on the basis of inability to meet real health needs.)

88. 'WHO moves closer to code', *Business International*

89. Arnold, R. B., speech to the 12th IFPMA Assembly, Paris, 17–19 Oct 1984, reproduced in 'IFPMA activities: present and future preoccupations: the pharmaceutical industry under attack', *Swiss Pharma*, No. 3, 1985

90. 'Rational use of drugs', *Lancet*, 8 Jun 1985, pp.1,344–5

91. In a press conference at the end of the meeting, Dr Mahler, WHO's Director General, said that there was 'no secrecy' and that it was the 'most extraordinary thing that the organisation has ever done to have even a discussion about this before and a discussion now, so let us have no insinuations about "veils of secrecy" or anything like that. WHO would never have been able to produce its remarkable things through expert committees if there were to be anything like an open kind of public participation, press or otherwise.'

92. Chetley, A., 'Veil of secrecy over international drugs meeting' (GH 37), Gemini News Service, London, 8 Nov 1985; Dinwoodie, R., 'WHO sedated to quell US anger', *Scotsman*, 27 Nov 1985, p.13; '100 delegates for Nairobi meeting', *Scrip*, No. 1,047, 30 Oct 1985, p.17

93. Fabricant, S.J. and Hirschhorn, N., 'Deranged distribution, perverse prescription, unprotected use: the irrationality of pharmaceuticals in the developing world', *Health Policy and Planning*, Vol. 2, No. 3, 1987, pp.204–13

94. International Organisations Monitoring Service (IOMS), 'World Health Organisation: results of Nairobi Conference on the rational use of drugs', New York, Dec 1985

95. Letter from Dr J. Cohen, adviser on health policy, Director General's Office, WHO, to Lars Broch, director, International Organisation of Consumers Unions, 16 Sep 1985

96. Chetley, 'Veil of secrecy'; Dinwoodie, 'WHO sedated'

97. Chetley, 'Veil of secrecy'

98. Cowhig, J., 'The drug industry meets its critics', *General Practitioner*, 22 Nov 1985, p.20

99. Medawar, 'International regulation'

100. Chetley, 'Veil of secrecy'

101. Comments attributed to Dr Mahler about the conference are drawn from tapes of press conferences at the beginning and end of the WHO Conference of Experts (25 and 29 Nov 1985). Comments attributed to other named individuals quoted in this section are based upon interviews with them during the conference. The background papers, a summary of the discussion, and Dr Mahler's summation of the conference are given in WHO, *The Rational Use of Drugs*, 1987. Other printed material which presents information about the conference includes: 'WHO meeting agrees on rational drugs strategy', *Lancet*, 14 Dec 1985, pp.1,350–1; IOMS, 'Results of Nairobi Conference'; 'Essential drugs seminar draws up new strategy. Ratification in May', *Africa Health*, Dec 1985/Jan 1986, p.7; Chetley, A., 'Better information a key to rational drug use', *Consumer Affairs*, No. 78, Nov/Dec 1985, pp.1–4, and 'WHO's way forward from Nairobi', *THS Health Summary*, Dec 1985, p.4; *Scrip*, 'WHO's Nairobi meeting: problems identified, solutions later?', No. 1,058, 9 Dec 1985, p.15, and 'Mahler sums up at Nairobi', No. 1,059, 11 Dec 1985, p.21; Schwartz, H., 'The Schwartz commentary on the Nairobi Conference', *Scrip*, No. 1,060, 16 Dec 1985, pp.20–1, and 'A further look at Nairobi – the Schwartz column', No. 1,069, 20 Jan 1986, p.17; Rawlins, M. D., 'Professor Rawlins replies to Harry Schwartz', *Scrip*, No. 1,065/66, 8 Jan 1986, p.19; Gicheru, C., 'Drugs talks end with "agreement"', *Daily Nation* (Kenya), 30 Nov 1985; WHO, 'Rational use of drugs: cooperation prevails at WHO conference in "spirit of Nairobi"' (press release WHO/32), 3 Dec 1985

102. IFPMA, 'IFPMA preliminary view on rational use of drugs conference', press release, 29 Nov 1985
103. Brooks, R. A., 'Saving the World Health Organisation from a poison pill', *Heritage Foundation Backgrounder*, No. 471, 19 Nov 1985. Despite its title, the Heritage Foundation is not a foundation: it makes no grants. Instead, it is dedicated to a single purpose: the distillation and dissemination of conservative ideas on contemporary issues. Its primary target audience is the US Congress and the US Administration. During the years of the Reagan administration, Heritage enjoyed a close working relationship with the White House. One Heritage staff member claims that the links with the Bush administration are even better. Over the past 10 years there has been a constant two-way flow of personnel between the US government and Heritage: former Attorney General Edwin Meese and former Deputy Secretary of State Elliott Abrams are among those who have settled into temporary or permanent assignments with Heritage; in the other direction, former Heritage staff such as William J. Bennett and Jack Kemp became the director of the anti-drug programme and Secretary of Housing and Urban Development in Bush's administration. Other Heritage personnel have moved into high level positions in the administration, and a 'Heritage Talent Bank' has been successful at recruiting several dozen strong conservatives for second- and third-level jobs in 'virtually every government agency'. The research done by Heritage is fast, topical and ideologically consistent; most papers produced are short and to the point. Most of it, however, is derivative and synthetic rather than original. Its $14 million dollar a year income is derived from grantmaking trusts (38 per cent), corporations (17 per cent) – including General Motors, Ford, IBM, Sears Roebuck, Chase Manhattan Bank – and the balance comes from contributions from some 140,000 'members'. For further information, see Williams, R. M., 'Capital clout', *Foundation News*, Jul/Aug 1989, pp.14–19.
104. PMA, *Health Consequences*
105. Medawar, C., *The 'Spirit of Nairobi'?* (mimeo), paper presented at the International Workshop at the Nordic School of Public Health, Gothenburg, Jun 1986, p.3
106. Tape of WHO press conference at the end of the WHO/UNICEF meeting on infant and young child feeding, Geneva, 12 Oct 1979
107. Mossinghoff, G., *Report on WHO Conference of Experts on the Rational Use of Drugs*, PMA, Washington, 1 Dec 1985, (report to PMA Board of Directors)
108. When Young resigned as FDA Commissioner in December 1989, differing opinions emerged about his five and a half years at the agency. Clearly his tenure coincided with a time of change at the FDA, in part a response to the deregulatory policies preferred by the Reagan administration. The AIDS scare and the pressure on the FDA to rapidly approve possible drugs of use for the illness has been both praised and criticised. The praise has been related to the way in which the agency has been able to give such products priority treatment; the criticism has been that such an approach has loosened too much the essential regulatory mechanisms. A major scandal emerged in 1989 around some FDA staff who allegedly acted in a cavalier fashion with regard to the approval of some generic drugs, which resulted in a scare about the quality and efficacy of many of these products. The agency also faced budgetary constraints which made its work difficult. The PMA was unreserved in its praise for Young: 'few Commissioners have faced such formidable challenges and acquitted themselves so well as Frank Young these past few years'. On the other hand, Dr Sidney Wolfe of the Public Citizen Research Group described Young as 'by far the worst' commissioner the Group had ever had to deal with. He said that Young's resignation 'can only improve the health of the American public by removing someone whose industry-oriented decisions have cost hundreds of lives and injuries to many more'. (See 'Frank Young to leave FDA', *Scrip*, No. 1,466, 22 Nov 1989, pp.17–18.)

164    *Notes*

109. IOMS, 'Results of Nairobi Conference'
110. 'PMA/FDA co-operation', *Scrip*, No. 1,096, 23 Apr 1986, p.19
111. '39th WHA Opens Today', *Health Now*, Vol. 2, No. 1, 5 May 1986, p.1
112. Mahler, H., letter to Lars Broch of IOCU, 18 April 1986
113. Broch, L., letter to Dr H. Mahler of WHO, 25 Apr 1986
114. IOMS, 'Consumer protection – World Health Organization – results of the 1986 World Health Assembly', No. 86-22, 23 May 1986, p.5
115. Pilon, J., 'For the WHO: the moment of truth', *Heritage Foundation Backgrounder*, 30 Apr 1986
116. IOMS, 'World Health Organization – Heritage Foundation Report on politicization of WHO – assessment of report and its impact on industry relations with WHO', No. 86-19, 12 May 1986
117. Bidwai, P., 'US offensive against UN: I – WHO the latest victim' and 'WHO under US attack: II – drug MNCs score a victory', *Times of India*, 4 Jul 1986 and 5 Jul 1986
118. Starrels, J. M., *The World Health Organization – Resisting Third World Ideological Pressures*, Heritage Foundation, Washington, DC, 1985
119. 'Much politics at this year's Assembly', *Lancet*, 31 May 1986, pp.1283–4
120. Nelson, D., 'Money talks louder than health in Geneva' (GH 47), Gemini News Service, 20 May 1986
121. Boyer, N., speech delivered 16 May 1986, in IOMS, 'Consumer protection', Attachment B
122. WHO, *WHO's Revised Drug Strategy: report by the Director General* (Doc No. A39/13), Geneva, 10 Feb 1986
123. IOMS, 'Consumer protection'
124. Chetley, A. and Gilbert, D., *Problem Drugs*, HAI, The Hague/Penang, 1986. (This is available in English, French and Spanish, and a revised edition is expected in 1990, at which time an Arabic edition will also be issued.)
125. 'Worldwide activist network keeps pace with pharmaceutical industry – wherever it is', *International Barometer*, Vol. 2, No. 10, Mar 1987, pp. 1, 3

**Chapter 6**

1. Bengzon, A. R. A., 'The evoloution of a national drug policy', abridged version of a keynote address to the International Consultation on Rational Drug Use in Undergraduate Medical/Pharmacy Education, Manila, Philippines, 13–16 Aug 1988. Reproduced as a supplement to *HAI News*, No. 43, Oct 1988
2. WHO, *Essential Drugs Monitor*, No. 8, 1989, p.1
3. Comments attributed to named individuals in this section about Bangladesh are from interviews conducted during January, July and August 1986, unless otherwise noted. Where possible, reference is also made to printed material in which the same or similar comments are made.
4. Bangladesh Drug Administration, *Report of the Expert Committee for Drugs on the National Drug Policy of Bangladesh 1982*, Government of Bangladesh, Dhaka, March 1986, p.1
5. Melrose, *Bitter Pills*, p.43, quoting Dr Humayun K. M. A. Hye, Director of Drug Adminstration
6. Ibid., p.62
7. Rolt, *Pills, Policies and Profits*, pp.70–2
8. Tiranti, D., *The Bangladesh Example: four years on*, IOCU/New Internationalist/War on Want, Penang/Oxford/London, 1986, p.18
9. Melrose, *Bitter Pills*, p.44

10. Tiranti, *The Bangladesh Example*, p.18
11. Bangladesh Drug Administration, *Report of the Expert Committee*, p.1
12. Ibid.
13. Ibid., p.2
14. Chowdhury, Z. and Chowdhury, S., 'Essential drugs for the poor: myth and reality in Bangladesh', *Ecodevelopment News*, No. 23, Dec 1982, p.43
15. Anon., '5 out of 6 die before reaching a doctor', *Bangladesh Times*, 5 Aug 1986
16. Melrose, *Bitter Pills*, p.22
17. Ibid., p.22
18. Anon., '5 out of 6 die'
19. UNICEF, *State of the World's Children 1989*, p.94
20. Bangladesh Health Profile prepared by WHO, 1977, cited in Chowdhury, A. K., *Community Oriented Problem Based Medical Education Programme* (mimeo), Savar, May 1986, p.6
21. UNICEF, *State of the World's Children 1989*, p.96
22. UNICEF, *State of the World's Children 1984*, p.35
23. UNICEF, *State of the World's Children 1989*, p.98
24 Ibid., p.102
25. Bangladesh Bureau of Statistics, *1984–85 Statistical Yearbook of Bangladesh*, Government of Bangladesh, Dhaka, Dec 1985, pp.820–1
26. Chetley, A., 'Medical students demand government jobs', *Lancet*, 20 Sep 1986
27. Anon., 'Issues of health', *New Nation* (Bangladesh), 3 Aug 1986, p.5
28. Rolt, *Pills, Policies and Profits*, p.2
29. Correspondence between Frank Duckworth, vice-president and general counsel of Pfizer and Rev. Michael H. Crosby of the Corporate Responsibility Program in the USA, 17 Nov 1982
30. 'Drug ban is Bangladesh blunder', *ABPI News*, Oct 1982
31. Chorlton, P., 'US is aiding drug companies in Bangladesh', *Washington Post*, 19 Aug 1982
32. Righter, R., 'Squeeze by drug lobby', *Sunday Times* (London), 9 Aug 1982
33. Letter from the Rt Hon Douglas Hurd, MP to the Rt Hon Roland Moyle, MP, 16 Aug 1982
34. See Rolt, *Pills, Policies and Profits*, pp.33–41 for a more comprehensive description of the way the media is organised in Bangladesh and an indication of some of articles that appeared. Appendix B (pp.48–56) of Jayasuriya, D. C., *The Public Health and Economic Dimensions of the New Drug Policy of Bangladesh*, PMA, Washington, 1985, summarises 74 articles which appeared in publications between May 1982 and January 1985, 26 of which are from *Pulse*.
35. Jayasuriya, *The Public Health and Economic Dimensions*
36. PMA, 'Bangladesh policy caused higher drug prices and lower quality, report finds' (press release), 24 Sep 1985
37. Interview with Zafrullah Chowdhury, November 1985. (See also: Chetley, A., 'An essential drugs policy in action', *Far East Health*, Sep 1986, pp.49–51; 'PMA report on Bangladesh criticised', *Scrip*, No. 1,067, 13 Jan 1986, p.17.)
38. Tiranti, *The Bangladesh Example*, p.14
39. Ibid., p.25
40. Laurance, R., 'Bangladesh: faith in the future', *Health Horizons*, No. 6, Jan 1989, pp.24–5
41. Tiranti, *The Bangladesh Example*, pp.11–12
42. Rolt, *Pills, Policies and Profits*, pp.78–88
43. Chetley, A., 'Operation Sidestep', *Health for the Millions*, Vol. 8, No. 6, Dec 1982, p.6

44. BASS, open letter to members of the Parliament of Bangladesh, 9 Nov 1986. See also Shahidullah, A. K. M., 'Pharmaceutical industries' view of Drug Control Ordinance 1982', *Bangladesh Times*, 9 Oct 1986

45. Chetley, A., *Bangladesh: finding the right prescription*, War on Want, London, 1982, p.9

46. Anon., 'WHO', *South*, Sep 1982

47. Rolt, *Pills, Policies and Profits*, p.90

48. Anon., 'Bangladesh launches model drug supply project', *Essential Drugs Monitor*, No. 7, 1988, p.13

49. Nordic Council on Medicines, *Nordic Statistics on Medicines 1981–1983* (Part 1), Nordic Council on Medicines, Uppsala, Sweden, 1986, pp.6–7

50. Jøldal, B., 'Selecting drugs on the basis of need', *World Health Forum*, Vol. 6, 1985, pp.67–9

51. Ibid., p.67

52. Sakshaug, S., et al (eds.), *Drug utilization in Norway during the 1970s – increases, inequalities, innovations*, Norwegian Medicinal Depot, Oslo, 1983, pp.37, 60, 87–8, 130, 157, 102–3, 117, 174, 209–10, 213, 143, 185, 198, 227

53. Ibid., p.242

54. IFPMA, *Making the Most of Medicines*, Geneva, 1985, p.13

55. Mossinghoff, G., PMA letter to organisations in the US, Jun 1986, p.2

56. Anon., 'Health groups oppose need criteria', *Health Horizons*, No. 4, May 1988, p.7

57. WHO, *The Rational Use of Drugs*, 1987, p.255

58. Anon., 'Rationalizing drug use in Costa Rica', *Essential Drugs Monitor*, No. 8, 1989, p.14

59. Costa Rican Ministry of Health, *Guía Terapeutica Nacional*, San José, 1985

60. Anon., 'Rationalizing drug use in Costa Rica'

61. WFPMM, *Self-Medication – Making It Work Better For More People* (proceedings of 8th General Assembly, 21–23 Sep 1986, Washington, USA), Bonn, 1987

62. Chetley, A., *Peddling Placebos: an analysis of cough and cold remedies*, HAI, Amsterdam, 1989

63. AMA, *Drug Evaluations* (6th edn), W.B. Saunders, Philadelphia, 1986, p.376

64. Amery, J. and López, R., *Medicamentos en el Perú*, Instituto de Promoción y Educación Popular/Oxfam, Chimbote/Lima, 1985, p.22

65. Ibid., pp.108–9

66. Ibid., p.111

67. López, R. (ed.), *Medicamentos: los casos de Bolivia, Brasil, Chile y Perú*, Acción Internacional por la Salud, Chimbote, 1988, p.96

68. Ibid., p.99

69. WHO, *World Drug Situation*, p.79

70. Chilmper, J., 'Peru: an essential drugs pioneer', *Essential Drugs Monitor*, No. 8, 1989, p.18

71. López, *Medicamentos*, p.102

72. Amery and López, *Medicamentos en el Perú*, p.120

73. Ibid., p.119

74. Anon., 'Kenya's system for supply of drugs to rural areas', *Lancet*, 21 Dec 1985

75. Moore, G., 'Developing drug distribution', *Africa Health*, Dec 1985/Jan 1986, pp.24–5

76. Anon., 'Kenya's system'

77. WHO, *Kenya: rural drug distribution programme*, WHO Action Programme on Essential Drugs and Vaccines, Geneva, 1985, p.7

78. Anon., 'Kenya's system'

79. Ibid.

80. IBON, *Philippine Drug Industry*, p.74

81. Bengzon, 'The evolution of a national drug policy', p.1

82. See: Mendoza-Escobar, V., 'Unnecessary drug expenditure' in: Reyes, D. A. (ed.), *The Philippine Health Situation and the Transnational Drug Companies*, AKAP, Manila, 1982, pp.22–6; IBON, *Philippine Drug Industry*; Tan, *Dying for Drugs*; Hardon, A. and van der Geest, S., *Hazards and Potentials of Self-medication: an example from a Filipino village* (mimeo), Anthropological Sociological Centre, University of Amsterdam, 1985; Hardon, A., *Fact Sheet on the Use of E-P Drugs in an Urban Poor Community*, Pharmaceuticals Research Project, Manila, 1986; Hardon, A., *An Analgesic for Every Ill: the use of analgesics in 80 families in an urban poor community*, Pharmaceuticals Research Project, Manila, 1986; Quanico, U., 'Antidiarrheals in the Philippines', *Drug Monitor*, Vol. 2, No. 6, Jun 1987; HAIN, 'Drug needs and utilization in four urban poor communities of Metro Manila', *Drug Monitor*, Vol. 2, No. 8, pp.16–20; Tan, M., 'Banned, withdrawn and restricted drugs in the Philippines', *Drug Monitor*, Vol. 2, No. 10, Oct 1987; Tan, M. et al, 'Drug needs and utilization patterns in four urban poor communities of Metro Manila', *Drug Monitor*, Vol. 3, No. 4, Apr 1988; Hardon, A., 'Towards rational drug use in urban primary health care', *Drug Monitor*, Vol. 3, No. 10, Oct 1988; 'Children's drugs in the Philippines' (special issue), *Drug Monitor*, Vol. 3, No. 12, Dec 1988.

83. IBON, *Philippine Drug Industry*, pp.8–9

84. Tan, *Dying for Drugs*, p.73

85. Gamboa, R., 'Changing the status quo: a report from the Philippines', *Essential Drugs Monitor*, No. 7, 1988, p.10

86. Anon., 'DAP cites position on drugs list', *Manila Times*, 29 Sep 1986, p.1

87. Wassmer, Jr., L. P., letter to the president of the Philippine Medical Association, 8 Oct 1986, pp.1, 3

88. Rodriguez, M. C., 'Doctors want list of essential drugs', *Manila Bulletin*, 6 Oct 1986, p.1

89. Aquino, C., speech delivered at the opening of new BFAD laboratory at Alabang, Muntinlupa, 30 Apr 1987, reproduced in *Drug Monitor*, Vol. 2, No. 4, Apr 1987, pp.4–6, and in Tan, *Dying for Drugs*, pp.189–92

90. Anon., 'National drug policy takes off?', *Drug Monitor*, Vol. 3, No. 1, Jan 1988 p.1

91. Anon, 'DOH delisting unsafe and ineffective drugs?', *Drug Monitor*, Vol. 3, No. 5, May 1988, p.53

92. Anon., 'DOH under siege with lawsuits', *Drug Monitor*, Vol. 3, No. 5, p.55

93. Anon., 'Aid, bases and drugs?', *Drug Monitor*, Vol. 3, No. 5, May 1988, p.52

94. Anon., 'Drug industry: on the defensive or on the offensive?', *Drug Monitor*, Vol. 3, No. 5, May 1988, p.55

95. Anon., 'Time to close ranks', *Drug Monitor*, Vol. 3, No. 5, May 1988, p.51

96. Westly, A. G., letter to Dr Alfredo R. A. Bengzon, 31 May 1988

97. Anon., 'Who says multinationals are moving out?', *Drug Monitor*, Vol. 3, No. 9, Sep 1988, p.103

98. Anon., 'Astra plays the game', *Drug Monitor*, Vol. 4, No. 1, Jan 1989, p.3

99. Bengzon, A. R. A., letter to A. G. Westly, 24 Jun 1988

100. Anon., 'President defends drug policy', *Drug Monitor*, Vol. 3, No. 6, Jun 1988, p.63

101. Anon., 'Generics Act signed into law', *Drug Monitor*, Vol. 3, No. 9, Sep 1988, p.95

102. Anon., 'PMA now using French to attack Generics Act' and 'Industry to fight DOH order?', *Drug Monitor*, Vol. 4, No. 1, Jan 1989, pp.2, 3

103. Anon., 'PMA goes to the Supreme Court over Generics Law', *Drug Monitor*, Vol. 4, No. 5, 1989, p.63

104. Anon., 'Generics Act under siege', *Drug Monitor*, Vol. 4, No. 8, Aug 1989, p.101

105. Quijano, R., 'From compromise to surrender (a DOH story)', *Drug Monitor*, Vol. 4, No. 3, Mar 1989, p.27; Logarta, J. D., 'Generics revisited: an overdose of expectations?', reprinted from *Philippine Currents*, Apr 1989, in *Drug Monitor*, Vol. 4, No. 4, Apr 1989, p.49

106. Anon., 'Patents will be protected – President Aquino', *Drug Monitor*, Vol. 4, No. 7, Jul 1989, p.90

107. Anon., 'US State Department intervention?', *Drug Monitor*, Vol. 4, No. 8, Aug 1989, p.103

108. Anon., 'DAP suit sparks strong reactions, including calls for nationalization', *Drug Monitor*, Vol. 4, No. 9, Sep 1989, p.119

109. Anon., 'DAP loses suit on generic labelling', *Drug Monitor*, Vol. 4, No. 9, Sep 1989, p.117

110. Bengzon, 'The evolution of a national drug policy'

## Chapter 7

1. Mahler, H., *Rational Drug Use in an Irrational World* (mimeo), speech given at the First International Conference on the Ethical and Moral Problems of Pharmacotherapy, Vatican City, 25 Oct 1986, p.7

2. WHO, *Guidelines for Developing National Drug Policies*, Geneva, 1988

3. WHO, *Ethical Criteria for Medicinal Drug Promotion*, Geneva, 1988

4. 'Changes to WHO Certification Scheme', *Scrip*, No. 1,360, 11 Nov 1988, p.28

5. WHO, *The Use of Essential Drugs – Model List of Essential Drugs (Fifth List)* (Technical Report Series No. 770), Geneva, 1988

6. WHO, *World Drug Situation*

7. 'Dr Mahler reports on WHO's Revised Drug Strategy', *Scrip*, No. 1,283, 17 Feb 1988, pp.26–7

8. Joyce, C., 'US withholds its subscription to the WHO', *New Scientist*, 18 Jun 1987, p.28

9. WHO, 'Finances of WHO receive a welcome boost – prospects of an end to financial crisis?' (press release WHA/9), 9 May 1988

10. Bloom, B. R., 'A new threat to world health', *Science*, Vol. 239, No. 4,835, 1 Jan 1988, p.9

11. Mahler, H., 'Address on the occasion of the celebration of the Fortieth anniversary of WHO and Tenth anniversary of the Declaration of Alma-Ata during the 41st World Health Assembly', WHA41/DIV/8, 7 May 1988

12. Chetley, A., 'New challenges for the World Health Organisation', *Lancet*, 28 May 1988, p.1,216

13. Mahler, 'Address'

14. Lewis, P., 'Divided World Health Organization braces for leadership change', *New York Times*, 24 Apr 1988

15. Ibid.

16. Anon., 'All change at the WHO' (editorial), *Lancet*, 28 May 1988, pp.1201–2

17. Chetley, 'New challenges'

18. HAI prepared an illustrated presentation, the text of which together with photocopies of the 39 overhead transparencies was subsequently published as: Medawar, C. and Chetley, A., *Promoting Health or Promoting Drugs?*, HAI, Amsterdam, 1988

19. Williams, J. D., editorial, *Health Horizons*, No. 4, May 1988

20. Interview with G. Lewandowski, Head of Pharma Policy, Ciba-Geigy, May 1988

21. 'US PMA draws strength from 1987', *Scrip*, No. 1,306, 6 May 1988, pp.18–20

22. Schwartz, H., 'The WHO and the pharma industry ... again – the Schwartz commentary', *Scrip*, No. 1,303, 27 April 1988, pp.22–3

23. HAI, *Controlling Drug Promotion*, Amsterdam, 1988

24. See: 'IOCU: offers challenges to the world health community', *Essential Drugs Monitor*, No. 7, 1988, p.3, for a summary of the speech.

25. Nakajima, H., address to 14th IFPMA assembly, Washington, DC, 5 Oct 1988, p.2

26. Arnold, R. B., '1988 – the landmark year', *Swiss Pharma*, No. 11a, 1988, p.24

27. 'Ms Westerholm and WHO controversy', *Scrip*, No. 1,368, 9 Dec 1988, p.21

28. 'Where now for WHO DAP?', *Scrip*, No. 1,396, 22 Mar 1989, p.29

29. Anon., 'Government, WHO, reiterate support for national drug policy', *Drug Monitor*, Vol. 3, No. 5, May 1988, p.54

30. Samsom, R. J., speech delivered at the WHA, 17 May 1989, p.2

31. APED, *Progress Report*, WHO/DAP/89.5, WHO, Geneva, May 1989, pp.2–3

32. APED, *Management Advisory Committee: report of the meeting, Geneva, 5–6 October 1989* (DAP/MAC(1)/89.8), WHO, Geneva, 1989, p.3

33. Samsom, speech

34. London School of Hygiene and Tropical Medicine and the Royal Tropical Institute, *An Evaluation of WHO's Action Programme on Essential Drugs*, DANIDA, Copenhagen, 1989, p.56

35. Ibid., p.53

36. Ibid., p.71

37. UNICEF, *State of the World's Children 1989*, p.50

38. Anon., 'The Bamako Initiative', *Lancet*, 19 Nov 1988, pp.1,177–8

39. World Bank, *Briefing Note: UNICEF's Bamako Initiative*, Washington, 23 Feb 1988

40. Memo from Dr F. Partow, Assistant Director General WHO, to Dr Nyi Nyi, director, Programme Division, UNICEF, 16 Feb 1988

41. Cross, P. N., et al, 'Revolving drug funds: conducting business in the public sector', *Social Science and Medicine*, Vol. 22, No. 3, 1986, pp.335–43

42. Foster, S. and Drager, N., 'How community drug sales schemes may succeed', *World Health Forum*, Vol. 9, No. 2, 1988, pp.200–6

43. WHO, *Basic Documents* (35th edn), Geneva, 1985

44. Dukes, M. N. G., 'Towards a healthy pharmaceutical industry by the year 2000', *Development Dialogue*, (special issue), No. 2, 1985, p.109

45. See for example: Teeling-Smith, G., 'The Golden Triangle', *Times Health Supplement*, 29 Jan 1982, p.17; PMA, *Health Consequences*; IFPMA, *The Need to Inform*, pp.22–3

46. Chetley, A., 'Experts suggest pharmaceutical advertising guidelines', *International Barometer* (special report), Dec 1985

47. The calculation is based on a cumulative total of 182,463 AIDS cases officially reported to WHO by 1 October 1989 (see 'Latest AIDS figures', *Lancet*, 25 Nov 1989, p.1,288). It is generally accepted that at least 50 per cent of cases reported could be considered fatalities at any given time, so at least 91,000 people have died from AIDS. Annual fatalities (estimated in 1987) for malaria were 1,000,000; from diarrhoeal diseases, 5,000,000, and from vaccine-preventable diseases, at least 3,000,000. (See UNICEF, *The State of the World's Children 1988*, pp.2–3.) Even taking the much higher WHO estimation of a possible 500,000 cases of AIDS worldwide, or the even larger estimate of 5 million people infected with human immunodeficiency virus (HIV), some of whom may well develop full-blown AIDS, clearly there are still other pressing health problems which are not being adequately dealt with.

48. Diwan, V. and Nordberg, E., 'AIDS in an African perspective: epidemiology and control', in Sterky, G. and Krantz, I. (eds.), *Society and HIV/AIDS: selected knowledge base for research and action*, Karolinska Institutet, Stockholm, 1988, p.13

49. 'AIDS and the World Health Organization – the Schwartz commentary', *Scrip*, No. 1,170, 14 Jan 1987, pp.24–5

50. Schwartz, H., 'The Schwartz commentary on "The Economist" on drug discovery', *Scrip*, No. 1,344/5, 16/21 Sep 1988, p.19. A different view is put by Dr Joseph Zammit-Lucia of Cambridge Pharma Consultancy who argues that rather than concentrating on innovative research, imaginative product development is more likely to contribute 'to the success of a drug'. And by success, he means more sales and profits, rather than necessarily filling an obvious therapeutic need (see 'The secret of pharma success?', *Scrip*, No. 1,411, 12 May 1989, p.18).

51. Anon., 'Another development in pharmaceuticals: summary conclusions', *Development Dialogue* (special issue), No. 2, 1985, p.137

52. Vane, J. and Gutteridge, W., 'TDR and the drug industry', *World Health*, May 1985, p.23

53. UNDP/World Bank/WHO, *Venture for Health*, WHO, Geneva, 1984

54. Fernex, M., 'Mefloquine and its allies', *World Health*, May 1985, p.6

55. Ibid., p.7

56. Johnstone, M., 'Malaria: prospects for new drugs and vaccines', *Health Horizons*, No. 1, May 1987, p.4

57. Reynolds, J. E. F. (ed.), *Martindale: the extra pharmacopoeia* (29th edn), Pharmaceutical Press, London, 1989, p.55

58. See: Anon., 'Ivermectin: new drug for river blindness', *Essential Drugs Monitor*, No. 6, 1988, p.14; Anon., 'Uniquely effective tropical disease drug available free of charge', *Health Horizons*, No. 3, Jan 1988, p.13; Anon., 'Eleven-country programme cleared to receive supplies of new drug to treat onchocerciasis', *Health Horizons*, No. 6, Jan 1989, pp.6–7

59. Anon., 'One million doses of hepatitis B vaccine donated to the World Health Organization', *Health Horizons*, No. 7, May 1989, pp.3–5

60. PMA, *The Gambia: a case study in improved primary health care through improved pharmaceutical management*, Washington, 1985; Lucas, C. P., 'Africare', *Health Horizons*, No. 2, Sep 1987, pp.8–10

61. ABPI, 'British pharmaceutical companies assist Commonwealth medicines projects' (press release), London, 3 May 1985

62. Lowndes, V., 'ABPI assistance in the Maldives', *Health Horizons*, No. 1, May 1987, pp.8–10; Loshak, D., 'The Maldives: a practical approach', *Wellcome Journal*, Apr 1986, pp.8–11

63. Anon., 'Médicaments et tiers monde', *Health Horizons*, No. 1, May 1987, p.16; Anon., 'Stage de perfectionnement professionnel au contrôle de la qualité dans les pays en développement', *Health Horizons*, No. 1, May 1987, p.13; Pharma Information, *Burundi's Drug Scheme*, Basle, 1986; Anon., 'Audio-visual training programme in preventive health practices launched in Colombia', *Health Horizons*, No. 5, Sep 1988, pp.16–17; Anon., 'Japanese pharmaceutical industry coordinates policy for health care in developing countries', *Health Horizons*, No. 8, Sep 1989, pp.22–3; Anon., 'IFPMA conducts first survey of pharmaceutical industry projects in developing countries', *Health Horizons*, No.9, Jan 1990, pp.4–5

64. 'Industry PR paying off?', *Scrip*, No. 1,151, 3 Nov 1986, p.16

65. '£1.488 million ABPI PR budget for 1987', *Scrip*, No. 1,148, 22 Oct 1986, p.1

66. 'PMA's communications programme', *Scrip*, No. 1,154, 12 Nov 1986, p.17

67. 'US PMA draws strength', *Scrip*, No. 1,306, p.18

68. 'BPI starts image campaign', *Scrip*, No. 1,403, 14 Apr 89, p.4

69. Hansson, O., *Inside Ciba-Geigy*, IOCU, Penang, 1989

70. Lewandowski, interview

71. Hansson, *Inside Ciba-Geigy*, p.128

72. Ibid., pp.114–126

73. Ibid., p.201

74. Ibid., p.202
75. Lewandowski, interview
76. Taylor, D. and Miller, D., RAD-AR: *an executive summary*, Ciba-Geigy, Basle, Mar 1988, p.1
77. Stearns, B., 'RAD-AR: homing in on risk', *Ciba-Geigy Journal*, No. 2, 1987
78. 'Ciba-Geigy risk initiative', *Scrip*, No. 1,301, 20 Apr 1988, pp.14–15
79. Ibid.
80. Anon., 'Perception and management of drug safety risks: the need for wide co-operation to find solution to drug safety issues, recognised by the industry', *Health Horizons*, No. 5, Sep 1988, pp.20–1
81. Anon., 'Drug company heal thyself. How one organisation has met the challenge of self-regulation', *Australian Doctor Weekly*, 29 Jul 1988, p.8; 'Ciba-Geigy reaffirms open policy', *Scrip*, No. 1,377, 24 Aug 1988, p.13
82. Anon., 'Drug company heal thyself'
83. 'Searle's patient education programme', *Scrip*, No. 1,459, 27 Oct 1989, p.8. In contrast, Janssen, when facing a problem of young infants in Pakistan suffering from severe adverse effects and possible death as a result of using Imodium (loperamide) drops to treat diarrhoea, said that 'use of the product not in line with the prescribing information and without proper medical supervision is clearly beyond Janssen's control' (see 'Janssen on loperamide ADRs', *Scrip*, No. 1,491, 23 Feb 1990, p.29).
84. 'Searle makes a profit', *Scrip*, No. 1,459, 27 Oct 1989, p.8
85. Anon., 'Another development in pharmaceuticals', pp.136–137
86. Coleman, V., *The Medicine Men*, Arrow Books, London, 1977, p.173
87. Dukes, M. N. G., 'Towards a healthy pharmaceutical industry' pp.118–19
88. Arnold, R. B., 'IFPMA activities: present and future preoccupations – the pharmaceutical industry under attack', *Swiss Pharma*, No. 3, 1985, p.12
89. 'Industry PR', *Scrip*, No. 1,151
90. Anon., 'Another development in pharmaceuticals', p.137
91. 'Pharmaceutical industry, police thyself, say HAI leaders', *International Barometer*, Supplement to Vol. 2, No. 10, Mar 1987
92. 'Where were the scientists at Montreux? – the Schwartz commentary', *Scrip*, No. 1,154, 12 Nov 1986, p.22
93. IFPMA, *The Need to Inform*, p.12
94. WEMOS, *Organon and Anabolic Steroids*, Amsterdam, 1987, p.4
95. Dukes, 'Towards a healthy pharmaceutical industry', p.119
96. Leisinger, K. M., *Poverty, Sickness and Medicines: an unholy alliance?*, IFPMA, Geneva, 1989
97. Arnold, '1988 – the landmark year', p.22
98. Anon., 'Need for industry and the Third World to reach an understanding: Mr Patrick Jenkin addresses manufacturers', *Pharmaceutical Journal*, 25 Oct 1980, pp.464–7
99. Cowhig, J., 'The drug industry meets its critics', *General Practitioner*, 22 Nov 1985, p.20
100. *Scrip Yearbook 1987*, p.3
101. Anon., 'Another development in pharmaceuticals', p.137

# Bibliography

The following works were consulted during the preparation of this report, although not all are referred to directly in the text.

Abosede, O. A., 'Self-medication: an important aspect of primary health care', *Social Science and Medicine*, Vol. 19, No. 7, pp.699–703

ABPI, *Action Programme on Essential Drugs: summary of progress 1985/86* (mimeo), London, 17 Apr 1986

——— 'British pharmaceutical companies assist Commonwealth medicines projects' (press release), London, 3 May 1985

——— *Medicines for the Developing Nations*, London, 1988

——— Minutes of the Half-Yearly General Meeting of the Association held at the Gleneagles Hotel, Auchterarder, 14 Oct 1982, Ref. No. 1267/82, 20 Dec 1982

Adams, S., *Roche versus Adams*, Jonathan Cape, London, 1984

Agarwal, A., *Drugs and the Third World*, Earthscan, London, 1978

Akhter, F., *Depopulating Bangladesh*, Ubinig, Dhaka, 1986

Alliance for the Prudent Use of Antibiotics, *Statement Regarding Worldwide Antibiotic Misuse*, 4 Feb 1982

Alvan, G., Öhman, B. and Sjöqvist, F., 'Problem-oriented drug information: a clinical pharmacological service', *Lancet*, 17 Dec 1983, pp.1,410–12

AMA, *Drug Evaluations* (4th edn), AMA, Chicago, 1980

——— *Drug Evaluations* (6th edn), W.B. Saunders, Philadelphia, 1986

Amery, J. and López, R., *Medicamentos en el Perú*, Instituto de Promoción y Educación Popular/Oxfam, Chimbote/Lima, 1985

Amidi, S., et al, 'Antibiotic use and abuse among physicians in private practice in Shiraz, Iran', *Medical Care*, Vol. 18, No. 4, 1975, pp.341–5

Anon., '5 out of 6 die before reaching a doctor', *Bangladesh Times*, 5 Aug 1986

Anon., '39th World Health Assembly', *Lancet*, 7 Jun 1986, p.1,338

Anon., 'ABPI begins campaign against "stupid and dangerous" proposal', *Pharmaceutical Journal*, 8 Dec 1984

Anon., 'ABPI "to fight tooth and nail" ', *Pharmaceutical Journal*, 17 Nov 1984

Anon., 'All change at the WHO' (editorial), *Lancet*, 28 May 1988, pp.1,201–2

Anon., 'The Bamako Initiative', *Lancet*, 19 Nov 1985, pp.1,777–8

Anon., 'Benzodiazepine dependence and withdrawal', *Drug Newsletter*, Wolfson Unit of Clinical Pharmacology, Newcastle upon Tyne, Apr 1983

Anon., 'The big lie about generic drugs', *Consumer Reports*, Aug 1987, pp.480–5

Anon., 'DAP cites position on drugs list', *Manila Times*, 29 Sep 1986, p.1

Anon., 'Drug ban is Bangladesh blunder', *ABPI News*, Oct 1982

Anon., 'Drug company heal thyself. How one organisation has met the challenge of self-regulation', *Australian Doctor Weekly*, 29 Jul 1988, p.8

Anon., 'Drug promotional problems', *Medical Journal of Australia*, Vol. 150, 17 Apr 1989, p.463

Anon., 'Drug use in the Third World', *Lancet*, 6 Dec 1980, pp.1231–2

Anon., 'Drugs fight renewed', *New Scientist*, 15 May 1986, p.28

Anon., 'Essential drugs seminar draws up new strategy. Ratification in May', *Africa Health*, Dec 1985/Jan 1986, p.7

Anon., 'Genetic engineering causes a revolution in medicine', *New Scientist*, 26 Feb 1987, p.29

Anon., *The Grafton Compact*, InterAction, New York, 1988

Anon., 'HAI report slams use of discredited drugs', *Far East Health*, Sep 1986, p.7

Anon., 'How to buy vitamins', *Which?*, Jan 1984, pp.6–9

Anon., 'Infant formula critics now planning big offensive against drug and health firms', *Business International*, 26 Jun 1981

Anon., 'International drug marketing code', *Lancet*, 30 Apr 1988

Anon., 'Issues of health', *New Nation* (Bangladesh), 3 Aug 1986, p.5

Anon., 'Kenya's system for supply of drugs to rural areas', *Lancet*, 21 Dec 1985

Anon., 'MLAM' (Round the World column), *Lancet*, 13 Oct 1984, p.861

Anon., 'Much politics at this year's Assembly', *Lancet*, 31 May 1986, pp.1283–4

Anon., 'Need for industry and the Third World to reach an understanding: Mr Patrick Jenkin addresses manufacturers', *Pharmaceutical Journal*, 25 Oct 1980, pp.464–7

Anon., 'Networking versus the multinationals', *Economist Development Report*, Dec 1985, pp.8–9

Anon., 'No money – no drugs', *Far East Health*, Nov 1986, pp.20–1

Anon., 'Paediatricians get their skates on', *Lancet*, 26 Sep 1987

Anon., 'Pharmaceutical industry, police thyself, say HAI leaders', *International Barometer*, Supplement to Vol. 2, No. 10, Mar 1987

Anon., 'Pharmaceutical industry takes varied approaches to threat to LDC sales', *Business International*, 9 Feb 1979, pp.43 and 46

Anon., 'Pharmaceutical policies for the Third World – whose responsibility?', *Lancet*, 16 Jul 1983, p.144

Anon., 'Rational use of drugs', *Lancet*, 8 Jun 1985, pp.1,344–5

Anon., 'Some problems with benzodiazepines', *Drug and Therapeutics Bulletin*, Vol. 23, No. 6, 25 Mar 1985, pp.21–2

Anon., 'WHO', *South*, Sep 1982

Anon., 'WHO meeting agrees on rational drugs strategy', *Lancet*, 14 Dec 1985, pp.1,350–1

Anon., 'WHO moves closer to code for drug industry: who will be next?', *Business International*, 25 May 1984, pp.164–5

Anon., 'Worldwide activist network keeps pace with pharmaceutical industry – wherever it is', *International Barometer*, Vol. 2, No. 10, Mar 1987, pp.1 and 3

Antezana, F. S., 'Essential drugs – whose responsibility?', *Journal of the Royal Society of Medicine*, Vol. 74, Mar 1981, pp.175–7

APED, *Management Advisory Committee: report of the meeting, Geneva, 5–6 October 1989*, (DAP/MAC(1)/89.8), WHO, Geneva, 1989

——— *Progress Report*, WHO/DAP/89.5, WHO, Geneva, May 1989

Arnold, R. B., '1988 – the landmark year', *Swiss Pharma*, No. 11a, 1988

———— 'IFPMA activities: present and future preoccupations – the pharmaceutical industry under attack', *Swiss Pharma*, No. 3, 1985, pp.7–12

Avorn, J., Chen, M. and Hartley, R., 'Scientific versus commercial sources of influence on the prescribing behavior of physicians', *American Journal of Medicine*, Vol. 73, Jul 1982, pp.4–8

Avorn, J., and Soumerai, S. B., 'Improving drug-therapy decisions through educational outreach: a randomized controlled trial of academically based "detailing" ', *New England Journal of Medicine*, Vol. 308, 16 Jun 1983, pp.1,457–63

Baistow, T., 'Point of departure', *Guardian*, 30 Apr 1985

Banerji, D., 'Population planning in India: national and foreign priorities', *International Journal of Health Services*, Vol. 3, No. 4, 1973

Bangladesh Bureau of Statistics, *1984–85 Statistical Yearbook of Bangladesh*, Government of Bangladesh, Dhaka, Dec 1985

Bangladesh Drug Administration, *Report of the Expert Committee for Drugs on the National Drug Policy of Bangladesh 1982*, Government of Bangladesh, Dhaka, Mar 1986

Bannenberg, W., 'Omnipotent industry?', *Health Now*, No. 3, 11 May 1984

Barral, E., *Prospective et santé*, No. 36, Winter 1985/86, pp.89–95

BASS, 'An appeal to the Martial Law Authority' (full-page advertisement in most Bangladesh newspapers, Jun 1982

———— Letter to members of Bangladesh Parliament, 9 Nov 1986

Bekele, M., 'Social and economic factors affecting women's health', *Assignment Children*, 49/50, Spring 1980, pp.77–8

Bennett, C., 'The remedy for drugs', *Marketing Week*, 8 Jun 1984, p.41–3

Bevan, J. A. (ed.), *Essentials of Pharmacology*, Harper and Row, New York, 1976

Bidwai, P., 'US offensive against UN: I – WHO the latest victim', *Times of India*, 4 Jul 1986

———— 'WHO under US attack: II – drug MNCs score a victory', *Times of India*, 5 Jul 1986

Bloom, B. R., 'A new threat to world health', *Science*, Vol. 239, No. 4,835, 1 Jan 1988, p.9

Blum, R. et al (eds.), *Pharmaceuticals and Health Policy*, Social Audit/IOCU/HAI, London/Penang/The Hague, 1983

Bowman, M. A., 'The impact of drug company funding on the content of continuing medical education', *Mobius*, Vol. 6, No. 1, Jan 1986, pp.66–9

BRAC, *Peasant Perceptions*, Dhaka, 1984

———— *Who Gets What and Why: resource allocation in a Bangladesh village*, Dhaka, 1983

Bradshaw, C., 'Treating children with diarrhoea and vomiting', *The Practitioner*, Vol. 228, Sep 1984, pp.834–5

Braithwaite, J., *Corporate Crime in the Pharmaceutical Industry*, Routledge and Kegan Paul, London, 1984

Brandt, W. et al, *North–South: a programme for survival*, Pan, London, 1980

*British National Formulary* (various numbers), BMA and Pharmaceutical Society, London, 1985–9

Bronstein, A., *The Triple Struggle*, War on Want, London, 1982

Brooks, R. A., 'Saving the World Health Organisation from a poison pill', *Heritage Foundation Backgrounder*, No. 471, 19 Nov 1985

BUKO, *Hoechst: a cause of illness?*, Bielefeld, 1987

Burkitt, D., *Don't Forget Fibre In Your Diet* (4th edn), Martin Dunitz, London, 1983

Burley, D. M. and Thomson, T. J., 'Doctors and the drug makers' (letter to the editor), *Lancet*, 18 Aug 1984, pp.403–4

Burstall, M. L., Dunning, J. H. and Lake, A., 'Multinational enterprises, governments and technology; pharmaceutical industry', OECD, Paris, 1981

Burstall, M. L., and Michon-Savarit, C., *The Pharmaceutical Industry: trade related issues*, OECD, Paris, 1985

Burstall, M. L. with Senior, I., *The Community's Pharmaceutical Industry*, EC, Brussels, 1985

*The Business Top Thousand*, Business People Publications, London, 1986


Cameron, M. and Hofvander, Y., *Manual on Feeding Infants and Young Children* (2nd edn), FAO, Rome, 1980

Caplan, R. and Malcomson, S. L., 'Giving the UN the business', *Nation* (USA), 16/23 Aug 1986, pp.108–12

Cassels, A., 'Drug supply in rural Nepal', *Tropical Doctor*, 13, Jan 1983, pp.14–17

Chen, M.A., *A Quiet Revolution: women in transition in rural Bangladesh*, BRAC, Dhaka, 1986

Cheng, E. et al, 'Asia develops the drug habit' (feature series), *Far Eastern Economic Review*, 11 Apr 1985, pp.45–61

Chennabathni, C. S. and Brown, D. J., 'Prescribing patterns in Seychelles', *Tropical Doctor*, Oct 1982, pp.228–30

Chetley, A., 'Baby milk, drugs, tobacco stir Geneva storms', *Bangkok Post*, 13 May 1986

———— *Bangladesh: finding the right prescription*, War on Want, London, 1982

———— 'Better information a key to rational drug use', *Consumer Affairs*, No. 78, Nov/Dec 1985, pp.1–4

———— *Cleared for Export*, CADE, The Hague/Brussels, 1985

———— 'Drugs "what a waste of money"', *Far East Health*, Apr 1984, p.15

———— 'An essential drugs policy in action', *Far East Health*, Sep 1986, pp.49-51

———— 'Experts suggest pharmaceutical advertising guidelines', *International Barometer*, Dec 1985

———— 'Health for all', *Bernard van Leer Foundation Newsletter*, No. 48, Oct 1987

———— 'Medical students demand government jobs', *Lancet*, 20 Sep 1986

———— 'New challenges for the World Health Organisation', *Lancet*, 28 May 1988, p.1,216

———— 'Operation Sidestep', *Health for the Millions*, Vol. 8, No. 6, Dec 1982, p.6

———— *Peddling Placebos: an analysis of cough and cold remedies*, HAI, Amsterdam, 1989

———— *The Baby Killer Scandal*, War on Want, London, 1979

———— *The Politics of Baby Foods*, Frances Pinter, London, 1986

———— *Towards Rational Drug Use*, HAI, The Hague, 1988

———— 'Veil of secrecy over international drugs meeting' (GH 37), Gemini News Service, London, 8 Nov 1985

———— 'WHO's way forward from Nairobi', THS *Health Summary*, Dec 1985, p.4

———— 'World Health Assembly draws coordinated activist campaigns', *International Barometer*, May 1986

———— and Gilbert, D., *Problem Drugs*, HAI, The Hague/Penang, 1986

Chilmper, J., 'Peru: an essential drugs pioneer', *Essential Drugs Monitor*, No. 8, 1989, p.18

Chorlton, P., 'US is aiding drug companies in Bangladesh', *Washington Post*, 19 Aug 1982

Chowdhury, Z. and Chowdhury, S., 'Essential drugs for the poor: myth and reality in Bangladesh', *Ecodevelopment News*, No. 23, Dec 1982, p.43

Chustecka, Z., 'Professor Sir John Vane on research and drug discovery', *Scrip*, No. 1,300, 15 Apr 1988, pp.20–2

Clark, E., *The Want Makers*, Coronet Books, London, 1989

Clemens, J., 'How to discover what your doctor is thinking', *Marketing Week*, 8 Jun 1984, pp.45–9

Coleman, V., *The Medicine Men*, Arrow Books, London, 1977

Collier, J., *The Health Conspiracy*, Century Hutchinson, London, 1989

—— and Foster, J., 'Management of a restricted drugs policy in hospital: the first five years' experience', *Lancet*, 9 Feb 1985, pp.331–3

Collier, J., and Medawar, C., 'Why fewer drugs is a prescription for a healthier Britain', *Guardian*, 17 Dec 1984

Collier, J., and New, L., 'Illegibility of drug advertisements', *Lancet*, 11 Feb 1984, pp.341–2

Coney, S., 'Pharmaceutical advertising', *Lancet*, 20 May 1989, pp.1,128–9

Cooper, W. and Smith, T., *Everything You Need to Know about the Pill*, Sheldon Press, London, 1984

Costa Rica Ministry of Health, *Guía Terapeutica Nacional*, San José, 1985

Costello, A. M. de L. and Tudor-Williams, G., 'Improvement of rural health services', *Lancet*, 21 Jun 1986, p.1,433

Cowhig, J., 'The drug industry meets its critics', *General Practitioner*, 22 Nov 1985, p.20

Cross, P. N. et al, 'Revolving drug funds: conducting business in the public sector', *Social Science and Medicine*, Vol. 22, No. 3, 1986, pp.335–43

Cunliffe, P. W., 'Drugs in the Third World' (letter to the editor), *Listener*, 3 Oct 1985

—— 'Pharmaceuticals in the Third World', *Pharma Topics*, No. 4, Mar 1982

Curry, P., 'Society tomorrow', *Guardian*, 1 Jul 1987, p.11


Dag Hammarskjöld Foundation, 'Another development in pharmaceuticals', *Development Dialogue* (special issue), No. 2, 1985

de Bruxelles, S. and Ferriman, A., 'Deadly "super bug" spreads through wards', *Observer*, 31 Aug 1986

Diczfalusy, E., Griffin, P. D. and Khanna, J. (eds.), *Research in Human Reproduction: biennial report (1986–1987)*, WHO Special Programme of Research, Development and Research Training in Human Reproduction, Geneva, 1988

Dinwoodie, R., 'WHO sedated to quell US anger', *Scotsman*, 27 Nov 1985, p.13

Djukanovic, V. and Mach, E. P. (eds.), *Alternative Approaches to Meeting Basic Health Needs in Developing Countries*, WHO, Geneva, 1975

Dowie, M., 'The corporate crime of the century', *Mother Jones*, Nov 1979

Doyal, L. and Pennell, I., *The Political Economy of Health*, Pluto Press, London, 1979

Dukes, M. N. G., 'Towards a healthy pharmaceutical industry by the year 2000', *Development Dialogue*, No. 2, 1985

—— (ed.), *Side Effects of Drugs Annual 11*, Elsevier, Amsterdam, 1987

—— and Beeley, L. (eds.), *Side Effects of Drugs Annual 12*, Elsevier, Amsterdam, 1988

Ebrahim, G. J., *Child Care in the Tropics*, Macmillan, London, 1978

Edwards, B. and Newens, S., *The Multinationals*, Liberation, London, 1979

Elarabi, I. I., 'Where drugs don't help', *World Health*, Apr 1986, p.10

Ennals, D., 'A socialist view of the government and industry', *Health Herald*, Jun 1984

Erlichman, J., 'Drug firm suspended over gifts', *Guardian*, 18 Dec 1986

——— 'No dilemma for Doctor Griffin', *Guardian*, 21 Jan 1985

——— 'The pill-makers bluster – but is it just bluff?', *Guardian*, 6 Mar 1984, p.23

——— 'Profit squeeze stifles drug research', *Guardian*, 28 Nov 1984, p.25

——— 'Third World drug plan seen as PR ploy', *Guardian*, 13 Apr 1984

——— 'Why the foreign drug firms will swallow the bitter pill of reduced profits', *Guardian*, 30 Apr 1984, p.16

Escobar, V., 'We spend too much for the wrong drugs', *CACP Journal*, 2nd Quarter, 1982


Fabricant, S.J. and Hirschhorn, N., 'Deranged distribution, perverse prescription, unprotected use: the irrationality of pharmaceuticals in the developing world', *Health Policy and Planning*, Vol. 2, No. 3, 1987, pp.204–13

Faich, G. A. et al, 'Reassurance about generic drugs', *New England Journal of Medicine*, Vol. 316, No. 23, 4 Jun 1987, pp.1,473–5

Farrar, W. E., 'Antibiotic resistance in developing countries', *Journal of Infectious Disease*, Vol. 152, No. 6, Dec 1985, p.1,105

Fattorusso, V., 'Essential drugs for the Third World', *World Development*, Vol. 11, No. 3, Mar 1983

Fazal, A., 'The right pharmaceuticals at the right prices: consumer perspectives', *World Development*, Vol. 11, No. 3, 1983

Fernex, M., 'Mefloquine and its allies', *World Health*, May 1985, pp.6–7

Ferriman, A., 'Exposed: drug giant's hard sell to doctors', *Observer* (London), 9 Jun 1985

Ferry, G., 'Drugs company buys brainpower at Oxford', *New Scientist*, 22 Oct 1987

Fitzsimons, C., 'Facing up to the bitter pill of addiction', *Observer*, 21 Feb 1988, p.7

*Fortune*, 'The Fortune 500', 24 Apr 1989; 25 Apr 1988; 27 Apr 1987

Foster, S. and Drager, N., 'How community drug sales schemes may succeed', *World Health Forum*, Vol. 9, No. 2, 1988, pp.200–6

Fraser, H. S., 'Rational use of essential drugs', *World Health Forum*, Vol. 6, 1985, pp.63–6


Gamboa, R., 'Changing the status quo: a report from the Philippines', *Essential Drugs Monitor*, No. 7, 1988, p.10

George, C. F. and Hands, D. E., 'Drug and therapeutics committees and information pharmacy services: the United Kingdom', *World Development*, Vol. 11, No. 3, Mar 1983

George, S., *A Fate Worse Than Debt*, Penguin, London, 1988

Gerlis, L., 'Complications for the drug industry', *New Scientist*, 15 Jan 1987, pp.61–2

Ghodse, H. and Khan, I, *Psychoactive Drugs: improving prescribing practices*, WHO, Geneva, 1988

Gicheru, C., 'Drugs talks end with "agreement"', *Daily Nation* (Kenya), 30 Nov 1985

Gilman, A. G., Goodman, L. S. et al (eds.), *The Pharmacological Basis of Therapeutics* (7th edn), Macmillan, London, 1985

Girolami, P., 'A European view', *World Link*, Dec 1988, p.70

Glucksberg, H. and Singer, J., 'The multinational drug companies in Zaire: their adverse effect on cost and availability of essential drugs', *International Journal of Health Services*, Vol. 12, No. 3, 1982, pp.381–7

Gofton, K., 'Drugs all in a twist', *Marketing*, 12 Apr 1984, pp.22–4

Goldfinger, S. E., 'A matter of influence', *New England Journal of Medicine*, Vol. 316, No. 22, 28 May 1987, pp.1,408–9

Gould, D., *The Medical Mafia*, Sphere, London, 1985

Graedon, J., *The People's Pharmacy – 2*, Avon Books, New York, 1980

Grant, E., *The Bitter Pill*, Corgi, London, 1986

Graves, J., 'Frequent-flyer programs for drug prescribing', *New England Journal of Medicine*, Vol. 317, 23 Jul 1987, p.252

Greenhalgh, T., 'Drug marketing in the Third World: beneath the cosmetic reforms', *Lancet*, 7 Jun 1986, pp.1,318–20

Griffin, J. P. and Diggle, G. E., 'A survey of products licensed in the United Kingdom from 1971–1981', *British Journal of Clinical Pharmacology*, Vol. 12, 1981, pp.453–66

Griffiths, K, et al, 'Therapeutic traditions in Northern Ireland, Norway and Sweden: 1. diabetes', *European Journal of Clinical Pharmacology*, Vol. 30, 1986, pp.513–19

Group for Defense of Consumers on Pharmaceuticals, *Antibiotics, Analgesics and Vitamins: use and abuse in Recife, Brazil*, Recife, 1984

Guest, I., 'America attacks drug code plan', *Guardian*, 21 Jan 1984

——— 'Which comes first – the purity of American capitalism or curing the sick?', *Guardian*, 23 Jan 1984

Guillebaud, J., *The Pill* (3rd edn), Oxford University Press, Oxford, 1984

Gustafsson, L. L. and Wide, K., 'Marketing of obsolete antibiotics in Central America', *Lancet*, 3 Jan 1981, pp.31–3

Gwinner, E., 'Nobel Prize for Medicine goes to three pharmaceutical industry research scientists', *Health Horizons*, No. 6, Jan 1989, pp.18–19


Haddon, C., *Women and Tranquillisers*, Sheldon Press, London, 1984

HAI, *Controlling Drug Promotion*, Amsterdam, 1988

——— *A Draft International Code on Pharmaceuticals* (2nd edn), The Hague/Penang, 1982

——— *HAI News*, various issues, 1981–9

——— *Not To Be Taken: at least, not to be taken seriously*, The Hague/Penang, 1981

——— *The Way Forward: the World Health Organisation's action programme on essential drugs and vaccines*, The Hague/Penang, 1984

Hailey, A., *Strong Medicine*, Pan, London, 1985

Hall, R. C., 'Drug regulation – a review of Australian procedures', *Health Reporter* (journal of the Commonwealth Department of Health, Australia), Vol. 3, No. 4, May/June 1986, pp.4–5

Hamilton, R. and Whinnett, D., 'A comparison of the WHO and UK codes of practice for the marketing of breastmilk substitutes', *Journal of Consumer Policy*, Vol. 10, 1987, pp.167–92

Hampton, J. R., 'The end of clinical freedom', *British Medical Journal*, Vol. 287, 29 Oct 1983, pp.1,237–8

Hansson, O., *Inside Ciba-Geigy*, IOCU, Penang, 1989

Hardon, A., *An Analgesic for Every Ill: the use of analgesics in 80 families in an urban poor community*, Pharmaceuticals Research Project, Manila, 1986

————— *Fact Sheet on the Use of E-P Drugs in an Urban Poor Community*, Pharmaceuticals Research Project, Manila, 1986

————— 'Towards rational drug use in urban primary health care', *Drug Monitor*, Vol. 3, No. 10, Oct 1988

————— 'WHO meeting on contraceptive steroids', *Drug Monitor*, Vol. 2, No. 3, Mar 1987, pp.8–12

————— and van der Geest, S., *Hazards and Potentials of Self-medication: an example from a Filipino village* (mimeo), Anthropological Sociological Centre, University of Amsterdam, 1985

Harpham, T., Vaughan, P. and Rifkin, S., *Health and the Urban Poor in Developing Countries*, Evaluation and Planning Centre for Health Care, London School of Hygiene and Tropical Medicine, 1985

Harrison, P., *Inside the Third World*, Penguin, London, 1979

Harvey, K., 'Antibiotic use in Australia', *Australian Prescriber*, Vol. 2, No. 4, 1988, pp.74–7

————— 'The influence of advertising over prescribing', *Australian Journal of Hospital Pharmacy* (supplement to Vol. 18, No. 3, Jun 1988) p.25

————— et al, 'Educational antibiotic advertising', *Medical Journal of Australia*, Vol. 145, 1986, pp.28–31

————— ————— 'Use of antibiotics in a large teaching hospital', *Medical Journal of Australia*, 1983, pp.217–21

Haslemere Group, *Who Needs the Drug Companies?*, Haslemere Group/War on Want/Third World First, London/Oxford, 1976

Hay, D. R., letter to the editor, *New Zealand Medical Journal*, Vol. 100, 8 Apr 1987, p.223

Hayer, F., 'Rational prescribing and sources of information', *Social Science and Medicine*, Vol. 16, 1982, pp.2,017–23

Hayes, A., 'What can the agrochemical industry learn from the pharmaceutical industry?', speech delivered at AgroChemical Conference, Zurich, Sep 1981

Health and Public Policy Committee, American College of Physicians, 'Improving medical education in therapeutics', *Annals of Internal Medicine*, Vol. 108, 1988, pp.145–7

*Health Now*, Vol. 1, Nos 1–5/6, 1984; Vol. 2, Nos 1–6, 1986

Heller, T., *Poor Health, Rich Profits*, Spokesman Books, Nottingham, 1977

Helsing, E., 'Malnutrition in an affluent society', *World Health*, Oct 1984

Herxheimer, A., 'Problem Drugs', *World Health Forum*, Vol. 4, 1983, p.245

————— (ed.), 'Manufacturer-sponsored symposia', *Drug and Therapeutics Bulletin*, Vol. 21, No. 6, 25 Mar 1983, p.24

————— and Collier, J., 'Self-regulation of promotion by the British pharmaceutical industry, 1983–1988: a critical analysis', *British Medical Journal*, 3 Feb 1990, pp.307–11

Hogerzeil, H. V. et al, 'Impact of an essential drugs programme on availability and rational use of drugs', *Lancet*, 21 Jan 1989, pp.141–2

Hossain, M., *The Assault that Failed: a profile of absolute poverty in six villages of Bangladesh*, UNRISD, Geneva, 1987

Hossain, M. et al, 'Antibiotic use in a rural community in Bangladesh', *International Journal of Epidemiology*, Vol. 11, No. 4, 1982, pp.402–5

Huq, J. et al, (eds.), *Women In Bangladesh: some socio-economic issues*, Women for Women, Dhaka, 1983

Hye, H. K. M. A., *Action Programme on Essential Drugs: the Bangladesh experience* (mimeo), Dhaka, Bangladesh Drug Administration, 1986
—— 'Essential drugs for all', *World Health Forum*, Vol. 9, No. 2, 1988, pp.214–17

IBFAN, *Fighting for Infant Survival*, Geneva/Penang/Minneapolis, 1989
IBON, *The Philippine Drug Industry*, Manila, 1986
IFPMA, *The Biological Industry and World Health*, Geneva, 1985
—— *Health Horizons* (various issues, 1987–9)
—— IFPMA *Code of Pharmaceutical Marketing Practices* (revised edn), Geneva, Mar 1987
—— *The Journey Forward*, Geneva, 1987
—— *Making the Most of Medicines*, Geneva, 1985
—— *The Need to Inform: the role of promotion in marketing medicines for the Third World*, Geneva, 1985
—— *Rational Drug Use in Developing Countries*, Geneva, 1985
—— *Statement as adopted by the* IFPMA *Council on the Report of a* WHO *Expert Committee on the Selection of Essential Drugs*, Zurich, Apr 1978
—— *Structure and Activities*, Geneva, 1986
Illich, I., *Limits to Medicine*, Penguin, London, 1977
IOCU, *Anabolic Steroids: availability and marketing*, Penang, Aug 1983
—— 'Chloramphenicol: recommended uses and warnings', *International Consumer*, Vol. 14, No. 3, Autumn 1973, pp.11–15
—— *Clioquinol: availability and instructions for use*, The Hague, June 1975
—— 'Food first, never anabolic steroids', *Consumer Interpol Focus*, No. 6, Dec 1983
IOMS, 'Consumer protection – World Health Organization – results of the 1986 World Health Assembly', No. 86-22, 23 May 1986
—— 'World Health Organization – Heritage Foundation report on politicization of WHO – assessment of report and its impact on industry relations with WHO', No. 86-19, 12 May 1986
—— 'World Health Organization: results of Nairobi Conference on the rational use of drugs', New York, Dec 1985
Islam, N., 'Health care in rural areas', *Bangladesh Quarterly*, Vol. 7, No. 4, Dec 1987, pp.42–3
—— 'Three years of Bangladesh drug policy', *Bangladesh Quarterly*, Vol. 6, No. 3-4, Mar and Jun 1986, pp.33–6

Janviroj, P., 'Pharmaceutical patents: fight without compromise', *The Nation* (Thailand), 9 Dec 1987
—— 'The politics of drugs', *The Nation* (Thailand), 8 Dec 1987
Jayasuriya, D. C., *The Public Health and Economic Dimensions of the New Drug Policy of Bangladesh*, PMA, Washington, 1985
Jenkins, R., *Transnational Corporations and Uneven Development: the internationalization of capital and the Third World*, Methuen, London, 1987
Johnstone, M., 'Malaria: prospects for new drugs and vaccines', *Health Horizons*, No. 1, May 1987
Jøldal, B., 'Selecting drugs on the basis of need', *World Health Forum*, Vol. 6, 1985, pp.67–9
Jørgensen, V., *Poor Women and Health in Bangladesh*, SIDA, Stockholm, 1983

Joyce, C., 'US withholds its subscription to the WHO', *New Scientist*, 18 June 1987, p.28

Kaech, R., *From Pharmaceutical Research to Medical Information*, Pharma Information, Basle, 1978

Kagimba, J., *The Problems of Drug Supply in Primary Health Care in Developing Countries* (mimeo), AMREF, Nairobi, Aug 1983

Kathe, H., Laschet, H. and Schuler, G. (eds.), *Drugs and the Third World: facts, figures and the future*, BPI, Frankfurt, 1982

Kennedy, I., *The Unmasking of Medicine*, Paladin, London, 1983

'Kill or cure', transcript of radio programme broadcast on BBC Radio,15 Sep 1985

Kingman, S., 'AIDS brings health into focus', *New Scientist*, 20 May 1989, pp.37–42

—— 'Medical research on trial', *New Scientist*, 18 Sep 1986, pp.48–52

Kotulak, R. and Van, J., 'They write, patients suffer: many doctors suffer "Rx fever"', *Chicago Tribune*, 9 Oct 1980, p.1

Lall, S., *Major Issues in Transfer of Technology to Developing Countries: a case study of the pharmaceutical industry* (TD/B/C.6/4), United Nations, New York, 1975

Lamb, W. H. et al, 'Changes in maternal and child mortality rates in three isolated Gambian villages over ten years', *Lancet*, 20 Oct 1984, pp.912–4

Lankester, T. E., 'The central dilemma: destroy or develop', *British Medical Journal*, Vol. 293, 26 Jul 1986, pp.260–1

Lappe, M., *When Antibiotics Fail*, North Atlantic Books, Berkeley, 1986

Laurance, R., 'Bangladesh: faith in the future', *Health Horizons*, No. 6, Jan 1989, pp.24–5

Laurence, D. R. and Bennett, P. N., *Clinical Pharmacology* (6th edn), Churchill Livingstone, London, 1987

Lauridsen, E., 'But some are more essential than others!', *World Health*, Jul 1984, pp.3–5

Ledogar, R. J., *Hungry for Profits*, IDOC, New York, 1975

Leisinger, K. M., *Poverty, Sickness and Medicines: an unholy alliance?*, IFPMA, Geneva, 1989

Lesser, F., 'Drug firm pays the price for deception', *New Scientist*, 8 Jan 1987, p.28

—— 'A drug on the market', *New Scientist*, 18 May 1978, pp.442–4

—— 'Drugs monitor needs sharper teeth', *New Scientist*, 17 Mar 1983

Levi, J., 'Patent side-effects hit Wellcome', *Business*, Jan 1988, p.32

Lewis, P., 'Divided World Health Organization braces for leadership change', *New York Times*, 24 Apr 1988

Lexchin, J., 'Doctors and detailers: therapeutic education or pharmaceutical promotion?', *International Journal of Health Services*, Vol. 19, No. 4, 1989, pp.663–79

—— 'The pharmaceutical industry in Canada', *HAI News*, No. 46, Apr 1989, p.2

—— 'Pharmaceutical promotion in Canada: convince them or confuse them', *International Journal of Health Services*, Vol. 17, No. 1, 1987, pp.77–89

Liebenau, J. M., 'Innovation in pharmaceuticals: industrial R&D in the early twentieth century', *Research Policy*, 14, 1985, pp.179–87

—— 'Medicine and technology', *Perspectives in Biology and Medicine*, Autumn 1983, pp.76–92

Lionel, W. and Herxheimer, A., 'Coherent policies on drugs', *World Health Forum*, Vol. 3, 1982, pp.285–96

Liskin, L. S. and Quillin, W. F., 'Long-acting progestins — promise and prospects', *Population Reports*, Series K, No. 2, May 1983

Litvack, J. I., Shepard, D. S. and Quick, J. D., 'Setting the price of essential drugs: necessity and affordability', *Lancet*, 12 Aug 1989, pp.376–9

London School of Hygiene and Tropical Medicine and the Royal Tropical Institute, *An Evaluation of WHO's Action Programme on Essential Drugs*, DANIDA, Copenhagen, 1989

López, R. (ed.), *Medicamentos: los casos de Bolivia, Brasil, Chile y Perú*, Acción Internacional por la Salud, Chimbote, 1988

Loshak, D., 'The Maldives: a practical approach', *Wellcome Journal*, Apr 1986, pp.8–11

Lowndes, V., 'ABPI assistance in the Maldives', *Health Horizons*, No. 1, May 1987, pp.8–10

Lucas, C. P., 'Africare', *Health Horizons*, No. 2, Sep 1987, pp.8–10

Lunde, I. and Dukes, M. N. G., 'On regulating regulation', *European Journal of Clinical Pharmacology*, Vol. 19, 1981, pp.1–2

Mabud, M.A., *Women's Development, Income and Fertility in Bangladesh*, External Evaluation Unit, Planning Commission/CIDA, Dhaka, 1985

Madden, S. J. and Slovak, J., 'A year of pain and promise', *Fortune* (international edn), 27 Apr 87, p.157

Madeley, J., 'Africa and the drug merchants', *Africa*, No. 101, Jan 1981, pp.74–5

Mahler, H., 'Address on the occasion of the celebration of the fortieth anniversary of WHO and tenth anniversary of the Declaration of Alma-Ata during the 41st World Health Assembly', WHA41/DIV/8, 7 May 1988

―――― 'Essential drugs for all', paper presented at the 11th IFPMA Assembly, Washington, 7–8 Jun 1982

―――― *Rational Drug Use in an Irrational World* (mimeo), speech given at the First International Conference on the Ethical and Moral Problems of Pharmacotherapy, Vatican City, 25 Oct 1986

Maitai, C. K., 'Overreliance on drugs', *East African Medical Journal*, Feb 1984, pp.93–4

―――― and Watkins, W. M., 'A survey of outpatient prescriptions dispensed in Kenyatta National Hospital', *East African Medical Journal*, Vol. 58, No. 9, Sep 1980, pp.641–5

Maitai, C. K., Guantai, A. and Mwangi, J. M., 'Self medication in management of minor health problems in Kenya', *East African Medical Journal*, Vol. 58, No. 8, Aug 1981, pp.593–600

Management Sciences for Health, *Managing Drug Supply*, Boston, 1981

Margo, J., 'A gift for persuasion', *Sydney Morning Herald*, 14 Jan 1989

―――― 'Medicine men bewitch doctors', *Sydney Morning Herald*, 14 Jan 1989

Marsh, P., 'Prescribing all the way to the bank', *New Scientist*, 18 Nov 1989, pp.50–5

*Martindale: the extra pharmacopoeia* (28th edn), Pharmaceutical Press, London, 1982

Marzagao, C. and Segall, M., 'Drug selection: Mozambique', *World Development*, Vol. 11, No. 3, 1983, pp.205–16

Mass, B., *Population Target*, Women's Press, Toronto, 1976

McComas, M., *Europe's Consumer Movement: key issues and corporate responses*, Business International, Geneva, 1980

McDonnell, D., 'Drug company in offer uproar', *Sun* (Australia), 30 Apr 1988

McDonnell, K. (ed.), *Adverse Effects: women and the pharmaceutical industry*, IOCU, Penang, 1986

McFadden, M., 'AIDS stocks worth the gamble', *Fortune* (international edn), 13 Apr 87, p.73

McKeown, T., *The Role of Medicine*, Blackwell, Oxford, 1979

McKinley, J. B. (ed.), *Issues in the Political Economy of Health*, Tavistock Publications, New York, 1982

McMahon, T., Clark, C. M. and Bailie, G. R., 'Who provides patients with drug information?', *British Medical Journal*, Vol. 294, 7 Feb 1987, pp.355–6

Medawar, C., *Drugs and World Health*, IOCU/HAI, The Hague, 1984

————— *Insult or Injury?*, Social Audit, London, 1979

————— 'International regulation of the supply and use of pharmaceuticals', *Development Dialogue*, No. 2, 1985

————— *One Drug At a Time*, IOCU, The Hague, 1984

————— 'The "Spirit of Nairobi"?', (mimeo) paper presented at the International Workshop at the Nordic School of Public Health, Gothenburg, Jun 1986

————— *The Wrong Kind of Medicine?*, Consumers Association and Hodder and Stoughton, London, 1984

————— and Chetley, A., *Promoting Health or Promoting Drugs?*, HAI, Amsterdam, 1988

Melrose, D., *Bitter Pills*, Oxfam, Oxford, 1982

————— 'Double deprivation: public and private drug distribution from the perspective of the Third World poor', *World Development*, Vol. 11, No. 3, 1983, pp.181–6

————— 'Unethical exports', *Development Forum*, Jul–Aug 1981

Mendoza-Escobar, V., 'Unnecessary drug expenditure' in Reyes, D. A. (ed.), *The Philippine Health Situation and the Transnational Drug Companies*, AKAP, Manila, 1982, pp.22–6

Meyer, B. R., 'Improving medical education in therapeutics', *Annals of Internal Medicine*, Vol. 108, No. 1, Jan 1988, pp.145–7

Michel, J.-M., 'Why do people like medicines? A perspective from Africa', *Lancet*, 26 Jan 1985, pp.210–11

*Midland Bank Review*, 'Prospects for the pharmaceutical industry', Summer 1985

Midtvedt, T., 'Increasing worldwide microbial resistance: a worldwide responsibility – for whom?', in Dukes, M. N. G. (ed.), *Side Effects of Drugs Annual 11*, Amsterdam, Elsevier, 1987, pp.223–4

————— 'Increasing worldwide microbial resistance: a worldwide responsibility for all, including the pharmaceutical industry and the World Health Organisation', in Dukes, M. N. G. and Beeley, L. (eds.), *Side Effects of Drugs Annual 12*, Elsevier, Amsterdam, 1988, pp.206–8

Mills, A. and Walker, G. J. A., 'Drugs for the poor of the Third World: consumption and distribution', *Journal of Tropical Medicine and Hygiene*, No. 86, 1983, pp.139–45

Mishell, D. R., 'Current status of intrauterine devices', *New England Journal of Medicine*, Vol. 312, No. 15, 11 Apr 1985, pp.984–5

Mohs, E., 'Infectious diseases and health in Costa Rica: the development of a new paradigm', *Pediatric Infectious Disease*, Vol. 1, No. 3, 1982, pp.212–16

Moore, G., 'Developing drug distribution', *Africa Health*, Dec 1985–Jan 1986, pp.24–5

Morley, D., *Paediatric Priorities in the Developing World*, Butterworth, London, 1977

————— Rohde, J. and Williams, G. (eds.), *Practising Health for All*, Oxford University Press, Oxford, 1983

Mossinghoff, G., *Report on who Conference of Experts on the Rational Use of Drugs*, PMA, Washington, 1 Dec 1985 (report to PMA Board of Directors)

Moulds, R. F. W., Bochner, F. and Wing, L. M. H., 'Drug advertising', *Medical Journal of Australia*, Vol. 145, 4–18 Aug 1986, pp.178–9

Muller, M., 'Roche in the Third World', *New Scientist*, 12 Aug 1976, pp.326–7

——— *The Health of Nations*, Faber and Faber, London, 1982

Murphy, P. A., 'One drug company's sales techniques', *New England Journal of Medicine*, Vol. 313, 25 Jul 1985, p.270


Nakajima, H., address to 14th IFPMA assembly, Washington, DC, 5 Oct 1988

NCIH, *Pharmaceuticals and Developing Countries: a dialogue for constructive action*, Washington, Aug 1982

Neill, J. R., 'A social history of psychotropic drug advertisements', *Social Science and Medicine*, Vol. 28, No. 4, 1989, pp.333–8

Nelkin, D., 'How to doctor the media', *New Scientist*, 20 Nov 1986, pp.51–6

Nelson, D., 'Money talks louder than health in Geneva' (GH 47), Gemini News Service, 20 May 1986

*New Internationalist*, *A Pill for Every Ill* (special issue), No. 165, Nov 1986

Nordic Council on Medicines, *Nordic Statistics on Medicines 1981–1983* (Part 1), Nordic Council on Medicines, Uppsala, Sweden, 1986

Nyazema, N. Z., 'An examination of the use of over-the-counter drugs in Harare', *Central African Journal of Medicine*, Vol. 29, No. 10, Oct 1983, pp.203–9


Ombega, J. N., 'Knowledge and comprehension of therapy by hospital outpatients at Kenyatta National Hospital', *Medicom*, Vol. 5, No. 6, Nov–Dec 1983, pp.165–8


PAHO, *Policies for the Production and Marketing of Essential Drugs* (CD29/DT/1), Washington, 18 Apr 1983

Parish, P., *Medicines: a guide for everybody* (6th edn rev.), Penguin, London, 1989

Parker, P., 'Sierra Leone', *Lancet*, 23 Aug 1986

Peretz, S. M., 'Patients, not political units, urgently need drugs', *Ciba-Geigy Journal*, No. 3, 1981

——— 'Pharmaceuticals in the Third World: the problem from the suppliers' point of view', *World Development*, Vol. 11, No. 3, 1983, pp.259–64

Pfizer, *Pfizer and Third World Health Issues*, New York, 1983

Pharma Information, *An Industry Like No Other*, Basle, 1982

——— *Burundi's Drug Scheme*, Basle, 1986

Phillips, A. and Rakusen, J. (UK eds.), *Our Bodies Ourselves*, Penguin, London, 1978

*The Pill Jungle* (transcript of film), Radio Nederland International, Hilversum, 1985

Pilon, J., 'For the who: the moment of truth', *Heritage Foundation Backgrounder*, 30 Apr 1986

PMA, 'Bangladesh policy caused higher drug prices and lower quality, report finds' (press release), 24 Sep 1985

——— *The Gambia: a case study in improved primary health care through improved pharmaceutical management*, Washington, 1985

——— *The Health Consequences of Restricted Drug Lists*, Washington, 1985

——— *Medicines and the Developing World*, Washington, 1984

——— *Pharmaceutical Product Information in Developing Countries* (mimeo), Washington, 1982

*Population Reports*, 'Immunizing the world's children', Series L, No. 5, Population Information Programme, Johns Hopkins University, Baltimore, 1986

Quanico, U., 'Antidiarrhoeals in the Philippines', *Drug Monitor*, Vol. 2, No. 6, Jun 1987

Rabeneck, S. and Stone, T., *Strategies for Nutrition in CIDA*, CIDA, Ottawa, 1982
Radolf, A., 'UN has bitter pill in mind for international drug firms', *Examiner* (San Francisco), 16 Sep 1981, p.3
Rawlins, M. D., 'Doctors and the drug makers', *Lancet*, 4 Aug 1984, pp.276–8
———— 'How to push the drug industry towards an ethical approach' (letter), *Guardian*, 5 Apr 1983
———— 'Professor Rawlins replies to Harry Schwartz', *Scrip*, No. 1,065/66, 8 Jan 1986, p.19
Ray, J. K., *Organizing Villagers for Self-Reliance: a study of Gonoshasthya Kendra in Bangladesh*, Orient Longman, Calcutta, 1986
Redwood, H., *The Pharmaceutical Industry: trends, problems and achievements*, Oldwicks Press, Felixstowe, 1988
Reich, M. R., *Essential Drugs: who, how and why?*, (mimeo), paper presented at the Notre Dame Program on Multinational Corporations and Third World Development, Conference on Third World Health Problems and the Role of Pharmaceuticals, 11–13 Dec 1985
Reynolds, J. E. F. (ed.), *Martindale: the extra pharmacopoeia* (29th edn), Pharmaceutical Press, London, 1989
Richards, T., 'Drugs and the Third World', *British Medical Journal*, Vol. 290, 5 Jan 1985, pp.52–3
———— editorial, *British Medical Journal*, 24 May 1986
Ridley, H., *Drugs of Choice*, Social Audit, London, 1986
Righter, R., 'Squeeze by drug lobby', *Sunday Times* (London), 9 Aug 1982
Rodriguez, M. C., 'Doctors want list of essential drugs', *Manila Bulletin*, 6 Oct 1986, p.1
Roepnack, C. G., 'Criticizing the critique: the international campaign against the pharmaceutical industry', *Drugs Made in Germany*, Vol. XXVIII, 1985, pp.64–7
Rohde, J. E., 'Selective primary health care: strategies for control of disease in the developing world. XV. Acute diarrhoea', *Reviews of Infectious Diseases*, Vol. 6, No. 6, Nov–Dec 1984, p.846
———— 'Why the other half dies: the science and politics of child mortality in the Third World', *Assignment Children*, No. 61/62, 1983, pp.35–68
Rolt, F., *Pills, Policies and Profits*, War on Want, London, 1985
———— and Learmonth, T., *Underdeveloping Bangladesh*, War on Want, London, 1982
Round, I. R., 'Marketing and advertising trends', *BIRA Journal*, Vol. 5, No. 2, Jul 1986, pp.9–10
Rylance, G. (ed.), *Drugs for Children*, WHO Regional Office for Europe, Copenhagen, 1987

Sakshaug, S., et al (eds.), *Drug Utilization in Norway during the 1970s: increases, inequalities, innovations*, Norwegian Medicinal Depot, Oslo, 1983
Samsom, R. J., speech delivered at the WHA, 17 May 1989
Sanders, D. and Carver, R., *The Struggle for Health*, Macmillan, London, 1986
Saunders, E., *Nestlegate: secret memo reveals corporate cover-up*, Baby Milk Action Coalition, Cambridge, UK, 1981

Saunders, P., 'Fewer drugs, better therapy: learning from the Third World', *Lancet*, 7 Nov 1987

Schwartz, H., 'ACP and the pharma industry – the Schwartz commentary', *Scrip*, No. 1,297/8, 6–8 Apr 1988, pp.18–19

——— 'A drug-code warm-up', *Pharmaceutical Executive*, Aug 1981

——— 'A further look at Nairobi – the Schwartz column', *Scrip*, No. 1,069, 20 Jan 1986, p.17

——— 'AIDS and the World Health Organization – the Schwartz commentary', *Scrip*, No. 1,170, 14 Jan 1987, pp.24–5

——— 'A war on drugs, "new order" style', *Wall Street Journal*, 24 Mar 1983

——— 'A world apart: physician attitudes here and abroad', *Pharmaceutical Executive*, Sep 1987, p.16

——— 'Great industry–WHO debate: the Schwartz column', *Scrip*, No. 1,114, 25 Jun 1986, pp.20–1

——— 'The Schwartz commentary on "The Economist" on drug discovery', *Scrip*, No. 1,344/5, 16/21 Sep 1988, p.19

——— 'The Schwartz commentary on the Nairobi Conference', *Scrip*, No. 1,060, 16 Dec 1985, pp.20–1

——— 'Where were the scientists at Montreux? – the Schwartz commentary', *Scrip*, No. 1,154, 12 Nov 1986, p.22

——— 'The WHO and the pharma industry … again – the Schwartz commentary', *Scrip*, No. 1,303, 27 Apr 1988, pp.22–3

*Scrip*, various issues

*Scrip Changes and Trends: an analysis of four years of Scrip's League Tables*, PJB Publications, Richmond, UK, July 1986

*Scrip Yearbook 1987*, PJB Publications, Richmond, UK, Dec 1986

Sekhar, C., Raina, R. K. and Pillai, G. K., 'Some aspects of drug use in Ethiopia', *Tropical Doctor*, Jul 1981, pp.116–18

Seligmann, J. and Glass, C., 'Overdosing on antibiotics', *Newsweek*, 17 Aug 1981

Senturias, E. N. et al, *A Preliminary Study on the Prescribing Habits of Physicians in Manila, Philippines* (mimeo), National Council of Churches in the Philippines, Manila, 1984

Sepulveda, C. and Meneses, E. (eds.), *The Pharmaceutical Industry in ASEAN Countries*, UN Asian and Pacific Development Institute, Bangkok, 1980

Shahidullah, A. K. M., 'Pharmaceutical industries' view of Drug Control Ordinance 1982', *The Bangladesh Times*, 9 Oct 1986

Shapiro, S., et al, 'Fatal drug reactions among medical inpatients', *Journal of the American Medical Association*, No. 216, 1971

Sheoin, T. M., 'Unethical behaviour in an ethical industry? critical coverage of the pharmaceutical industry, 1985–1986', *International Journal of Health Services*, Vol. 18, No. 3, 1988, pp.495–517

Shulman, J., 'Limited list: a personal view', *Pharmacy Update*, Apr 1985, p.45

Sidahmed, A., 'Medicine: a healthy business?', *Sudanow*, Jun 1981, pp.52–3

Silverman, M., *The Drugging of the Americas*, University of California Press, Berkeley, 1976

——— Lee, P. R. and Lydecker, M., 'Drug promotion: the Third World revisited', *International Journal of Health Services*, Vol. 16, No. 4, 1986, pp.659–67

——— *Prescriptions for Death: the drugging of the Third World*, University of California Press, Berkeley, 1982

Smith, D., 'When misleading ads can kill', *National Times* (Australia), 17–23 May 1985, p.24

Sonenclar, R., 'Prescription for profits: be selective, be careful', *Financial World*, 17–30 Oct 1984, p.14

Soumerai, S. B. and Avorn, J., 'Economic and policy analysis of university-based drug "detailing"', *Medical Care*, Vol. 24, No. 4, Apr 1986, pp.313–31

Starrels, J. M., *The World Health Organization – resisting Third World ideological pressures*, Heritage Foundation, Washington, DC, 1985

St George, D., 'Life expectancy, truth, and the ABPI' (letter), *Lancet*, 9 Aug 1986, p.346
———— and Draper, P., 'A health policy for Europe?', *Lancet*, 29 Aug 1981, pp.463–5

Stearns, B., 'RAD-AR: homing in on risk', *Ciba-Geigy Journal*, No. 2, 1987

Sterky, G., 'Towards Another Development in health', *Development Dialogue*, No. 1, 1978
———— and Krantz, I. (eds.), *Society and HIV/AIDS: selected knowledge base for research and action*, Karolinska Institutet, Stockholm, 1988

Stimson, G. V., 'Information contained in drug advertisements', *British Medical Journal*, 29 Nov 1975, pp.508–9

Strom, B. L., 'Generic drug substitution revisited', *New England Journal of Medicine*, Vol. 316, No. 23, 4 Jun 1987, pp.1,456–62

Sutton, J., McEwin, K. and Kwok, Y. S., *Women and Tranquillisers*, Women's Co-ordination Unit, Sydney, Apr 1986


Tan, M., 'Banned, withdrawn and restricted drugs in the Philippines', *Drug Monitor*, Vol. 2, No. 10, Oct 1987
———— *Dying for Drugs*, HAIN, Manila, 1988
———— 'A short primer on rational drug policy', *Drug Monitor*, No. 9, 15 Oct 1986
———— et al, 'Drug needs and utilization patterns in four urban poor communities of Metro Manila', *Drug Monitor*, Vol. 3, No. 4, Apr 1988

Taylor, D., *Development, Health and the Need for Pharmaceuticals*, ABPI, London, 1985
———— 'Drugs in the Third World' (letter to the editor), *Listener*, 3 Oct 1985
———— *Medicines, Health and the Poor World*, Office of Health Economics, London, 1982
———— 'Why the medicine men feel misunderstood', *Guardian*, 2 Nov 1983
———— and Griffin, J. P., *Orphan Diseases, Orphan Medicines and Orphan Patients*, ABPI, London, 1985

Taylor, D. and Miller, D., *RAD-AR: an executive summary*, Ciba-Geigy, Basle, Mar 1988

Teeling-Smith, G., 'The golden triangle', *Times Health Supplement*, 29 Jan 1982, p.17
———— 'The politics of pharmaceutical prices in Britain', *Health Herald*, Jun 1984
———— and Wells, N. (eds.), *Medicines For the Year 2000*, OHE, London, 1979

Temple, R. J., 'The DESI Programme', in *Proceedings of the Third International Conference of Drug Regulatory Authorities*, Swedish National Board of Health and Welfare/WHO, Uppsala, 1984, pp.13–18

Thomas, H., 'When family planning is necessary', *Guardian,* 18 Jul 1984

Timmins, N., 'Psychologists can cut GPs' drug bills, survey shows', *The Times*, 16 Jan 1984, p.3

Tiranti, D., *The Bangladesh Example: four years on*, IOCU/New Internationalist/War on Want, Penang/Oxford/London, 1986

Tisdall, P., 'Medicinal maelstrom', *Marketing*, 12 Apr 1984, pp.27–30

Tomson, G. and Sterky, G., 'Self-prescribing by way of pharmacies in three Asian developing countries', *Lancet*, 13 Sep 1986, pp.620–1

Totaro, P., 'Row as drug firm offers doctors prize', *Daily Telegraph* (Australia), 29 Apr 1988

Townsend, P. and Davidson, N., *Inequalities in Health*, Penguin, London, 1982

Toynbee, P., 'The patients who get hooked on tranquillisers', *Guardian*, 25 Nov 1985

Tucker, D., *The World Health Market*, Euromonitor Publications, London, 1984

Tudge, C., 'Pills? You ain't seen nothing yet!', *New Scientist*, 28 May 1987, p.62

Turner, J., 'World Health Assembly', *Lancet*, 3 Jun 1989, pp.1,277–8


UN, *Towards a World Economy That Works*, United Nations, New York, 1980

UNCTAD, *Case Studies in the Transfer of Technology: the pharmaceutical industry in India* (TD/B/C.6/20), United Nations, New York, 1977

———— *Guidelines on Technology Issues in the Pharmaceutical Sector in the Developing Countries* (UNCTAD/TT/49), United Nations, New York, 1982

———— *Technology and Development Perspectives of the Pharmaceutical Sector in Ethiopia* (UNCTAD/TT/58), United Nations, New York, 1984

UNCTC, *Transnational Corporations and the Pharmaceutical Industry* (ST/CTC/9), United Nations, New York, 1979

———— *Transnational Corporations in the Pharmaceutical Industry of Developing Countries* (ST/CTC/49), United Nations, New York, 1984

UNDP/World Bank/WHO, *Newsletter* (Special Programme for Research and Training in Tropical Disease), No. 23, May 1986

———— *Science at Work*, WHO, Geneva, 1986

———— *Tropical Disease Research*, 7th Programme Report, WHO, Geneva, 1985

———— *Venture for Health*, WHO, Geneva, 1984

UNFPA, *1984 Report*, New York, 1985

UNICEF, *The State of the World's Children 1984*, Oxford University Press, Oxford, 1983

———— *The State of the World's Children 1986*, Oxford University Press, Oxford, 1985

———— *The State of the World's Children 1987*, Oxford University Press, Oxford, 1986

———— *The State of the World's Children 1988*, Oxford University Press, Oxford, 1987

———— *The State of the World's Children 1989*, Oxford University Press, Oxford, 1988

———— *The State of the World's Children 1990*, Oxford University Press, Oxford, 1989

————/WHO/UNESCO, *Facts for Life*, New York, 1989

UNIDO, *Assessment of the Pharmaceutical Industry in Developing Countries, its Potential, and the National and International Action Required to Promote its Development* (ID/WG.292/2), 1978

———— *The Development of the Pharmaceutical Industry in Six Countries in Latin America*, 1978

———— *The Growth of the Pharmaceutical Industry in Developing Countries: problems and prospects*, 1978

———— *Lima Declaration and Plan of Action on Industrial Development and Co-operation*, Second General Conference of UNIDO, 1975

———— *Report of the Inter-regional Meeting to Prepare for Consultations on the Pharmaceutical Industry*, Cairo, (ID/WG.293/3/Rev.1), 1979

———— *The Steps Involved in Establishing a Pharmaceutical Industry in Developing Countries* (ID/WG.267/3), 1978

———— *Summary of the World-wide Study of the Pharmaceutical Industry, Preliminary Draft*, 1978

US Senate, *Examination of the Pharmaceutical Industry, Subcommittee on Health of the Committee on Labor and Public Welfare*, Washington, 1974

van der Geest, S., 'The illegal distribution of Western medicines in developing countries: pharmacists, drug peddlars, injection doctors and others. A bibliographic exploration', *Medical Anthropology*, Fall 1982, pp.197–219

Vane, J. and Gutteridge, W., 'TDR and the drug industry', *World Health*, May 1985, p.23

Veitch, A., 'Arthritis drug Suprol withdrawn', *Guardian*, 24 Oct 1986

———— 'BMA wants action against misleading drug adverts', *Guardian*, 30 Nov 1984

———— 'Civil servant to head drug firms', *Guardian*, 9 Jul 1984

———— 'Company objected to report critical of drug', *Guardian*, 14 Mar 1986

———— 'Criticism of tests on new drug by doctors', *Guardian*, 5 Nov 1984

———— 'Drug industry chief criticised promotion tactics', *Guardian*, 9 Mar 1983

———— 'Half drug adverts break firms' code of practice, says survey', *Guardian*, 13 Sep 1984

———— 'Ministry man takes top drug industry job', *Guardian*, 12 Jul 1984

———— 'Standard bearer', *Guardian*, 5 Sep 1984

Victora, C. G., Facchini, L. A. and Filho, M. G., 'Drug usage in Southern Brazilian hospitals', *Tropical Doctor*, Vol. 12, Oct 1982, pp.231–5

Victorian Medical Postgraduate Foundation, *Antibiotic Project Committee 1985 Report* and *Antibiotic Project Committee 1986 Report*, Adelaide

von Wartensleben, A., 'Major issues concerning pharmaceutical policies in the Third World', *World Development*, Vol. 11, No. 3, Mar 1983

Wade, V. A., Mansfield, P. R. and McDonald, P. J., 'Drug companies' evidence to justify advertising', *Lancet*, 25 Nov 1989, pp.1261–3

Walden, R. J., 'Doctors and the drug makers' (letter to the editor), *Lancet*, 18 Aug 1984, p.405

Waldholz, M., 'Pill promoters: marketing often is the key to success of prescription drugs', *Wall Street Journal*, 28 Dec 1981

Walton, H., 'Ad recognition and prescribing by physicians', *Journal of Advertising Research*, Vol. 20, No. 3, Jun 1980, pp.39–48

Washington Business Information, *The Food and Drug Letter*, 17 Jul 1981

Wassermann, U., 'Pharmaceuticals for the Fourth World', *Journal of World Trade Law*, Vol. 13, No. 2, Mar–Apr 1979, pp.178–81

Wein, P. J. and Hoffmann, R. P., 'What really sells a drug today?', *Hospital Pharmacy*, Vol. 23, May 1988, pp.478–9

Weitz, M., *Health Shock* (rev. edn), Hamlyn Paperbacks, London, 1982

Weller, T. H., 'Too few and too little: barricades to the pursuit of health', *Reviews of Infectious Diseases*, Vol. 5, No. 6, Nov–Dec 1983, pp.994–1002

WEMOS, *Organon and Anabolic Steroids*, Amsterdam, 1987

WFPMM, *Self-Medication – Making It Work Better For More People* (proceedings of 8th General Assembly, 21–23 Sep 1986, Washington), Bonn, 1987

WGBH Educational Foundation, 'Prescriptions for profit', *Frontline*, WGBH Transcripts, Boston, 1989, transcript of TV documentary broadcast on 28 Mar 1989

Wheelwright, E. L., 'Consumers, transnational corporations and the developing world in the 80s. I. The Drug Industry' and 'IV. The Corporate Response', papers presented at the 11th World Congress of the International Organization of Consumers Unions, Bangkok, 9–14 Dec 1984

White, A., *British Official Aid in the Health Sector*, IDS Discussion Paper No. 107, University of Sussex, Brighton, 1977

WHO, *Abuse of Narcotic and Psychotropic Substances* (progress report by the Director General, Doc. No. A39/10 Add.1), Geneva, 5 May 1986

—— *Basic Documents* (35th edn), Geneva, 1985

—— 'Certification scheme on the quality of pharmaceutical products moving in international commerce', *WHO Chronicle*, Vol. 31, No. 12, 1977

—— *Conference of Experts on the Rational Use of Drugs, Report by the Director-General, Part IV* (Doc. No. A39/12 Part IV), Geneva, 10 Feb 1986

—— *Essential Drugs Monitor*, various issues, 1985–9

—— *Ethical Criteria for Medicinal Drug Promotion*, Geneva, 1988

—— *Expanded Programme on Immunization* (progress report by the Director General, Doc. No. A39/15), Geneva, 6 March 1986

—— 'Finances of WHO receive a welcome boost – prospects of an end to financial crisis?' (press release WHA/9), 9 May 1988

—— *Guidelines for Developing National Drug Policies*, Geneva, 1988

—— *Handbook of Resolutions and Decisions, Vol. II, 1973–1984*, Geneva, 1985

—— *International Code of Marketing of Breast-milk Substitutes*, Geneva, 1981

—— *Kenya: rural drug distribution programme*, WHO Action Programme on Essential Drugs and Vaccines, Geneva, 1985

—— *A Manual for the Treatment of Acute Diarrhoea* (Doc. No. WHO/CDD/SER/80.2), Geneva, 1980

—— 'Medicinal products for all who need them', *WHO Chronicle*, Vol. 32, 1978, pp.280–2

—— *Primary Health Care* (report of the International Conference on Primary Health Care, Alma-Ata, USSR, 6–12 Sep 1978), Geneva, 1978

—— *Progress*, No. 1, Feb 1987

—— *Prophylactic and Therapeutic Substances* (report by the Director General, Doc. No. A28/11), 3 Apr 1975

—— *Rational Use of Drugs* (resolution WHA37.33), 17 May 1984

—— 'Rational use of drugs: cooperation prevails at WHO Conference in "spirit of Nairobi"' (press release WHO/32), 3 Dec 1985

—— *The Rational Use Of Drugs: report of the conference of experts, Nairobi, 25–29 November 1985*, Geneva, 1987

—— *Report of the Director-General on the Work of WHO in 1986 and Progress Report on the Global Strategy for Health For All By The Year 2000* (Doc. No. A40/3), Geneva, 18 Feb 1987

—— *Report of the WHO Meeting on Collaboration between the Pharmaceutical Industry and International Agencies in Reducing Drug Abuse* (Doc. No. MNH/PAD/87.1), Geneva, 1987

—— *The Selection of Essential Drugs* (Technical Report Series No. 615), Geneva, 1977

—— *Special Programme of Research, Development and Research Training in Human Reproduction: 40th annual report*, Geneva, 1985

—— *Summary of Progress in the WHO Action Programme on Essential Drugs and Vaccines*, Geneva, Apr 1987

—— *Surveillance for the Prevention and Control of Health Hazards due to Antibiotic-resistant Enterobacteria* (Technical Report Series No. 624), Geneva 1978

――― *The Treatment and Prevention of Acute Diarrhoea: practical guidelines* (2nd edn), Geneva, 1989

――― *The Use of Essential Drugs – Model List of Essential Drugs (Fifth List)* (Technical Report Series No. 770), Geneva, 1988

――― *The Use of Essential Drugs* (Technical Report Series No. 722), Geneva, 1985

――― WHO's Revised Drug Strategy: report by the Director-General (Doc. No. A39/13), Geneva, 10 Feb 1986

――― WHO's Revised Drug Strategy: report by the Director-General (EB81/25 Annex i), Geneva, 22 Dec 1987

――― *The World Drug Situation*, Geneva, 1988

WHO and UNICEF, *But Some Drugs Are More Essential Than Others*, WHO, Geneva, 1986

Wilkinson, J., 'Genetic engineering', *Business Life*, Apr/May 1987, pp.11–14

Willard, N., 'Antibiotics: the resistance problem', *WHO Features*, No. 89, Oct 1984

Williams, G., 'WHO: reaching out to all', *World Health Forum*, Vol. 9, No. 2, 1988

Williams, I., 'Pills are not the doctor's orders', *Sunday Times* (London), 24 Feb 1985

Williams, J. D., editorial, *Health Horizons*, No. 4, May 1988

Williams, R. M., 'Capital clout', *Foundation News*, Jul/Aug 1989, pp.14–19

Wood, M., *Pharmaceuticals in the Third World*, AMREF, Nairobi, Jun 1982. Text of a speech delivered at the IFPMA assembly in Washington, DC, Jun 1982

World Bank, *Briefing Note: UNICEF's Bamako Initiative*, Washington, 23 Feb 1988

――― *World Development Report 1980*, Oxford University Press, New York, 1980

Yarrow, M., 'Doctors and the drug makers' (letter to the editor), *Lancet*, 18 Aug 1984, p.405

Yudkin, J. S., 'Provision of medicines in a developing country', *Lancet*, 15 Apr 1978, pp.810–12

# Glossary of drugs

The information in this glossary is drawn from *The British Medical Association Guide to Medicines & Drugs*, the *British National Formulary*, the American Medical Association's *Drug Evaluations*, Goodman and Gilman's *The Pharmacological Basis of Therapeutics* and *Martindale: the extra pharmacopoeia*. Common brand names are often included within brackets.

**acetaminophen** – (*See* analgesics/paracetamol)

**anabolic steroids** – drugs which stimulate the growth protein in body tissues. They possess some of the actions of male sex hormones. They are promoted as an aid in recovery from serious illness as well as in debilitating disease, but evidence is scanty about their effectiveness. They have also been promoted as both growth and appetite stimulants for children, a use which cannot be justified, as they can actually stunt the growth of young children, and can interfere with sexual development

**analgesics** – pain killers (*See also* NSAIDs)
- **amidopyrine/aminopyrone** – a drug which can cause a fatal blood disorder (agranulocytosis), which makes it unsuitable for use
- **aspirin** – kills pain, reduces inflammation and fever; probably the most widely-used pain killer in the world. In large doses, it is also considered effective in treating arthritic conditions. It can cause gastric irritation, its most common side effect. It should be avoided in children under 12 years of age as it has been associated with Reye's syndrome.
- **benzydamine hydrochloride** (Benzitrat) – kills pain, reduces inflammation and fever; usually used as a cream in rheumatic disorders; occasionally used as a mouth wash or spray to treat inflammation in the mouth or throat
- **cocaine** – once used as a local anaesthetic; because of its side effects and potential for abuse, it now has little use in medicine
- **codeine** – a mild to moderate pain killer, also useful as a cough suppressant; may cause constipation, and can be habit-forming, although not usually if taken for a limited period and at recommended doses
- **dipyrone** – a salt of amidopyrine, possessing similar properties
- **ibuprofen** – both a pain killer and anti-inflammatory agent which has fewer side effects than many of the other NSAIDs
- **morphine** – a narcotic pain killer, derived from opium, usually used under strict medical supervision for the relief of severe pain

- **opium** – a narcotic pain killer, with slower action than morphine; occasionally used in small doses in combination cough or antidiarrhoeal preparations. Prolonged use may lead to dependence
- **paracetamol** (Tempra) – useful in the treatment of mild pain and to reduce fever; few side effects, but overdose is dangerous as it can cause serious damage to the liver and kidneys
- **phenacetin** – pain killer and fever reducing drug which is now little used due to its potentially serious adverse effects on the blood and kidneys

**antibiotics** – drugs (originally derived from moulds and fungi) which either kill bacteria or prevent them from multiplying. Antibiotics are useless in viral infections. (*See also* sulphonamides)

- **amoxycillin** (Augmentin) – from the penicillin family of antibiotics, useful in the treatment of ear, nose and throat infections, respiratory tract infections, cystitis, uncomplicated gonorrhoea and some skin and soft tissue infections
- **ampicillin** – from the penicillin family
- **cephalosporins** – broad spectrum antibiotics similar to the penicillins, and often used when penicillin treatment has proved ineffective
  - **cephalexin** (Ceporex, Keflex) – useful in the treatment of bronchitis, cystitis and some skin and soft tissue infections, but may be considered inconvenient as it has to be taken four times a day due to its short duration of action. Diarrhoea is a common side effect
- **chloramphenicol** – may cause serious or even fatal blood disorders; for this reason, oral or injectable chloramphenicol is reserved for life-threatening infections that do not respond to safer drugs
- **chlortetracycline** – a tetracycline antibiotic
- **cotrimoxazole** (Bactrim, Septrin) – a combination of trimethoprim and sulphamethoxazole used for urinary tract, respiratory or gastrointestinal infections, as well as infections of the skin and ear. Concern has recently been expressed about increasing bacterial resistance to the drug and to the fact that side effects are a combination of the two ingredients. Trimethoprim on its own has fewer side effects and is equally effective in many conditions
- **erythromycin** – one of the safest and most widely used antibiotics, it is useful as an alternative to penicillins and tetracyclines for people who are allergic to those drugs; although courses of longer than 10 days may increase the risk of liver disaese
- **flucloxacillin** (Floxapen) – effective in penicillin-resistant *Staphylococci* infections
- **neomycin** – considered too toxic to be administered by injection, and oral doses are poorly absorbed; can cause damage to the kidneys and to the eyes
- **oxytetracycline** – a tetracycline antibiotic
- **penicillin** – one of the first and still an important antibiotic
- **streptomycin** – now generally reserved for the treatment of tuberculosis

- **tetracycline** – among the most widely prescribed of antibiotics; should be avoided in children and pregnant women as it leads to the discolouration of children's teeth. Should also be avoided in people with poor kidney function

**anti-cancer drugs** – powerful drugs used to kill cancer cells which can also kill healthy cells, and particularly affect the blood producing cells in bone marrow

**anti-coagulants** – help to maintain normal blood flow in people at risk from blood clot formation. The most widely used are heparin (by injection) and warfarin (orally)

**antidiarrhoeals** – a wide variety of different agents is used to prevent diarrhoea. The main types of drugs used to relieve non-specific diarrhoeas are: narcotics such as codeine, diphenoxylate or loperamide; or bulk-forming agents or adsorbents. Antispasmodics, such as atropine, may be used to relieve accompanying pain. None of these products should be used without first determining that the diarrhoea is neither infectious nor toxic. And none of these products deal with the major medical problem caused by diarrhoea: the loss of body fluids and minerals and subsequent dehydration. For this, oral rehydration therapy is recommended

- **adsorbents** – absorb water and irritants present in the bowel so producing larger and firmer stools less frequently
  - **kaolin** (usually with pectin) (ADM) – although widely used in anti-diarrhoeal products, there are no well controlled studies which demonstrate any benefit or effectiveness
  - **atropine** – in addition to its antispasmodic action, because of its unpleasant effects in overdose, it is used in combination whith diphenoxylate which is a potentially dependence-inducing drug, to deter excessive dosage
  - **clioquinol** (Entero-Vioform) – described by the *British National Formulary* as 'valueless'; should be avoided as it is neurotoxic
  - **diphenoxylate** (with atropine) (Lomotil) – a narcotic which reduces muscle contractions which allows more time for water to be absorbed from food residues in the bowel and reduces the fluidity and frequency of bowel movements. Should be avoided if the diarrhoea is caused by an infection, since it may slow the elimination of the infecting micro-organisms from the intestine; should not be used in young children
  - **oral rehydration solution** (ORS) – provides a balanced amount of sodium, potassium and glucose to enhance the absorption of water and essential minerals, is simple to use and prepare and is effective in treating dehydration caused by diarrhoea

**anti-epileptic drugs** – drugs which neutralise excessive electrical activity in the brain. As they also affect normal brain activity, the dose has to be carefully adjusted to the individual. Additionally, most of these drugs affect the liver's ability to break down other drugs

**antihypertensives** – drugs used to lower blood pressure

- **angiotensin-converting enzyme** (ACE) **inhibitors** – drugs which block the activity of an enzyme which encourages constriction of the blood vessels, therefore the blood vessels dilate, improving blood flow and reducing the force with which the heart needs to pump blood
  - **captopril** (Capoten) – may cause a variety of minor gastrointestinal side effects. Rashes, which occur frequently, ususally disappear soon. Large doses have been associated with altered kidney function
- **beta-blockers** – drugs which interrupt the transmission of stimuli throughout the body by ineterfereing with the action of the hormone nor-adrenaline. They therefore reduce the force and speed at which the heart pumps blood
  - **propranolol** (Inderal LA) – also used to reduce the physical symptoms of anxiety
- **nifedipine** (Adalat Retard) – a calcium channel blocker which prevents the movement of calcium in the muscles of blood vessels and so encourages them to dilate. The action helps to reduce blood pressure and relieves the strain on the heart muscle in angina by making it easier for the heart to pump blood

**antiparasitics** – (or anthelmintics) often kill or paralyse parasitic worms (helminths) and they pass out of the body
- **ivermectin** – now the drug of choice for the treatment of river blindness (onchocerciasis)

**anti-ulcer drugs** – the most commonly used anti-ulcer drugs are $H_2$ blockers which prevent histamine from triggering the production of stomach acid, thereby allowing the tissue under the ulcer to heal. They are among the most widely prescribed drugs in the world
- **cimetidine** – side effects are rare, but continuous use of the drug for longer than one year is not recommended
- **ranitidine** – unlike cimetidine, it does not affect the action of certain enzymes in the liver where other drugs are broken down; however, like cimetidine, continuous use for longer than one year is not recommended

**appetite stimulants** – a large variety of products have been promoted as appetite stimulants. They are seldom required and most independent medical experts advise identifying and treating the cause of loss of appetite or growth failure rather than focusing on this symptom, which is common in many illnesses
- **pizotifen** – an antihistamine which is generally used for the prevention of migraine headaches; prolonged use often causes weight gain, and it has been promoted as an appetite stimulant mainly in developing countries

**arsphenamine** (Salvarsan) – an arsenic derivative formerly used in the treatment of syphillis

**azidothymidine/zidovudine** (Retrovir) – an antiviral drug which prolongs life expectancy in patients with acquired immune deficiency syndrome (AIDS), although it does not cure the disease

**cardiac glycosides** – drugs which improve the heart's pumping action
- **digitalis** – for the drug to be effective, the dose must be very near the toxic dose and treatment must be monitored carefully

**chloroquine** – used for the prevention and treatment of malaria, although it is not suitable for use in all countries due to resistance. Also used in the tratment of rheumatoid arthritis. Should not be used in combination with products containing kaolin, as the kaolin may reduce the absorption of the chloroquine

**contraceptives** – drugs or devices which prevent pregnancy

- **Depo-Provera** – a long-acting progestogen (female sex hormone) given by injection; provides a contraceptive effect for about three months. A major disadvantage is disruption to the menstrual cycle, often with heavy and irregular bleeding. A further disadvantage is that the contraceptive effect may last for several months after discontinuation of treatment
- IUDs (**intra-uterine devices**) – usually copper devices inserted into the uterus. They increase the risk of pelvic inflammatory disease and possible infertility
  - **Dalkon Shield** – an IUD which, because of its design, has been highly associated with pelvic inflammatory disease; withdrawn from sale worldwide in 1975
- **oral** – pills containing either a synthetic form of the female sex hormone progestogen or progestogen with another female sex hormone, oestrogen. They disrupt the normal menstrual cycle by either preventing the release of the egg in the female, or by thickening the mucus lining of the cervix, making it impenetrable to sperm. The main risks are an increase in circulatory disorders, particularly in women who smoke

**cough and cold remedies** – most proprietary cough and cold 'remedies' have little effect on the course of the illness; at best, they supress some of the more annoying symptoms, at worst, they trigger off unpleasant side effects

- **bromhexine** (Bisolcillin, also contains ampicillin) – a mucolytic which makes phlegm and lung mucus more fluid, thereby supposedly making it easier to spit out. Most independent experts agree that few patients derive any real benefit from this effect. Studies have shown that when used in combination with an antibiotic, the bromhexine improves the ability of the antibiotic to penetrate the secretions in the lungs; however, antibiotic treatment in ordinary cough and colds is generally unnecessary

**iron** – an essential mineral; most average diets supply adequate amounts, however larger amounts are necessary during pregnancy; overdosage is extremely dangerous

**isoniazid** – drug used in the prevention and, in combination with other drugs, for the treatment of tuberculosis. May cause vitamin $B_6$ deficiency

**laxatives** – stimulant drugs which either encourage the contraction of the bowel muscle which speeds the passage of faecal matter through the large intestine, thus allowing less time for water to be absorbed and making the faeces more liquid; or bulk-forming agents which absorb many times their own volume of water, increase the bulk of the faeces and encourage bowel action. Prolonged use leads to dependence on the drugs for normal bowel action; they should be avoided in children

**mefloquine** – an antimalarial drug, generally reserved for the treatment (or prevention) of chloroquine-resistant malaria

**nitroglycerin** (Transderm Nitro) – used for the treatment of angina

**NSAIDs** – drugs used to relieve pain, stiffness and inflammation, particularly in muscles, bones and joints. They are particularly used in the treatment of rheumatoid arthritis, osteoarthritis and other rheumatic conditions; however they do not alter the progress of those diseases. The main danger is that they can occasionally cause gastric bleeding. The main difference among them is the incidence and severity of side effects

  • **benoxaprofen** (Opren/Oraflex) – withdrawn worldwide in 1982 because of a high incidence of side effects, including deaths

  • **diclofenac** (Voltaren) – similar to ibuprofen (*see* analgesics), with a slightly higher risk of side effects

  • **ketoprofen** (Orudis SR) – similar to ibuprofen but with more side effects; the slow-release preparation is claimed to cause less gastro-intestinal irritation

  • **oxyphenbutazone** (Tanderil) – because of its risk of causing severe and sometimes fatal side effects related to the bone marrow's ability to produce blood cells, this is no longer considered a useful drug

  • **phenylbutazone** (Butazolidin) – can impair the bone marrow's ability to produce blood cells. Now generally restricted to treating severe spinal arthritis under careful medical supervision

  • **piroxicam** (Feldene) – there is an increased risk of bleeding from peptic ulcers and in the bowel with prolonged use

  • **suprofen** (Suprol) – withdrawn in many countries because of adverse side effects

**quinine** – the first antimalarial drug; now rarely used because it frequently causes side effects

**sulphonamides** – antibacterial drugs whose importance has decreased as the result of increased bacterial resistance and the development of antibiotics which are generally more active and less toxic

  • **sulphanilamide** (Prontosil) – the first sulphonamide; now rarely used, other than in vaginal creams (with little evidence of efficacy in the treatment of vaginitis), or in veterinary medicine

**thalidomide** (Contergan) – a sedative, generally withdrawn in the 1960s when it was found to cause severe birth defects if administered to pregnant women; now used in controlled conditions for the treatment of some forms of leprosy and experimentally in transplant operations to suppress the immune system's rejection mechanism

**tranquillisers** – drugs which relieve anxiety and/or sleeplessness

  • **benzodiazepines** – the most commonly used class of sleeping drug, benzodiazepines are also used in the treatment of anxiety and depression. Their main risk is that people who take them regularly may become psychologically and physically dependent upon them

    • **chlordiazepoxide** (Librium) – can be habit forming if taken regularly over a long period of time, and the effectiveness diminishes

    • **diazepam** (Valium) – can be habit forming if taken regularly over a long period of time. Severe withdrawal reactions have occurred

**vaccines** – agents which stimulate the body's immune system to create antibodies to resist specific infectious diseases; usually formulated from weak live viruses or from dead viruses
- **BCG** – a vaccine against tuberculosis prepared from an artificially weakened strain of cattle tuberculosis bacteria
- **hepatitis B** – either prepared from the blood of human carriers or made synthetically by biotechnology
- **malaria** – still at the experimental stage
- **polio** – generally given as an oral vaccine

**vitamins** – complex chemicals that are essential for a variety of body functions. Vitamin supplements should not used as a general tonic to improve well-being – they do not do so – nor should they be used as a substitute for a balanced diet. Fat-soluble vitamins such as A, D, E and K are stored in the liver and and excessive amounts may lead to serious side effects
- **$B_{12}$** – apart from dietary deficiency, all other causes of vitamin $B_{12}$ deficiency are due to malabsorption so there is little place for the use of vitamin $B_{12}$ orally
- **sulbutiamine** – a vitamin $B_1$ substance with the general properties of thiamine (vitamin $B_1$)

# Index